Divided Britain

Divided Britain

Ray Hudson
and
Allan M. Williams

Belhaven Press
(a division of Pinter Publishers)
London and New York

First published in Great Britain in 1989 by
Belhaven Press (a division of Pinter Publishers),
25 Floral Street, London WC2E 9DS

British Library Cataloguing in Publication Data
A CIP catalogue record for this book is available from the
British Library

ISBN 0–85293–110–8 (cased)
    0–85293–111–6 (paper)

Library of Congress Cataloging in Publication Data
Applied for

Filmset by Mayhew Typesetting, Bristol, England
Printed and bound in Great Britain by
Biddles Ltd, Guildford and King's Lynn

Contents

List of figures

Preface

In 1985 Prince Charles spoke publicly about his fears of the United Kingdom becoming a 'divided realm'. In this, he was no more than reflecting the feelings that many others had expressed, some publicly, others privately, about growing divisions within the UK in the 1980s and the dangers to social cohesion that they contained. Nevertheless, we believe this royal intervention in the public debate to be a significant one. Indeed, our original title for the book simply was 'The Divided Realm'. As this clearly did not have the same connotations for others as it did for us, we altered the title to the present one. But the book is still infused with the spirit of the divided realm, even if this is no longer its title.

There is no doubt that divisions within the UK, on a wide variety of dimensions, have deepened in the 1980s, though at the same time in other respects the gap has narrowed. The pattern of change, then, has often been a complex one, so that the UK is differently divided, as well as more deeply divided, in 1989 than it was in 1979. There is a tendency to attribute all this simply to the effects of Thatcherite policies. By implication, a reversal of these policies would produce a less divided Britain. In passing, however, we would argue that a combination of Thatcherite policies and changes in the global political economy preclude any easy return – perhaps any return at all – to consensus politics of the type that characterised the three decades prior to Mrs Thatcher.

Accepting this latter caveat, this is fine as far as it goes. But it neglects the fact that for a very long period before Mrs Thatcher became Prime Minister, the United Kingdom had in fact been a deeply divided and profoundly unequal society. The transition from feudalism to capitalism had laid the basis for the most fundamental transformation in the structure of divisions within the UK (although significant feudal traces remain today, as we show). Moreover, within the last couple of centuries the lineaments of division within a predominantly capitalist UK have changed in significant ways, as class structures have altered, gender divisions have been re-defined, ethnic divisions have been created, and spatial divisions have been re-cast in various moulds. The state has often been integrally involved in such changes as the form, content and extent of its own involvement have varied. Perhaps the central point is that as a capitalist society the UK is – and *must* be – divided on class lines. Any attempt to deny this is based on a misunderstanding of capitalism or represents an attempt to mystify the fundamental basis on which capitalist societies are constituted. Divisions via gender, place and race are related to – but are not reducible to – those of class, but they are not necessary in the same structural sense as those of class. Divisions and the inequality that flows from them are thus built into the way in which UK society is constituted.

What we therefore seek to do in this book is to explore the interplay between these various ingrained dimensions of division in UK society – class, gender, place and race – and the specific politics of Thatcherism. We would argue that it is only by locating Mrs Thatcher's divided realm in the historical context of the creation and reproduction of divisions within the UK that both Thatcherite policies and their effects can be properly understood. Thatcherism is as much symptomatic of such divisions, as it is a cause of them.

In what follows, we use the terms (Great) Britain and United Kingdom synonymously, unless we make it specifically clear that the former excludes Northern Ireland. This is not intended as a slight to the inhabitants of the latter area, but is simply a way of introducing some variety in terminology.

Finally, in this Preface we wish to acknowledge various forms of advice and help in producing this book: to the numerous individuals who persuaded us to change the title; to Catherine Reed, Elizabeth Pearson and Tracy Reeves for typing various drafts of the text; to Terry Bacon for drawing the maps and figures; to Mark Cohen, for his initial advice and support, and with our best wishes for the future; and finally, but not least, to Iain Stevenson, for his positive response to the text and for a speed of production that is quite remarkable! As ever, however, the usual disclaimers apply: the shortcomings in what follows are ours alone.

Ray Hudson, Durham
Allan M. Williams, Exeter
April 1989

1
Introduction: a divided realm?

Where there is discord may we bring harmony.
Where there is error may we bring truth.
Where there is doubt may we bring certainty.
Where there is despair may we bring hope.
[Mrs Thatcher, entering No 10 Downing Street on Friday, 4 May 1979]

When Mrs Thatcher entered 10 Downing Street for the first time as Prime Minister in the early hours of 4 May 1979, she chose her words for the media carefully. Quoting from St Francis, she aimed to bring harmony, truth, certainty and hope to the United Kingdom after Labour's winter of discontent.

What was the condition of the United Kingdom in the late 1970s and what is it now in the late 1980s? Is the United Kingdom really united or is it a divided realm? Some half a century after the beginning of post-war reconstruction and the creation of the welfare state this is a particularly acute criterion by which to judge the achievements of the post-1945 years. With 1989 marking the first decade in power of the Thatcher government, the need to address such questions is even more pressing. In what ways have the policies of Mrs Thatcher's governments lessened, increased or modified social inequalities in the UK? Has harmony replaced discord, has hope replaced despair?

Margaret Thatcher and the Conservative Party were elected to power in May 1979 with a radical reforming programme. This emphasised the need for enterprise, 'freedom' and efficiency, with no more than a sideways glance at equity and justice. Many commentators at the time dismissed the programme as little more than a series of paper tigers. After all almost every single post-war government had been elected with a reforming, if not a radical, programme. Once in power – and faced with economic and political constraints on their actions – their policies, with seeming inevitability, conformed to the norms of a broad social-democratic consensus.

There were the same expectations in 1979. On the day after the election, the *Daily Telegraph* editorial urged on the Prime Minister the need for only a few modest reforms. Mrs Thatcher's government was different, however, in that it actually set out to implement a large part of its agenda. The consequences of this can be assessed in many different ways, ranging across economic growth, unemployment, justice and liberty. However, one of the most important yardsticks is the extent to which its policies have contributed to making the UK a more or a less divided society.

It is not difficult to make out the case that the UK at the end of the 1980s continues to be a prosperous society. In the preceding two years it had experienced some of the highest growth rates in the developed world although gross domestic product per head lags behind the UK's major international rivals (Table 1.1). It is also an influential member of one of the three global super-powers, the EC. Moreover, 1988 had witnessed record car sales, soaring house prices in the South and the North, and a virtually unprecedented credit boom.

If there is such a being as the average UK citizen, then in 1989 he or she was probably better off than they had ever been – leastways in material terms. This was copiously documented in the official handbook, *Britain 1989*, published by the government early in that year. Nearly two-thirds of households own their homes and 73 per cent have central heating. There is also widespread ownership of consumer goods with, for example, 74 per cent owning freezers. Not only have such items become almost universal possessions but the consumer boom has encompassed an ever increasing range of household goods. For example, almost a half of all households possess video recorders. It is no longer simply a question of owning such items as much as the number of cars or televisions owned. The same applies to holidays, with about one fifth of the population taking at least two vacations in 1988.

The surge in economic prosperity in the mid-1980s was very real, even if in part it was no more than a recovery from the severe economic recession of the early 1980s. It had profound political consequences in helping to ensure the re-election of Mrs Thatcher's third government. Whereas the 1979 election victory had been preceded by the 'winter of discontent' and the 1983 election by the Falklands War, it was the post 1985 economic recovery and the consumer boom which was critical in the 1987 general election. Hence it was little wonder that the 1989 New Year's Honours list was lavish in its recognition of the business community. Of the twenty-seven new knights of the realm, nine were representatives of the financial and business world. Amongst the companies whose executives and chairmen were recognised in this way were Rover, Rothschild, Tesco and the Wates Building Group. An even greater honour was reserved for Sir John Sainsbury who was raised to a life peerage.

While the national economy was certainly experiencing a boom of sorts, it was equally evident that the benefits were not being spread equally within the UK. It is as easy to draw a portrait of a divided and impoverished UK as it is of a prosperous nation. Indeed, this was the objective of the Divided Britain declaration issued by the Child Poverty Action Group in 1986. It stated that 'Britain is divided into different worlds by extremes of wealth, income and prospects. In north and south there is a widening gap between rich and poor, women and men, black and white, sick and healthy, employed and unemployed'.

More than one hundred thousand homeless families, more than two million officially unemployed, and the continuing disadvantages experienced by women and by black people are indicative of the divisions. This is not to say that homelessness or unemployment are essentially creations of the Thatcher years, but whether these divisions have been widened or narrowed during the Thatcher decade is one of the major themes of this book.

Poverty and inequality are not features which are particular to either the Thatcher years or the post-war period as a whole. Persistent if changing inequalities are enduring features of life in the UK. For example, for the late nineteenth century there are copious chronicles of social inequalities. General Booth in 1890 referred to a 'Darker England' as being submerged portions of 'Greater England'.[1] He and his namesake Charles Booth graphically described the depths of poverty and despair which characterised late-Victorian Britain even at the height of the UK's dominance of the world economy. Another of these chroniclers was Disraeli who portrayed the 'Two Nations' – the Privileged and the People.

We would certainly not wish to argue that the absolute levels of poverty recorded by Booth, Rowntree and others are matched by those of modern Britain. The conditions experienced by the millions of people in the UK living at below supplementary benefit level in the mid-1980s cannot be equated directly with those of the inhabitants of East London as described by Charles Booth. But poverty is not to be measured simply by the ability of people to clothe and feed themselves. Poverty is both a relative and an absolute concept. Relative poverty can be interpreted as the ability to participate in the consumption of material and non-material goods and activities to the level which forms the expected standard of living in any time and place. Therefore the poorest may become better off in an absolute sense while becoming impoverished in a relative sense. Consequently the nation as a whole may become better off and the poor may become better off, while the gap between the two nations deepens. Whether Disraeli's concept of the 'Two Nations' remains relevant during the Thatcher years is a theme to be considered in the pages which follow.

Relative poverty does matter. Its extent provides a measure of social justice and a moral comment on contemporary society. But it is more than this, for relative poverty also frames the felt needs of the poor. This is especially pertinent in the age of mass advertising. The modern advertising industry is expressly geared to raising popular expectations as to what constitutes 'normal' consumption of goods and services. At one extreme this gives rise to a 'my little pony' culture, but it also heightens the awareness of the have-nots of what they do not have.

Inequality should be measured in terms of access to the goods, services and power that are currently available in society rather than to any arbitrary absolute standards. Nowhere is this more evident than in those places where the rich and poor are brought into juxtaposition. In recent years the North–South divide represents one of the more publicised geographical divides. But the relative sense of social inequality is probably greatest where communities stare at each other 'across the tracks'. One such example is to be found in the narrow Wirral peninsula in Cheshire: on the western side there are double- and treble-garaged homes looking out across the Dee estuary at mid-Wales, while on the eastern side stands Birkenhead, where even the second-hand shops are barred and shuttered.

The people of Birkenhead are certainly deprived in that they lack many goods and services which contribute to the 'good life' which is so visible on the other side of the Wirral. They are also disadvantaged compared to their neighbours on the Wirral.[2] The difference between deprivation and disadvantage is an important one. Deprivation may be the outcome of bad luck or personal failings and it can affect anyone in any social group. In contrast, disadvantage results from facing systematic handicaps in access to life chances. It may result from simply belonging to a particular social group.

Structural disadvantage is firmly rooted in the way in which society is constituted. In the UK age, gender and race all constitute important dimensions of structural disadvantage. Being old, being black or being a woman have important implications for the way in which society regards individuals and makes opportunities and access to resources available to them. Of even greater consequence is social class. This remains the key to understanding social disadvantage in modern Britain.

The UK As a Class Society

Divided by Class: But how?

The conceptualisation of class has re-emerged as one of the most controversial and interesting areas of contemporary social science. Disputes over theorising class are not new, however. There has been a long-running debate between adherents of, broadly speaking, Marxian and Weberian views about class. The current variety of theoretical positions cannot easily be reduced to one of these alternatives and this poses a problem.[3] Whilst we are not writing a chapter, let alone a book, on class theories, any discussion of classes in, and the changing class structure of, the UK, presupposes some theorisation of class (even if only implicitly).

The UK is still a class society. We take as a theoretical departure point Marx's identification of the decisive class relation between capital and labour as lying at the heart of capitalist societies. This is an asymmetrical relationship in terms of power. Members of the working class have to work for a wage in order to live whilst capitalists reap the rewards of their labour. It is important to appreciate that this two-class model represents a powerful abstraction to reveal the inner dynamism and the pivotal class structural relationship of capitalism.

But – and it is an important but – any particular capitalist society, such as that of the UK, is constructed around more complex sets of social relationships than just a dichotomous direct antagonism between capital and labour. Put another way, the existence of capital and labour as a fundamental structured class relationship does not mean that the principal social actors are always, or even often, the sole and unified collective representatives of these interests. Actual capitalist societies are more complicated than the two-class model.

What are the implications of this in conceptualising class structure in the UK? Two points can be made at this stage. First, the transition from feudalism to capitalism in the UK did not mean that all traces of feudal social relationships were eradicated. Significant 'relict' relationships, especially in terms of landownership and landed property and the social practices associated with them, persist to this day. Moreover, the initial development and subsequent evolution of industrial capitalism were often shaped in important ways by the feudal heritage. There is much to be said for the view that capitalism was established in the UK in a strangely compromised form.

Secondly, within capitalist societies, the simple dichotomy between capital and labour influences but does not determine class formation. It is rather like peeling an onion from the inside, beginning from the centre and the fundamental class structural relationship, then successively working back layer by layer to the surface, revealing the actual complexities of class relations in the process.

There are several dimensions to this complexity. Firstly, there are divisions within the bourgeoisie, the owners of capital. There are conflicts between financial and manufacturing sectors; there are conflicts between branches of these sectors, for example between chemicals and electronics; and there are conflicts between companies in the same branch of the economy – for example, in chemicals between ICI, Bayer and BASF (typically as competition on world markets).

There are also divisions amongst those who have to work for a wage, both between and within the working class and the middle class. These are divisions on the bases of industry, occupation, region and so on. The relative sizes of the working class and middle class, and the criteria by which they are defined, are matters of some debate. Indeed, the growth and changing composition of the middle class is perhaps the most contentious issue in recent theoretical debates.[4]

For one thing, the 'old' middle class – the petite bourgeoisie – has not disappeared. There are still many people who are self-employed, or owners of small firms but who do not employ waged labour. Similarly, there are still many owners of small firms who do. This old middle class has not only persisted but, in some respects, has grown. Its further growth is a central objective of Mrs Thatcher's political strategy.

There has also been a growth of a new middle class – called a service class by some. This is linked to two processes: the growing size of major private companies and the growth of state intervention in the economy and society. As capital became increasingly centralised in a relatively small number of firms, a separation emerged between owners and managers. The former derived incomes from profits whilst the latter were paid a salary, exercising control without ownership. This change was closely tied to the growth of institutional share-ownership in the UK. The second source of growth of this new middle class lay in the considerable post-war expansion of the welfare state. This created an increase in the number of professional employees (in education, health, social services, local government etc.) reliant upon the state for their incomes.

One further point can be made at this stage. There has also been some limited growth in property ownership amongst the lower-middle and working classes. Some of this has been direct, mainly through house purchase – simultaneously providing a place in which to live and the prospects of future appreciation in prices. More recently, the promotion of wider share-ownership has become an important element in Mrs Thatcher's 'popular capitalism', a project which deliberately seeks to restructure class relations in the UK. This remains much less important for many people, however, than 'indirect' share-ownership via their participation in pension schemes. Savings for future retirement provide a pool of money capital for major institutional investors. In this way, people's future incomes depend on the investment decisions of fund managers. As the Stock Market crash of October 1987 showed, this is not necessarily a secure future.

Analysing Class in the UK

The preceding discussion indicates the need for a sensitive approach to class analysis. Classes in the UK are not static. Their composition and structure are constantly evolving. In the forty plus years since the end of the Second World War the nature of the working and the middle classes has been moulded and remoulded. But class is still the key to interpreting differential access to power, income and life chances.

We are not arguing that consumption or political beliefs stem in any simplistic manner from the class structure of the UK.[5] There are cleavages within social classes in terms of life style, incomes and wealth. Not least, owner occupation has grown so that it is now the majority tenure amongst the skilled working class. This has had a profound influence on many aspects of traditional working-class values and behaviour as is evident in, for example, voting behaviour in the 1980s. While the working class as a whole still largely votes for the Labour Party, some sections of it have given substantial support to the Conservatives during the last decade.

Whether individuals or households own or rent their homes also conditions whether they – and perhaps more importantly their children – have shared in the redistribution of wealth resulting from the post-war inflation of property prices. This and other examples lead us to the view that many aspects of behaviour and consumption are not simply dependent on class. Instead class can be said to spill over into consumption and to shape if not determine behaviour.

While there is a lively theoretical debate about how to conceptualise class and where to draw class boundaries, there is no consensus on this. There is also a further problem. This is the correspondence between available empirical data and theoretical categories. Much of the available official data from sources such as the *Census of Population* refer to socio-economic groups (SEGs) which, at best, only partially correspond to theoretical categories of class. If, for example, we consider all those within a given occupational group (on which SEGs are based), such as 'electrician', it will contain members of different classes: wage labourers, the self-employed and capitalist employers. Nevertheless, many social scientists, as well as government statisticians, would accept that classes delimited in terms of occupational groupings are as reasonable a definition as one can produce, given the available data. An empirical investigation of class divisions in the UK cannot avoid such problems but at least we can be aware of them.

Beyond Class: Other Forms of the Divided Realm

Class is not the only fundamental social divide in the UK. In different ways gender, race and place are also sources of structural inequality and disadvantage. Indeed an impressive feature of the political scene in the 1970s and 1980s has been the efforts of women, black people and particular regions to gain greater recognition for these inequalities. While these topics are reviewed separately in later chapters, some brief comments are appropriate at this point.

Turning to gender first, there has been some narrowing of the gap between men and women in the post-war UK. More women have entered the labour force and more positions of responsibility have been opened up to them. At the same time there have been advances in the legal recognition of the rights of women and in anti-discrimination laws. Consequently – as a recent television programme expressed it – women have come 'out of the doll's house'. However, it would be more accurate to state that women are in process of passing out of the doll's house.

There continue to be glaring inequalities in the types of jobs to which men and women gain access This affects their incomes and their abilities to control their lives. It is also the case that women and men have not yet achieved complete equality in the eyes of the law, let alone in reality. There are significant differences in their retirement ages and access to state pensions, in their treatment by many occupational pension schemes and – until 1991 – in the taxation treatment of men and women. While not all the differences are in men's favour, the majority are.

Even if all legal and formal barriers to equality had been removed – which they have not – considerable informal barriers would still remain. Social expectations as to the roles of mothers and wives still largely determine who does what jobs in the household and who stays at home to look after children. This gender division of labour severely constrains the opportunities which are open to women as opposed to men. It affects job and career prospects, and access to a wide range of services and leisure activities. In the 1980s the Conservative government has emphasised the virtues of Victorian family life, involving greater reliance on the family to support dependants, unemployed teenagers and the sick. It remains to be seen whether this will improve or weaken the position of women in society at large.

Positive discrimination would be one way to improve the opportunities open to women. This could take a number of forms ranging from greater nursery school provision to specific job quotas being reserved for them. These and other forms of positive discrimination were the next logical step forward for women's rights after their legislative victories against discrimination in the 1970s. The extent to which any such advance has occurred will be reviewed later in the book. One obvious sphere to consider is politics. Has Mrs Thatcher's personal success in becoming Prime Minister been reflected in greater participation by women as a whole in the control of power?

Race is another dimension of inequality in the divided realm. Again the objective indicators are to be found in the data on jobs, education, incomes and housing. The more subjective – and often more dramatic – indicators are to be found on the streets of the United Kingdom. The inner cities have witnessed violent civil disturbances in the 1980s. While these are not all necessarily race riots, they have been linked to the grievances of the young black residents of these areas. They are symptoms of the deep mistrust which exists between many black people and the police in the UK's cities, and of the alienation of several generations of black people from white society.

The civil disturbances are also symptomatic of the structural inequalities in these cities. Formal discrimination has mostly been made illegal, but black people still tend to do less well in schools, and in housing and job markets. There is a need to consider the reasons for this: does it reflect the deprivation of individuals or the disadvantages faced by racial and ethnic groups as a whole?

Poor jobs, education and housing are not confined to black people. The inner cities, for example, are peopled by deprived black and deprived white people. Both black and white youths took part in the civil disturbances in Brixton, Toxteth and elsewhere in 1981 and 1984. Conversely there are many individual examples of black people achieving economic success. Frank Bruno, Lenny Henry and Joan Armatrading have all in their own way achieved great success. There is also the often-quoted success of Asians as owners of small businesses. Although this tends to conceal the continuing economic difficulties faced by most Asians, individual successes are not to be denied. However, with both race and gender the issue is whether or not there are systematic handicaps faced by social groups. Individuals may succeed while social groups remain severely disadvantaged.

The same point can be made with respect to locational differences in the UK. Do people born into particular places face disadvantages by virtue of this? The most obvious locational cleavage in the UK is that between the 'North' and the 'South'. There are clear differences in incomes, unemployment and house prices between these two parts of the UK. In addition to the statistical data which can be marshalled on this topic, and which are reviewed later, there are a number of more poignant indicators of the differences between North and South. Amongst these are 'the Tebbit specials', the early Monday and late Friday trains bringing workers from places such as Liverpool and Middlesbrough to and from the London job market. These are the unemployed workers who can find jobs in the South but cannot afford Southern house prices. They therefore have become long-distance commuters and in London they live in the cheapest possible lodgings or sleep on-site in vans and huts. It is estimated[6] that there are more than 10,000 such 'industrial gypsies' and they include both middle-class and working-class commuters.

Another indicator of the prosperity of the South is the changing geographical distribution of first division football clubs. While once-mighty clubs such as Sunderland, Bolton and Burnley languish in the lower divisions, their places in the premier division have been taken by such clubs as Charlton, Norwich, Millwall and Wimbledon. The paradox is not the Londonisation of the first division but the fact that, despite this, economically-depressed Merseyside has still retained a near monopoly on the championship!

North-South inequalities are no more exclusive than are those based on race or gender. There are areas of affluence within the North in such places as Harrogate and Chester and these are matched by concentrations of poverty in the South, especially in the inner cities. Having the correct address influences life chances, but this is as much a matter of being the 'right' side of town as it is of being in the 'right' region.

Geography is also strongly evident in the way in which the UK votes. It is well known that the 'South' has voted Mrs Thatcher into power in the last three elections. What is perhaps less well-known is that the electoral polarisation between regions has increased at each of these elections. Is this a fair reflection of how the two parts of the UK have fared as a result of Conservative policies?

Certainly the Scottish Nationalists and some Scottish Labour supporters have no doubts about the economic and political divides in the UK. They argue that the Conservative administration in London has no mandate to rule north of the border. Nationalist sentiments are certainly not the creation of the Thatcher government but its policies have given a fresh urgency (as in the Govan by-election) to a political cause that seemed to have foundered in the late 1970s. They also place in question whether the 'United' Kingdom is a misnomer. Nowhere is that question more relevant, of course, than in Northern Ireland. Few, if any commentators, can see a united kingdom in John Bull's 'other island'.

The preceding comments serve to remind us that the United Kingdom is divided in many different ways. It could therefore be argued that class has become less relevant for interpreting social cleavages. Such an argument would emphasise that classes have been fragmented along the lines of race, gender and location. Furthermore it could be suggested that sectional interests within the working, middle and upper classes have further undermined the usefulness of these categories as bases for analysis. Hence, conflict over the distribution of resources – such as health care, housing or jobs – has become inter-sectional rather than inter-class. We would reject such a view.

Class is not and never has been the only basis of social divisions in the UK. An individual's life chances and life-style are not just determined by social class. The precise nature of the life chances and the opportunities open to a black working-class girl in London are obviously very different to those for a white working-class boy living in Glasgow. Nevertheless they are both affected by virtue of having been born into the working class rather than the middle class. This basic fact has conditioned the range of schooling, job and other opportunities available to them. It has also probably influenced the expectations that their parents and teachers, and above all they themselves, have about the jobs they will get and the houses they will live in.

While class is not the only dimension of inequality it does impinge strongly on all the others. The theoretical framework of this argument was noted earlier and our intention in the remainder of the book is to consider the empirical evidence for social inequality in the UK. In the course of this we will investigate the extent of these inequalities and the ways in which they are related to social class. One important question is whether there is an underclass in the UK. An underclass is locked rigidly into a position of social disadvantage or, more likely, multiple disadvantage; possibly this may apply to black people or to the unemployed living in the inner cities. Our major question, however, is how various forms of social inequality have changed in Mrs Thatcher's Britain.

The State in The UK: Its Role in Redistribution

The link between class and consumption is also profoundly affected by the role of the state in the redistribution of resources. This is to be seen both in income-related policies, such as taxation and welfare payments, and in other policies related to, for example, the provision of health, education and housing.

The state is not a monolithic instrument unproblematically serving the interests of capital. Instead it operates as a series of different agencies at the national, regional and local levels. They have powers and resources available and there is a continuing struggle to influence the ways in which the latter are allocated between social groups and areas. Decision-making is influenced in a number of ways: by the elected representatives, usually acting along party lines, by the permanent bureaucracies, and by pressure groups and interested parties.

Neither the Labour nor the Conservative Party is exclusively a representative of a particular social class, although both have their class affiliations. Similarly, pressure and interest groups do not all operate exclusively in the interests of any one social class. The Consumers' Association has a cross-class basis while the Country Landowners Association and the Child Poverty Action Group have class affiliations. Along with the political parties and the bureaucracies they are engaged in a struggle to influence the ways in which government intervenes in society and also the ways in which it distributes its resources.

Although the struggle to control the state may not always be constituted along overtly class lines, many of its policies have clear class implications. Amongst these are decisions on the taxation of income, property and inheritances. Other examples are the balance of public 'expenditure' on council housing as opposed to mortgage subsidies, or decisions on comprehensive or selective schooling. The outcome of the struggle over the state therefore has important implications for inequality in the UK.

One of the most notable features of the post-war period is that the struggle over the state was confined within relatively narrow limits until the mid-1970s. There were important differences between the policies of the Labour and the Conservative Parties, but there was also a marked consensus between them with respect to many issues. In particular there has been consistent agreement on the need for a welfare state to care for the needy, and for most educational and health provision to be undertaken by the public sector. There has also been broad agreement that the public sector should have a major role in housing provision.

This political consensus over the role of the state was rooted in the Second World War. Before the war social security was still founded on the nineteenth century Poor Law. It was based on the practice of making life difficult for the recipients of state assistance, whether they were unemployed, elderly or sick. The underlying principle – in so far as there was one – was that the poor were undeserving and their needs arose from their personal failings. The undeserved stress and deprivation this caused for many millions of people in the 1930s Depression has been vividly described in such novels as Walter Greenwood's *Love On The Dole*.

After the bitter experiences of the 1930s, the Second World War raised some awkward social contradictions. This was a total war which required total commitment by all sections of the nation. The efforts of Jarrow were as essential as those of Hampstead, if not more so, if the war was to be won. Women's labour was also required in the wartime factories. However, if the war was to be won, then it would not be to maintain the inequalities of the 1930s. Future governments would have to introduce measures to reduce deprivation and disadvantage in the post-war period.

The blueprint for a less divided United Kingdom was laid down in a number of war-time reports. The most important of these was the Beveridge report. Although it was never fully implemented, it had a profound effect on post-war policies. Above all the Beveridge Report stated a commitment to break the link between income and access to decent health, education and life-styles. Its proposals included the establishment of the National Health Service, a fiscal system to ensure full employment, pensions to be paid as of right not after a means test, and a national insurance system to be paid for jointly by workers, employers and the state.

Many of these proposals were implemented by the 1945–51 Labour government. For example the National Health system was established and a programme of legislation introduced a reform of secondary education and systems of economic controls and land use planning. A dual system of income support was also introduced: a contributory social insurance scheme for those in paid employment and a non-contributory scheme for those who were not. The guiding principle – if not always adhered to – was that of universal provision available at the point of need.

The welfare state was in place and there was broad party political consensus concerning its role and relevance. With growing national affluence in the 1950s, it was to ensure that a large minority was not left behind in the scramble for individual prosperity. There was a belief that the benefits of economic growth could be redistributed to reduce relative inequalities while maintaining the absolute living standards of the better-off.

The welfare state has not achieved all its set objectives. It has certainly not eradicated poverty. In practice, benefit levels tended to be kept low so as not to undermine low wages in parts of the economy. There was also a low rate of take-up of benefits, with about 40 per cent remaining unclaimed. The social security system was also patriarchal, with families being treated as a single unit for most purposes. Furthermore, no allowance was made in contributory schemes for women taking career breaks to bring up children.

By the 1960s the gloss of post-war affluence was beginning to look faded. Television programmes such as 'Cathy Come Home' and reports by, amongst others, Abel-Smith and Townsend showed that there was still considerable absolute and relative poverty in the UK. The response of Harold Wilson's Labour government was to try and make the welfare state more efficient. At this stage neither the Labour nor the Conservative Parties considered – leastways in public – that there was any alternative to the welfare state. Instead, reports such as those by Robbins and Seebohm recommended ways in which access to education and social services could be widened and improved. At the same time the major parties were committed to increasing the resources devoted to the welfare state.

The challenge to the welfare state came in the mid-1970s. Faced with a global recession, Wilson's Labour government committed itself to cutting public expenditure. In the April 1975 Budget statement Dennis Healey, Chancellor of the Exchequer, announced that 'This is not a matter of choice or political decision. It is a fact of the world we live in, a fact for which I must budget'. This signal led to the end of the commitment to full employment and the beginning of rounds of cuts in public expenditure. The cuts were substantial. If the share of GDP devoted to public spending had been maintained then it would have been £7,500 million higher in 1979 than it turned out to be.[7] The welfare state would be one of the victims of these cuts. Labour, which had initiated much of the welfare state, was now the party which – however reluctantly – was weakening it.

Despite the severity of the cuts, Labour never abandoned its commitment to the welfare state or its commitment to ensuring that significant minorities were not excluded from national prosperity. However, radical changes were under-way in the Conservative Party. Margaret Thatcher had replaced Edward Heath as party-leader and she was intent on a new vision of UK society. Ultimately this would crack and arguably break the post-war political consensus.

The UK under Margaret Thatcher

Margaret Thatcher and the Conservative Party were returned to power in 1979, in the wake of the 'winter of discontent' and the evident failure of the corporatist strategy of the Labour government. The pact with the trade unions had ended in bitterness and prolonged and widespread disputes during the winter of 1978–79. The television and press carried powerful images of firemen on strike, uncollected refuse in the streets and of dissatisfaction amongst nurses. This contributed to a Conservative government coming to power with a radical agenda to change the economic and social face of the UK. The strengthening of market forces and the 'restoration of freedom' were high on this agenda. Unlike many preceding governments, Mrs Thatcher's actually set about implementing a large part of its electoral programme.

Economic policies under Mrs Thatcher were dominated by three prime considerations: mastering inflation, trade union reform and privatisation. Each of these objectives was pursued relentlessly, although always with a political eye on the electoral consequences.

During the first of Mrs Thatcher's governments, anti-inflation policy was based on tight monetarist policies and an attempt to reduce public expenditure. These policies had been formulated in opposition during the 1970s and were implemented in the early 1980s, even though there was by then a global recession. The result was an economic crisis in the UK – far more severe than occurred in its major competitors, as can be seen from the unemployment rates shown in Table 1.1. Britain's industrial base actually shrank and unemployment rose to over three million. This, the division between those in and those out of work, was to be one of the major elements in a divided UK.

Table 1.1 Unemployment rates and GDP per capita in the European Community, Japan and the USA

	% unemployed		GDP per capita at current prices and purchasing power parities, 1986
	1981	*1986*	
West Germany	4.8	8.1	15,702
France	7.7	10.7	15,042
Italy	8.1	13.7	14,037
Netherlands	8.8	12.4	14,527
UK	9.1	12.0	14,158
EC 12 Average	–	*10.8*	*13,639*
USA	7.5	6.9	21,307
Japan	2.2	2.8	15,155

Source: Commission of the EC, *Basic Statistics of the Community*, 25 Ed. (Luxembourg: Office for Official Publications of the EC, 1988)

The second element in the economic strategy was the weakening of trade union power. This was achieved in two ways. First via laws reducing the rights of trade unions, especially with respect to secondary picketing. Secondly, and especially in the case of public sector unions, by coercion. Both the steel workers' unions and the National Union of Mineworkers were taken on by Mrs Thatcher's administration. The strikes were carefully engineered to occur at a time when circumstances favoured the government. The miners' strike was particularly significant. Acute political acumen was shown by the government in avoiding a confrontation in 1982 and, instead, waiting until 1984 when conditions (including large stockpiles of coal) were more difficult for the NUM. The strike was long, bitter and divisive. The determination of the government and the schisms within the union, and between the NUM and other unions, ensured that the former was victorious. Its hand was also strengthened by reducing the amount of weekly benefit paid to strikers' families by £12. In both the steel and the coal industries union defeats were followed by drastic cuts and radical reorganisation as a prelude to privatisation.

Privatisation was the government's third major policy objective. This has been persistently pursued by all three Thatcher governments. The list of privatised or reprivatised companies is a long one. It includes British Telecom, British Aerospace, Jaguar Cars, Leyland, British Gas, BP, the British Steel Corporation and Cable and Wireless. At the time of writing, coal, electricity and water were amongst the industries for which privatisation was being planned, though not without considerable protest. Privatisation has had two principal aims: raising revenue for the government and strengthening market forces. The first is very real and has brought substantial gains for the government. Privatisation receipts (almost £4000 million just from the sale of 50% of British Telecom in 1984) have played an important role in financing tax cuts and in holding down the public sector borrowing requirement. The contribution to increasing market competition is far less clear. In many instances – notably those of British Telecom and British Gas – public monopolies have simply been converted into private ones. The proposals to introduce competition into the privatised electricity industry are generally regarded as cosmetic whilst water price increases ahead of privatisation are raising fears as to the future costs that consumers will have to bear.

Despite the realities of privatisation, Mrs Thatcher has been anxious to link this process with her commitment to 'freedom'. 'Freedom' is one of the favourite words of Conservative governments, but Mrs Thatcher's has redefined its meaning. Freedom was a central concept of the post-1945 political consensus and, although imprecisely defined, it involved both freedoms to and freedoms from. For example, freedom from unemployment and freedom from hunger were seen to be important as were the freedoms to criticise government and to belong to trade unions.

Mrs Thatcher largely takes her definition of freedom from the writings of F.A. Hayek.[8] This is a much more precise and narrow definition based on the notion of freedom from coercion. Its appeal to Mrs Thatcher is clear for, in essence, Hayek argues that government intervention tends to diminish true freedom. Freedom has therefore become the right of people to make their own decisions about how to live their lives. One part of this is the freedom to spend one's money as one wishes, that is free of government intervention. Taxation to fund welfare spending is therefore no longer seen as an essential redistributive mechanism but as a denial of freedom. Furthermore, not only are markets supposedly freer but they are also supposedly far more efficient than the state in allocating resources.

These philosophical premises have been transformed by Mrs Thatcher's government into its radical programme of selective de-intervention. As already noted, it encompasses privatisation. 'Freedom' also involves an attempt to end national wage negotiation – both within the public sector and in the abolition of some of the wages councils. Other arms of the strategy encompass council house sales and a reduction in subsidies to private industry to move into depressed economic regions, such as the North and Wales. The reforms of education and health care announced in 1988 and 1989 have also emphasised 'freedom' – whether for schools to opt out or for patients to choose their doctors.

Of course Mrs Thatcher is as much a perceptive politician as she is a radical reformer. Hence she has been tactically astute in timing the introduction of measures to bring about the implementation of economic freedom. The privileges and monopolies of the professions were initially barely touched, though by the late 1980s professionals in law, medicine and higher education felt the full weight of Thatcherite policies on their employment conditions and status. The most striking exception has been her refusal to contemplate ending the tax relief on mortgages, which is surely the greatest distortion to the operation of market forces in the UK.

The example of mortgage relief is an important one for it underlines the essentially political rather than philosophical or economic aims of Mrs Thatcher. Council house sales may increase the freedom of some individuals but this is also a way to appeal to greed or self-interest. Large discounts on the sales to the public of shares in privatised companies have a similar appeal. The barely hidden, and sometimes explicit appeal is obvious: vote Conservative and you can buy your council home cheaply and make a profit from buying shares in British Gas or British Telecom.

Above all, Mrs Thatcher's government has encouraged the cult of the individual and the need to give him or her greater freedom. This of course has its darker side. Individuals are seen to succeed or fail by their own efforts and, as such, there is no recognition of structural inequalities. Therefore individuals are not seen to fail, to be deprived or to be poor because they are black or because they are women or to face discrimination as a result of this. Similarly social class is not seen as a barrier to personal advancement, for the enterprise culture is supposedly open to everyone. Whether or not this is the case is a matter for empirical verification later in this book rather than a matter of opinion. However, acceptance of this particular view of the world does have important policy implications. It means that, for example, race-related civil disturbances in the inner cities are seen as the outcome of individual criminal acts rather than of alienation and structural inequalities. It also affects the way in which the welfare state is perceived, and helps legitimate its partial deconstruction.

Mrs Thatcher's view of the welfare state is that it is necessary but requires reform and reduction. In particular it absorbs too many resources and therefore hinders the broad strategy of deregulation and de-intervention. It also means that fewer resources are available for distribution as tax cuts. In addition, the welfare state is seen to have failed even in terms of its own remit; it is considered inefficient in the use of resources and as not offering choice to the consumer. The response of Mrs Thatcher's government to these problems is 'to roll back the frontiers of the state'. However, public opinion surveys continue to reveal strong support for the welfare state – even at the personal cost of forgoing tax cuts. As a result, Mrs Thatcher's actual approach to the welfare state is much more politically than ideologically inspired. It has three elements and – thus far – collectively they fall far short of outright dismantling of the welfare state.

First there is considerable political rhetoric about the need for individual and family responsibility – with a mythical caring Victorian family frequently being invoked as a model for modern families. There are many hidden assumptions in this model, not least that women will give up jobs and careers to look after elderly or sick relatives. The caring family is therefore supposed to assume some of the functions previously carried out by the welfare state but at lower or nil costs. In practice this amounts to little more than government rhetoric but real cuts in health and welfare provision do gradually increase the pressure on individuals to adopt such a role. Similarly, charities in particular and the community in general are constantly encouraged to assume some of the caring roles of the welfare state. Sometimes the community is not even consulted in such moves as, for example, the shifting of mental health care from institutions to the community.

The second element in the treatment of the welfare state is a gradual squeezing of the real resources available relative to the growth in need. In practice it has been very difficult to achieve this. Overall public expenditure as a proportion of Gross Domestic Product actually increased from 39.5 per cent in 1979–80 to 42.5 per cent in 1983–84. Cuts in spending on nationalised industries, public sector housing and some parts of the welfare state were outstripped by increased spending on pensions and defence. The costs of unemployment benefits also soared as the number out of work rose to more than three million. Nevertheless there have been successive cuts in the range of services offered by the welfare state. Ministerial budgets have been trimmed by the Cabinet's 'star chamber'. The result is seen in longer hospital waiting lists, fewer school textbooks, eye-test and dental check-up charges, and vastly increased prescription charges. Against this, the bulk of the welfare state has been left intact, no doubt for political reasons. Even so, this does not mean that the cuts which have been implemented have not been harmful to individuals and to particular social groups.

The third element of the Thatcher approach to welfare policy has been to try and introduce market choice into the production and allocation of services. In the provision of services this has mainly involved privatising parts of the operations, such as catering or cleaning in public institutions. Introducing market principles into the allocation of resources has been even more contentious. It has been seen in various guises in different services: examples include council house sales, and 'parental choice' and schools opting out of local authority control. By 1989 there were also proposals that students' choice of universities and doctors' choice of hospitals for their patients could also be made subject to market principles.

The introduction of market-based provision is also being fostered by more insidious methods. Limiting spending on public sector provision of health, education and welfare services is increasing the pressure on individuals to make their own private arrangements. Hence – as will be shown in chapters two and three – it is no coincidence that private medicine, private schools and private pension schemes have flourished in the 1980s. The government then uses this as an indicator of a preference for private services and as a critical comment on the ineffectiveness of public provision. This, of course, disregards the underlying reasons for the shortfall in public sector provision in the first place. Such a strategy also makes no allowance for structural inequalities in society. Provision on the basis of the ability to pay excludes, by definition, certain social groups. One of our objects in this book is to assess whether such exclusion has increased or decreased during the 1980s.

Reform of social security was ushered in by the Fowler Review. This shifted the debate about the welfare state, setting out reform as a means of 'freeing individuals from welfare dependency'. Welfare dependency is seen to have negative consequences for individuals, encouraging them to take state handouts and so becoming less 'free'. This leads to benefits being viewed as a form of social pathology. Poverty is the fault of individuals in not accepting jobs rather than being due to structural causes such as a lack of jobs at decent wages.

This view of welfare is not completely new and Labour's 1976 Social

Security Review had looked at how to redistribute benefits to the more needy. However, the 1986 Social Security Act went further and sought to reduce sharply state assistance, limiting it to those in 'real' need. The definition of real need was very narrow. For example, it excluded 16–18 year-olds from benefits. Income support was also reduced for additional items such as fuel, while one-off payments were abolished. Instead there was to be a new Social Fund but the poor could only seek assistance from this after they had first exhausted the possibilities of getting help from charities or from their families. Benefits were also to be withheld for six months from those who were considered to have been responsible for losing their last jobs. At heart, this was a policy to force people into low-wage jobs, and as such it must be seen alongside the abolition of wages councils.

Policies are the products of governments rather than of individuals. Nevertheless it is appropriate to refer to the 'Thatcher' governments because of the way in which the Prime Minister has imposed her personal touch on almost all matters of importance. Contentious changes in policy are typically made by ad hoc cabinet committees, chaired by the Prime Minister. While the party and the Cabinet have to provide at least passive – and in practice often active – support for her policies, the 1980s have been characterised by prime ministerial government. This degree of personalisation of power and leadership has no precedent in the post-war era of Cabinet government. As a result, the achievements and the failures of government in the 1980s are strongly associated with one individual, acting in the context of the political and economic constraints which have given her a near-monopoly of power.

What are the hallmarks of Mrs Thatcher's style of government? Above all these are centralism and abrasiveness. The two qualities have been strongly entwined. Drawing on imagery from the Falklands campaign, striking miners in 1984–85 were labelled 'the enemy within'. We also see these characteristics in the aggressive hostility of the government to all its critics and to constitutional restraints on its power. Dissenting ministers such as Prior – 'not one of us' – have been dismissed from the Cabinet, the powers and finances of local authorities have been 'rate-capped' and neutered, university autonomy has been limited and bishops have been castigated. These institutions provide some balances and checks to the power of central government, yet their rights to criticise have been attacked and in some cases curtailed.

Our primary objective in this book is not to pass judgement on the policies of the Thatcher government as such. First and foremost, we wish to establish the extent and the forms of inequalities in the United Kingdom. The source of these lies in the nature of the UK as a capitalist and class society. Poverty, deprivation and inequality have been persistent features of the UK throughout the post-war years, whether of boom or of recession. As the economy and society have been transformed in the post-war period, so the nature of these inequalities has changed. However, government policies can have an important influence in modifying the extent of such inequalities. Hence our second objective is to establish whether these inequalities have increased or diminished during the first ten years of Thatcherism. Is the UK a more divided realm in 1989 than it was in 1979? Will it be more divided in 1999 than in 1989?

Notes

1. W. Booth, *In Darkest England and the Way Out* (London: Salvation Army, 1890).
2. For a discussion of deprivation and disadvantage see M. Brown, 'Deprivation and social disadvantage', in M. Brown (ed), *The Structure of Disadvantage* (London: Heinemann, 1983) pp. 1–13.
3. See, for example, A. Giddens, *A Contemporary Critique of Historical Materialism* (London: Macmillan, 1981); A. Giddens, *The Constitution of Society* (Cambridge: Polity Press, 1984); J. Urry, *The Anatomy of Capitalist Societies* (London: Macmillan, 1981); and E.O. Wright, *Classes* (London: Verso, 1984). Modern class theorists tend to blend strands drawn from a variety of theoretical positions.
4. See, for example, N. Abercrombie and J. Urry, *Capital, Labour and the Middle Classes* (London: George Allen & Unwin, 1983); J. Goldthorpe, 'On the service class, its formation and future', in A. Giddens and G. Mackenzie (eds), *Social Class and the Division of Labour* (Cambridge: Cambridge University Press, 1982) pp. 162-85; R. Scase, 'The petty bourgeoisie and modern capitalism: a consideration of recent theories', in A. Giddens and G. Mackenzie (eds), *Social Class and the Division of Labour*, op. cit. pp. 148–61; and E.O. Wright, *Class, Crisis and the State* (London: New Left Books, 1978).
5. This debate is reviewed in chapter 1 of G. Marshall, H. Newby, D. Rose and C. Vogler, *Social Class in Modern Britain* (London: Hutchinson, 1988).
6. T. Hogarth and W.W. Daniel, *Britain's New Industrial Gypsies* (London: Policy Studies Institute, 1989).
7. P. Ormerod, 'The economic record', in N. Bosanquet and P. Townsend (eds), *Labour and Equality* (London: Heinemann, 1980), pp. 47–62.
8. For example, see F.A. Hayek, *The Fatal Conceit* (London: Routledge & Kegan Paul, 1988).

Further Reading

The nature of deprivation and disadvantage are discussed in M. Brown (ed), *The Structure of Disadvantage* (London: Heinemann, 1983).

There is a considerable literature on class but useful starting points are provided by A. Giddens, *The Constitution of Society* (Cambridge: Polity Press, 1984); E.O. Wright, *Classes* (London: Verso, 1984); N. Abercrombie and J. Urry, *Capital, Labour and the Middle Classes* (London: George Allen & Unwin, 1983); and J Goldthorpe, 'On the service class, its formation and future', in A. Giddens and G. Mackenzie (eds), *Social Class and the Division*

of Labour (Cambridge: Cambridge University Press, 1982).
For reviews of the welfare state, see P. Corrigan, 'Social Welfare', in P. Abrams and R. Brown (eds), *UK Society* (London: Weidenfeld and Nicolson, 1984), pp. 310–25; I. Gough, *The Political Economy of the Welfare State* (London: Macmillan, 1979).
A good general introduction to modern Britain can be found in N. Abercrombie and A. Warde, *Contemporary British Society* (Cambridge: Polity Press 1988) and R. Hudson and A. Williams, *The United Kingdom* (London: Harper & Row, 1986).

2
Divided by class I: wealth and income

Introduction: class, income and wealth

Capitalist societies are inevitably characterised by inequalities between classes in income and wealth, although the precise form of these depends upon social and political conditions specific to particular societies. Such inequalities were endemic in the UK before 1979, but since the election of Mrs Thatcher's government they have widened further. Following some redistribution from rich to poor in the immediate post-war years the next three decades were ones of relative stability in the distribution of income with a slight tendency to reduced income inequalities. Growing equality in pre-tax personal incomes between 1949 and 1977 largely involved a redistribution within the top 30 per cent of income earners, away from the top 10 per cent and particularly the top 1 per cent (whose share of incomes more than halved). An important reason why income inequalities remained substantially unaltered is that the proportions of tax paid at different income levels above the bottom 20 per cent of the population (who received most of their income in state benefit payments) varied little. Any progressive tendency in direct taxation was largely cancelled out by the effects of indirect taxation.

In contrast, in the 1980s income inequalities widened (Table 2.1). This process began under the preceding Labour government but accelerated sharply in the 1980s. The share of the top 20 per cent (and especially that of the top 1 and 5 per cent) increased whilst that of the bottom 60 per cent fell. The magnitude of inequalities was less for disposable and final incomes, reflecting some continuing redistributive element in government taxation policies. But since 1979 Conservative policies on taxation and benefits have become sharply regressive. Further taxation changes introduced after 1985, particularly in the March 1988 Budget, further cut the top rate of income tax to 40 per cent and the tax bill of the top income earners by huge amounts. These have further increased inequalities.

Table 2.1 Distribution of income, United Kingdom, 1976–85.
Percentage share of national total

	Quintile groups of households				
	Bottom fifth	*Next fifth*	*Middle fifth*	*Next fifth*	*Top fifth*
Original income					
1976	0.8	9.4	18.8	26.6	44.4
1981	0.6	8.1	18.0	26.9	46.4
1983	0.3	6.7	17.7	27.2	48.0
1985	0.3	6.0	17.2	27.3	49.2
Disposable income					
1976	7.0	12.6	18.2	24.1	38.1
1981	6.7	12.1	17.7	24.1	39.4
1983	6.9	11.9	17.6	24.0	39.6
1985	6.5	11.3	17.3	24.3	40.6
Final income					
1976	7.4	12.7	18.0	24.0	37.9
1981	7.1	12.4	17.9	24.0	38.6
1983	6.9	12.2	17.6	24.0	39.3
1985	6.7	11.8	17.4	24.0	40.2

Note:
Original income comes from various sources such as wages and dividends
Disposable income is defined as original income plus benefits and less direct taxes
Final income is defined as disposable income adjusted for the effects of indirect taxes
Source: Central Statistical Office, various dates, *Social Trends* (HMSO)

The growing concentration of income amongst the top 20 per cent has been paralleled by growing poverty amongst those at the other end of the income distribution. From 1960 to 1977 it is estimated that around two million people were, at any one point in time, living below the government's own supplementary benefit level (the officially defined level of inadequate income). By 1981 this had risen to 2.6 million. By 1983 there were an estimated 8.6 million people living at or below the supplementary benefit level, an increase of 43 per cent since 1979. Using a different definition of poverty, based on a measure of a minimum standard of living widely agreed among the population, Mack and Lansley[1] suggest that there were between 6 and 12 million poor people in Britain in the 1980s, of whom 2.6 million faced intense poverty. These include a disproportionate representation of the unemployed, the disabled, one-parent families and the elderly retired. Since the incomes of many in these groups depend directly on state

Table 2.2 Distribution of wealth in Great Britain, adults over 18 (percentage) 1971–85

		1971	1979	1985
Marketable wealth Percentage owned by most wealthy x% of population:	1% of	31	22	20
	5%	52	40	40
	10%	65	54	54
	25%	86	77	76
	50%	97	95	93
Marketable wealth plus occupational pension rights Percentage owned by most wealthy x% of population:	1% of	27	19	n.a.
	5%	46	24	n.a.
	10%	59	45	n.a.
	25%	78–83	70–74	n.a.
	50%	90–96	88–92	n.a.
Marketable wealth plus occupational and state pension rights Percentage owned by most wealthy x% of population:	1% of	21	13	11
	5%	37	25	25
	10%	49	35	36
	25%	69–72	56–59	57–60
	50%	85–89	79–93	81–85

Note: *Marketable wealth* refers to assets such as houses or shares that could be sold. Assets such as pension schemes will yield a future income but cannot be sold.
Source: Central Statistical Office, various dates, *Social Trends* (HMSO)

benefit payments, the creation of poverty at one end of the income distribution is as much a product of government policies as is affluence at the other end. Whereas a two-child family in the bottom 20 per cent of the income distribution experienced a 6 per cent decrease in income (including benefits) between 1979 and 1985, a two-child family in the top 20 per cent had a 9 per cent increase. Figures such as these led Mr Malcolm Wicks, Director of the Policy Studies Centre, succinctly to sum up the position: '. . . the poor are getting poorer and the rich are getting richer' (cited in the *Financial Times*, 4 January 1988).

In many ways, inequalities in wealth are related to but are more deeply entrenched and extensive than those in income. By wealth, we mean the assets that people own, either as money or in forms that can be converted to money (such as houses). Over the last fifty years or so, there would appear to have been a marked redistribution of wealth; for example, the share of the top 1 per cent fell from 55 per cent in 1938 to 32 per cent in 1972. This was largely a redistribution within the top 20 per cent however; over the same period their share only fell from 91 per cent to 85 per cent. This pattern continued throughout the 1970s (Table 2.2). Although the share of the top 1 per cent declined further, by the end of that decade the least wealthy 50 per cent of the population had only increased its share of marketable wealth from 5 to 7 per cent. Including occupational and state pensions lessens the inequalities in marketable wealth but by no means removes them. The continuing redistribution of wealth within the top quarter of the population partly reflects the strategies of the wealthy to set up trusts or distribute assets amongst members of their families prior to death, precisely to avoid the higher taxes payable on death. This suggests a need to consider wealth in relation to families rather than individuals.

Inequalities in wealth have stabilised in the 1980s: 1 per cent of the population still owned 20 per cent of marketable wealth and 5 per cent owned 40 per cent of it in 1985. A more favourable tax regime has been created since 1979 for the wealthy, making it easier for them to preserve wealth within their families.

How then are trends in income and wealth inequalities in the 1980s to be interpreted? To some extent, changes in the distribution of wealth and incomes from the late 1940s to the late 1970s resulted from redistributive taxation policies. The three decades before Mrs Thatcher became Prime Minister were, by and large, years of the post-war consensus around Keynesianism and a commitment to the welfare state. It is indicative of the limits to these reformist policies that the distribution of income and wealth changed so little. To the 'economic evangelicals' of the new right, however, the class compromises around which the post-war consensus was built caused the UK's economic decline. In contrast to its predecessors, from 1979 the new government deliberately set out to widen income inequalities. In particular, it reduced higher tax rates and the burden on those with high incomes. It saw a more divided society as central to regenerating the economy via creating an 'enterprise culture' that rewarded success and punished failure.

The causes of the reversal of previous weak trends towards a more equal distribution of income and wealth lie in the specific politics of Thatcherism. But these began to take effect in a society where the distribution of income and wealth was already markedly uneven. There are clear relationships between forms of property ownership, sources of money income and size of incomes. For most people, ownership of wealth is minimal. For most of those for whom it is more substantial, it is held in forms that relate to individuals' and household's consumption patterns: for example, houses as places in which to live, or bank and building society deposits or insurance policies to provide future income. Ownership of wealth in these forms largely depends upon money earned through wage labour, though income levels and the conditions under which they are earned vary greatly between and within classes. An important change for some, undoubtedly, is the one-off inflow of money from the inheritance of parental homes. Increasingly, however, wage earners are acquiring small amounts of share capital in private (usually privatised) companies which provide marginal unearned income. For a small minority, however, concentrated ownership of wealth provides access to very considerable unearned income in the form of dividends, profits and rents from money invested in government stocks, shares or land, for example.

In summary, then, access to different forms and amounts of income and wealth is related (though not reducible) to class relations. To simplify matters for the moment – some complications are introduced later – we can suggest that:

(i)   for a few, profits provide a source of income because of their ownership of property as industrial capital;

(ii) for a few, rents provide a source of money income (often related to the persistence of land ownership from an earlier feudal era);

(iii) for a minority, who are self-employed, money income depends upon their ability to sell goods or services produced by their own labour;

(iv) for most people, whether categorised as 'working' or 'middle' class, wages form the main source of money income upon which they depend;

(v)   for many people, some of whom are unemployed and others of whom for various reasons are too young or too old to form part of the wage labour force, state payments form the main source of money incomes.

Who owns the land?: Land, wealth and incomes

Who then are the major landowners today? An indication of this is given in Fig. 2.1. Perhaps the most surprising aspect is the extent to which traces of pre-capitalist ownership persist. The Crown estates, the monarchy, the Church of England and the universities (principally Oxbridge) remain important landowners. Even more striking, despite a sustained decline in their holdings, over 31 per cent of land is owned by the aristocracy. Other non-titled individuals own over 19 per cent of land.

Different categories of landowner have differing reasons for owning land. For many, owning a small piece of land is simply a condition for living in a particular house. For non-financial companies, land holdings are typically a necessary condition for carrying out their main economic activities (although selling sites in urban areas has often proved extremely profitable for them). For many other individuals and

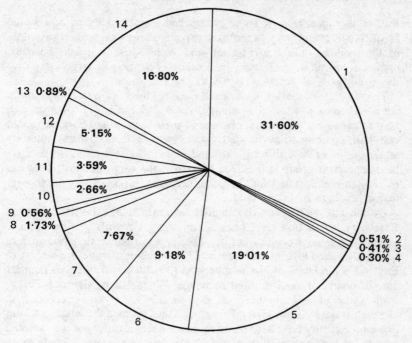

1 Landed aristocrats
2 Crown estates
3 Monarchy
4 Church of England
5 Other (non-titled) individuals
6 Central government
7 Local authorities

8 Nationalized industries and public services
9 Universities
10 Charities
11 Trusts
12 Non-financial companies
13 Financial institutions
14 Other

Figure 2.1 Who owns the land?
Source: after Massey and Catalano 1978.

organisations, however, land holdings are themselves a – even the – major sources of income via rents or profits.

Major private owners

Some big private estates result from the activities of successful capitalists who made their fortunes and wished to mimic the lifestyle of the landed aristocracy. These range from *nouveaux riches* industrialists in the nineteenth century to property developers in the second half of the twentieth. In part, this has involved a transfer of land from the aristocracy. Yet despite reductions, with capital transfer taxes leading to a break-up of some estates and the shrinking of others, the aristocracy remain very significant private owners of land. Two-thirds of the landed nobility in England and Wales, just over 200 families, own *at least* 5000 acres each; in Scotland, retention of large estates by the nobility is, if anything, stronger.

Twenty-six aristocrats have combined holdings of over one million acres. About a third of the peerage, some 350 lords, still own enough land to provide a significant element in their income and outlook; about one half combine their landed estates with active business interests while the other half live off the land alone. Consequently, an entirely land-dependant group still exists. Moreover the surge in land prices has more than compensated for shrinking acreages, especially for those with major holdings of urban land.

By the late 1970s very substantial landowners like Lords Leicester, Roseberry and Sefton were once again among Britain's wealthiest men, as they had been a century before. The largest aristocratic landowner in Scotland is the Duke of Buccleuch (277,000 acres), while the largest in England is the Duke of Northumberland (90,786 acres); the two families are, of course, linked through marriage. When Hugh Algernon Percy, tenth Duke of Northumberland, died in 1988, he was succeeded as eleventh Duke by Lord Harry Percy, who thus became the latest in a long line whose family have held land ever since a remote ancestor was granted estates for services to William the Conqueror. His estates include more than 80,000 acres in Northumberland, administered from the ancestral home in Alnwick Castle: this yields a variety of forms of income from tenanted farms, farms in hand, villages, stretches of moorland, parkland, grouse moor and rivers. In the past it also yielded huge returns from royalty payments on coal to his predecessors. He also owns 3,500 acres of rolling farm, forest and downland in Surrey, along with Syon House and the 200-acre Syon Park by the Thames in West London.

Other Dukes also remain major landowners, mostly of rural land but with some very valuable urban holdings. The Duke of Westminster, for example, has extensive urban holdings of prime land in London and other towns (held of course in family trusts); these include most of Oxford Street, Mayfair and Belgravia. He also owns agricultural land in England and estates in Scotland. The Queen personally is also a major landowner, with the 47,000 acres of the Balmoral and Sandringham estates. Land ownership on this scale provides access to considerable monetary incomes.

Incomes from land holdings take various forms. Rents are derived from the profits of farmers or, more recently, from expenditure by the bourgeoisie on leisure activities such as grouse shoots and salmon fishing. Profits are derived from farming and forestry, especially since 1945, in response to the inducements of State grants and subsidised prices. At the same time the aristocracy have diversified their sources of income away from land in the narrow sense. Many have, for example, cashed in on the leisure boom, opening the doors of their stately homes to the public. Great houses and their contents have become attractions that people will pay to see. Often these developments have been linked to the activities of the National Trust and have preserved a particular definition of the national heritage. In some cases, taking advantage of the growth in leisure has involved innovations that have little to do with history: Longleat wild life park is a good (or bad) example of this tendency.

Another major group of landowners, also originating in the pre-capitalist era, is the landed gentry, a uniquely British phenomenon. It ranges from yeoman farmers, to the titled nobility, often with marriage connections between gentry and nobility. In the mid-1980s about 1,000 families in the landed gentry owned 1,000 or more acres each, with another 500 families owning a few hundred acres each. They remain heavily reliant upon income from their estates but there have been important changes in the way in which land generates money for them. They have gradually moved from reliance upon rents to dependence upon profits from owner-occupied farming. They have ceased to be landowners who also produce, and have become agricultural producers who also own land. Moreover, since 1945 they have tended to adopt a more 'economic' approach towards land-ownership; not least, sales of land have often provided an alternative source of money.

In some respects, the transformation of part of the landed gentry overlaps the third main group of private landowners: owner-occupier farmers. For them, land ownership is central. It usually represents the bulk of their total invested capital and acquisition of more land is usually the simplest means (however difficult) of expanding production. Furthermore, land-based production is likely to be their sole economic interest.

Owner-occupied farming increased markedly after 1945, partly because of state support for agriculture. By 1960 over 50 per cent of farms – almost 190,000 holdings – were owner-occupied. Most – about 80 per cent – were small, with less than 100 acres. The number of small owner-occupied farms has since fallen. But size is not the main feature distinguishing this group of owners from the nobility and gentry. Fundamentally, such farmers are industrial capitalists for whom land is essential to production. Many employ wage-labourers, extracting surplus value from them. Many, however, only employ such labour on a part-time or casual basis, especially on smaller farms. Others are wholly reliant upon their own and/or family labour and more accurately are conceptualised as self-employed.

In one sense, however, *all* owner-occupier farmers have seen a great increase in their wealth as a result of land price increases. In the 1970s ownership of 1,800 or more acres of land made hundreds of farmers into paper millionaires. As land prices escalated in the 1980s, the acreage necessary to create a millionaire fell. Selling two or three acres for residential development in the right place was itself sufficient to raise a million pounds by the late 1980s. For small, owner-occupier farmers who wished to expand, however, escalating land prices caused problems as acquisition of more land became more difficult. In these circumstances, the rational capitalist solution of selling an existing holding at inflated prices became a more attractive proposition. This helped reduce the number of small owner-occupied units and farmers.

Institutions as landowners

Some institutions have long histories as land owners, such as the Oxbridge Universities (160,000 acres) and the Church of England (170,000 acres). Rents from land are an important element in their income whilst the land itself represents a considerable accumulation of wealth. Since 1945 established organisations such as the National Trust have become important landowners (over 400,000 acres), as a result of gifts or purchases. More recently, other institutions have become significant landowners. Financial institutions – life insurance companies and pension funds – became important landowners from the 1960s, in large part due to the 1965 Finance Act. In the 1960s and early 1970s, this mainly involved small acreages of highly-priced urban land; rising rents provided income for these institutions and, because of the way land values were calculated (as capitalised rents), it also translated into spiralling paper wealth. Following the property market slump of the early 1970s, the financial institutions sought to diversify their investments from urban to rural land. As early as 1973, they purchased 28 per cent of all agricultural land that came on the market, a trend that subsequently continued.

Property companies have become increasingly linked to financial institutions. By 1973 insurance companies and pension funds owned almost one quarter of the share capital of property companies. Property companies specialise in land: their economic activity consists almost exclusively in purchasing and/or developing land or property in order to collect rental incomes. Their activities are essentially speculative and consequently they provide opportunities for a few individuals to amass great personal wealth very quickly. For example, Harry Hyams, one of the more (in)famous property developers, was credited, at the height of the property boom of the early 1970s, with a personal fortune of between £500 million and £1,000 million. During the 1980s the privatisation policies of the Thatcher governments, forcing sales of land by local authorities and nationalised industries such as British Rail, created fresh spaces in which these speculative property companies could operate.

Land ownership is an important source of wealth and income. It has a wider social significance, however, that is important in relation to class. Some owners regard land purely and simply as a route to rents or profits. They are indifferent as to which land they own – as long as it 'does the business', literally. For others this is not the case. Many small farmers feel a strong bond to 'their' land (whether owned or rented). The landed aristocracy and gentry are also often deeply attached to *particular* pieces of land, with which they have historical and/or social connections and which hold a deeper symbolic value. Ownership of specific tracts of land also helps define the status of particular social groups and delineates the social relationships around which life in the countryside revolves – though perhaps this was more true of the 1950s than the 1980s when powerful forces of change have impinged on rural life. Ownership of specific areas of land helped define the 'traditional' social order in the countryside by virtue of the status that it conferred upon the gentry and aristocracy. Reflecting this, land-ownership became a status symbol for successful urban bourgeoises, seeking to mimic the life-styles of the landed aristocracy. This persistent, if socially changing, group of influential rural landowners helped shape the conservative character of much of the post-war planning system, designed to prevent or contain change.

Who owns the companies?: Capital, share-ownership, wealth and incomes

As the foundation of private enterprise capitalism, company share-holdings are crucially important; thus ownership of the companies is a politically sensitive issue in capitalist societies. It is often seen as decisively shaping the trajectory of national economic development. Sustained debates as to the merits of privatisation and nationalisation, and over multinational companies undermining national governments' economic strategies, bear testimony to this. Ownership of these companies is equally crucial in structuring links between class, power and income. Ownership and control of such companies is, therefore, central to understanding inequality.

Individual or institutional share-ownership?

Share-ownership and corporate control

Broadly speaking, the twentieth century has seen a change from personal to institutional shareholding in the UK. Personal shareholding was dominant until the early years of the twentieth century. As late as 1963, personal ownership of shares still stood at almost 59 per cent. Since then it has fallen substantially to 37 per cent in 1975 and 22 per cent in 1984 (see Fig. 2.2). The break-up of personal and family share-holdings created the space for a reconcentration of shareholdings via the growth of institutional shareownership: from 21 per cent in 1957, to 47 per cent in 1975 and 60 per cent in 1984 (Fig. 2.2). This has involved financial institutions mobilising the small savings of milions of people

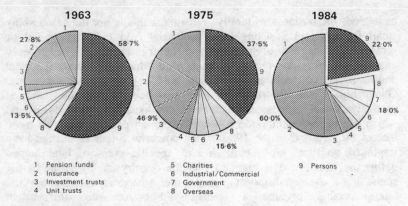

Figure 2.2 Who owns company shares, 1963–84?

Source: *Financial Times* 11.1.86

Unit trusts have vied with building societies to attract savings whilst for many others the decisions have been taken for them by pension fund managers. In this sense they have become involuntary and indirect shareholders.

There has undoubtedly been a dilution of family control over private companies. Many of the remaining family participants in such companies became passive *'rentier'* shareholders, content to withdraw from active control over corporate strategies and to draw their unearned incomes in the form of dividends etc. Many continue to do so. There is equally no doubt that growing institutional share ownership has been associated with growing centralisation of control and concentration of output in a fairly small number of major conglomerates that have become increasingly internationalised. Small firms (and their owners) have by no means disappeared but the strategic significance of multi-nationals in determining the trajectory of national economies has increased enormously.

For some, the growth of major transnational conglomerates, with a less concentrated pattern of share-ownership, was interpreted as bringing a more diffuse distribution of power and control. This, supposedly, heralded the demise of buccaneering figures such as 'Tiny' Rowland, with his personal 12 per cent stake in Lonrho. To some extent, this is true but it is important not to overstate the point. For example, the growing internationalisation of the economy helped create space for entrepreneurs such as Richard Branson, Robert Maxwell and Rupert Murdoch to increase the scale and variety of their activities. Private share ownership may have fallen but it remains very highly concentrated amongst a small number of powerful individuals and families: in 1975, the top 1 per cent of wealth holders held 54 per cent of all privately owned shares; the top 5 per cent held 80 per cent of them. Little has changed since.

It is, then, important not to underestimate the *continuing* significance of either personal and family control or of the entrepreneurial capitalists. What is remarkable is not so much that there has been a decline in active family control – in 44 per cent of the top 250 companies in 1904 compared to 29 per cent in 1976 – but that family control and influence remains so pervasive. This indicates the continuing existence of a small group of individuals and families which possess enormous power and derive great monetary incomes and wealth from company profits.

In some cases, continuing personal or family control depends upon majority or total share holding. Companies such as Barings, Littlewoods and Rothschilds are 100 per cent family-owned. In some – Pilkington, Marley and Mercury Securities – family share ownership was less than 10 per cent. In others exclusive control was achieved with minority shareholdings. Dispersed institutional shareholding has created the space for what Scott[2] terms controlling 'constellations of interest' to emerge. These are based on minority shareholdings and a web of interconnections between the largest enterprises. By 1976, 100 of the largest 250 UK firms were controlled by such 'constellations of interest'. There has been a growing concentration in strategic decision-making power precisely because of this trend. We would agree with Scott[3] that:

> . . . the growth of 'institutional shareholding' has resulted in the rise to dominance of a relatively small group of enterprises involved in fund management. Clearing banks, merchant banks, insurers and investment groups, together with a handful of large industrial pension schemes, *have achieved a virtual monopoly over the mobilization of capital.*

This 'monopoly' over key investment and disinvestment decisions lies not only with a small group of companies but with a small group of key decision-makers within them. Moreover there are considerable links between these key 'controllers'. Several pivotal merchant banks and investment groups remain under family control. Thus a very small elite take decisions that, directly and indirectly, affect the (earned and unearned) incomes of the great majority of the population.

The criteria on which these investment and disinvestment decisions are taken are, therefore, critically important. Pension fund managers, for example, are legally obliged to seek the maximum rate of return on their investments' to maximise returns to those drawing pensions. Despite some revival in profits in the UK, this led to further internationalisation of their investments in the 1980s. Their success in this was reflected in booming profits and contributions 'holidays' (periods when contributions were waived) for some pension funds in 1986–87. There is a clear conflict between seeking to maximise the incomes of pensioners (or at least some of them, as there are class differences which affect *which* pensioners benefit from the activities of these companies) and the numbers of jobs, and the wages and conditions attached to them, in the UK.

Growing foreign investment by pension funds in the 1980s should not just be interpreted as a UK-specific 'Thatcher effect'. It also reflected a broader global tendency to deregulation, though one that Thatcherism helped set in train and has encouraged. Moreover, there is a long history of foreign investment by UK capital and investment in the UK by foreign capital. This was historically related to the UK's imperial role. Since 1979, however, the scale of these activities has increased, with an expansion of overseas investment and of foreign investment in the UK in direct response to government policies. Investment abroad by UK-based banks, finance houses and manufacturing concerns soared after 1979, especially in the USA, while there was a smaller inflow of multinational investment into the UK. A survey of investment patterns in 1988 by the KPMG international accountancy firm revealed that investment outside the UK by UK-based companies was still increasing. It greatly exceeded, both absolutely and relatively, international investment by the UK's main competitors – Japan, F.R. Germany, the USA, France (*Financial Times*, 13 March 1989).

This growing two-way movement of capital was seen by Mrs Thatcher's government as important in reinforcing the role of the City of London as a global banking and financial centre. Underpinned by high interest and sterling exchange rates, and encouraged by the restructuring of financial markets driven by the catalyst of the 'big bang', foreign capital flowed in. This was also seen as central to 'solving' the problems of manufacturing in the UK. In particular, inward direct investment by Japanese capital was intended to engender new working practices and increased productivity, whilst UK companies were free to locate abroad in search of greater profits. In turn, these could be repatriated to help alleviate pressures on the balance of payments once the visible account slid into deficit, especially as North Sea oil revenues declined. For others, however, an increasingly deregulated, open and internationalised economy posed problems rather than offered solutions; profits were repatriated from the UK, technological dependence deepened, and more jobs and wages became dependent upon decisions by 'foreign' transnationals.

It is perhaps too early to reach a conclusive judgement as to the merits of the Thatcherite strategy. The burgeoning balance-of-payments deficit by mid-1988 (well before any major decline in North Sea oil production), growing import penetration and falling competitiveness of exports raise serious question-marks about its effectiveness, even in its own terms. What is less debatable is that growing international capital flows have implications as to where unearned incomes arise, how and between whom they are distributed, for the income levels of those reliant upon pension fund performance, and for opportunities for waged work in the UK. A growing number of companies and individuals are dependent upon a very small number of key decision-makers for the forms and levels of their money incomes. These key decision-makers are influential in the creation and remoulding of inequalities.

Big firms, small firms and their owners

An important part of this *political* strategy of Thatcherism was, partially and selectively, to reverse previous trends towards big companies and institutional ownership. This was to be achieved via the encouragement of new small firms and mass share ownership as part of a new enterprise culture. Although the economy has increasingly been dominated by 'big' companies, small firms and their owners, though reduced in importance, have not disappeared. Nurturing them has been central to the politics of Thatcherism. The petite bourgeoisie has important ideological effects, if only because it is the custodian of certain 'core' capitalist values. Proprietors tend to emphasise the desirability of the market, personal ownership and profit as rational resource allocation mechanisms. This is reflected politically by right-wing parties which, in turn, shape the parameters of political debate, and so the core elements of the political culture.

The petite bourgeoisie is, however, a very heterogeneous group.[4] This has implications for the class positions of its members and also for how they obtain their incomes. It also raises another point. There is considerable emphasis in the political economy of Thatcherism upon policies to encourage the formation and growth of small firms. Specific initiatives, such as the Enterprise Allowance Scheme, and changes in taxation, have been introduced to encourage this. Undoubtedly, creating an 'enterprise culture' is a project that simultaneously involves economic and class restructuring within the UK. But the very heterogeneity of the mélange of groupings which comprise petite bourgeoisie imply that it is not obvious what promoting 'small firms' would in practice mean.

Against this background, we consider some empirical evidence about small firms and the petite bourgeoisie. In 1980 about 5 per cent of the population were self-employed workers (mostly non-professionals) and 2 per cent were small-business owners (employing 1–24 employees). Small-business owners and the non-professional self-employed were drawn from a narrow range of social backgrounds. There is considerable inter-generational transfer of small firms and sources of self-employment. Moreover, manufacturing was conspicuous by its absence from the activities of both small-business owners and the self-employed. Services of various types were by far the dominant areas of activity. This situation in 1980 markedly contrasts with the political claims that technologically-sophisticated manufacturing forms the core of the small firm sector.

To what extent have more and new sorts of small firms sprung up in the 1980s? This is not an easy question definitively to answer, for government statistics simply do not provide an up-to-date picture of self-employment. Data from the *Labour Force Survey* have become available which estimate growth as follows: 1981–83, 51,000; 1983–84, 275,000; 1984–85, 115,000; 1985–86, 17,000. This led to suggestions that there was a 'one off' burst of growth in 1983–85, as an adjustment to the new political economy of Thatcherism, with self-employment levelling out at around 2.6 million people, 11 per cent of the labour force. Preliminary results from the 1987 *Labour Force Survey* suggest a renewed increase of 234,000 in self-employment between 1986 and 1987, heavily concentrated in transport (reflecting deregulation), construction (a booming house market) and various services, like hairdressing and dry cleaning. Thatcherite policies have, therefore, in many ways reinforced pre-1979 patterns of small firm growth rather than radically altered them.

Claims that a new spirit of enterprise is making its mark on the economy ought to be treated with considerable scepticism. Some government policies do encourage small firm formation and growth. Others, however, such as high interest rates, contribute to the existing difficulties of small firm survival, let alone growth. As yet, at least, the evidence does not suggest a dramatic revival and expansion into new innovative activities of the petite bourgeoisie in the UK in the 1980s. Rather it suggests a limited growth of service sector activities, providing low monetary incomes both to employees of small firms, their employers and the self-employed alike.

There are good reasons for questioning the sort of economy that such small firm growth produces and for believing that it is unlikely to become very different in future. The concentration of small firms and self-employment into particular segments of the service sector is not accidental; rather it is structured by the niches into which they are able to fit within the economy. There are definite relations between big and small capitals which structure the sorts of activities and sectors of the economy to which the latter are confined.

The 'independence' and 'autonomy' provided by becoming a small business person is, typically, more illusory than real. Many small businesses are set-up as a defensive response to the reality or threat of unemployment or to the terms and conditions of employment in big business. In this sense, the 1980s may have witnessed a broadening of the social base of new small firm owners, reducing the importance of inherited wealth as the criteria for becoming a small business person. These small firms are typically established in sectors of the economy where the monetary rewards will not necessarily be great. Indeed, study after study has revealed that maximising income may well not be the prime motivation for setting up such businesses. In most cases, establishing a small business is part of an individual or household survival strategy, and one that has definite limits to it, even though it holds out the promise of great wealth for some, such as professionals. Although the economic impact of small firms may be marginal, there are considerable ideological effects which make the promotion of independent, self-reliant small businesses central to Mrs Thatcher's *political* project.

Popular capitalism in a share-owning democracy?

Encouraging the growth of mass share ownership and reversing the trends of previous decades – which saw a decline from 2.5 million individual shareholders in the 1950s to 1.75 million in 1981 – is another important element in this project. Mrs Thatcher's governments set out via legislation and privatisation (offering shares at very attractive prices), to alter the climate for individual shareholding. As with so many aspects of Thatcherism, however, the seeds for this were sown by the preceding Labour government, as a result of the Lib.–Lab. pact in 1977–78. The Liberals secured the introduction of profit-sharing legislation with tax incentives, part of their price for supporting Mr Callaghan's government.

The succeeding Conservative government rapidly reinforced this initial breakthrough. In 1980 it granted tax incentives to a Save As You Earn employee share option scheme and, in 1984, brought in a share option scheme for executives. The introduction of the Personal Equity Plan (PEP) scheme at the beginning of 1987 represented a further mechanism to try to 'deepen' wider share ownership. Up to £2,400 per annum may be invested and, subject to a short qualifying period, no tax is payable on re-invested dividends or capital gains. By September 1987, 200,000 people had taken out PEPs, investing £350 million – on an average of £1,750. It is mostly those who are already relatively wealthy who take advantage of such schemes.

As well as these specific measures, more general tax changes were designed to boost individual share ownership by the more wealthy: for example, cutting the top rate of income tax from 83 per cent to 60 per cent and then to 40 per cent; abolishing the 15 per cent investment income surcharge; and halving the rate of stamp duty to 1 per cent. As a result of introducing inflation adjustment for capital gains tax, and increasing the tax threshold sixfold, only the wealthiest or most successful shareholders now pay it. Furthermore, the government's privatisation programme has played the decisive role in its attempt to encourage mass share ownership and not just a revival of personal shareholding amongst the affluent middle and upper classes. This becomes clear if we examine changes in patterns of personal shareholding.

First, consider the extent to which the 1984 share option scheme increased shareholdings by senior managers and company executives. It allows companies to offer them options worth up to four times their salary. The beneficiaries of the scheme are liable only to Capital Transfer Tax, not income tax, on any gains that they make, provided they wait three years before exercising their options. It has increased the already considerable shareholdings of these groups. In its first twenty-one months, the Inland Revenue approved 1,134 option schemes. By 1988 a majority of senior executives participated in such

Table 2.3   Executives holding share options, 1987

Company turnover £m	Percentage of:	
	Main board directors	Senior managers
1–40	62	21
40–150	76	28
150–300	88	20
300–1000	77	38
1001 +	97	70

Source: M. Skapinker and N. Tait, 'Worth taking the knocks', *Financial Times*, 28 November 1988

Table 2.4   Management buy-outs, 1967–88

	Number	Value £m	Average value, £m
1967–76	43	na	na
1977	13	na	na
1978	23	na	na
1979	52	26	0.50
1980	100	40	0.40
1981	170	120	0.71
1982	190	235	1.21
1983	200	230	1.15
1984	190	260	1.37
1985	230	1,030	4.48
1986	270	1,230	4.56
1987	300	2,820	9.40
1988 (1st 9 mths)	210	2,330	11.10

N.B. These data are estimates.
Source: W. Dawkins (1967–79 data), 'Buy-outs in 1985 put at £930m', *Financial Times*, 5 July 1986; N. Tait (1980–88 data), 'Specialists eye UK', *Financial Times*, 13 October 1988

schemes. For comparison, in over seven years, only 507 profit-sharing schemes were introduced and in over five years only 494 Save As You Earn schemes were taken up. Growing shareholding amongst senior managers as well as board directors, especially in bigger companies (Table 2.3), has resulted in their growing reliance upon a share of profits rather than merely their (often considerable) wages for their monetary incomes. These newly-acquired options are not without some risk, as the October 1987 stock market crash revealed. Even so, the potential gains, for some, are enormous. Sir Ralph Halpern, Chairman of the Burton Group, exercised options on 545,000 shares at 23p. and then sold the shares at 321p. – making £1.6 million profit.[5]

For many managers a logical extension of increased shareholding has been a management buy-out, especially when 'their' company has been faced with closure. These too have grown rapidly in the 1980s (Table 2.4). Clearly many buy-outs represent a form of small firm formation under new ownership but the average size of buy-out is increasing; October 1987 witnessed the largest (to date) management buy-out in the UK, with the sale of the MFI furniture group by ASDA for £715 million. There is a growing tendency for bought-out companies to be floated on the stock market, especially the unlisted securities market, to fund future growth. Those who become new owners via management buy-outs – not all of whom would necessarily have previously been shareholders – undergo a transition that has profound implications for their class position and source of monetary income.

Without doubt, however, privatisation has been the main mechanism for encouraging and, in some respects, successfully attaining more widespread share ownership and the growth of 'popular capitalism'

Table 2.5 Britain's shareholder profile, 1983–87

(a) Total share ownership		%	number (approx)
	1983 (pre BT)	5	2.0
	1984 (post BT)	8	3.2
	1986 (post TSB)	17	7.0
	1987 (post Gas)	23	9.4
(b) Number of companies invested in		%	number (approx) millions
	one	56	5.4
	two	22	2.1
	three	9	0.8
	four	8	0.8
	five	3	0.3

(c) Percentage of shareholders in different socio-economic groups	1983	1987	83/7 change
Professionals, employers and managers	56	29	– 27
Intermediate and junior non-manual	26	34	+ 8
Skilled manual	12	26	+ 14
Semi-skilled and unskilled manual	6	11	+ 5
Total	100	100	

Source: M. Marckus, 'Whither Maggie's army of capitalists?', *Observer*, 25 October 1987

(Table 2.5). Between 1983 and 1987 the proportion of the population owning shares rose from 5 per cent to 23 per cent; shareholding became much more evenly spread over both age groups and socio-economic groups. Forty per cent of shareholders in the newly-privatised companies were manual workers, for example. Clearly the government has successfully convinced many people, via its massive advertising campaigns, of the merits of taking up underpriced shares. This has often been in monopolistic companies such as British Telecom or British Gas which have a direct impact on their daily lives. Syd has not been without influence.

On the other hand, mass share ownership remains a thin veneer rather than something that is deeply embedded in the fabric of the nation. The government is acutely aware of the need to 'deepen' share ownership if 'popular capitalism' is to be firmly established. It still has a long way to go, however. In particular, 56 per cent of shareholders hold shares in only one company, and 22 per cent in only two, mostly acquired via privatisation. The greatest volume and value of shares remains heavily concentrated in a small number of individuals and families. Moreover, despite the widening of the share-owning base, the proportion of shares that were personally owned fell further to 1986.

Whilst wider share ownership marginally alters the source of monetary income for many people, great inequalities remain in share ownership, strategic decision-making power and access to unearned incomes. To some extent, the government would like to narrow these inequalities. Deepening share ownership and 'sedimenting' it more widely throughout the population is vital to securing the permanent establishment of the 'enterprise culture' and to bringing Mrs Thatcher's own cultural revolution to fruition. The government is under no illusions as to the importance of 'deepening' share ownership. Mr Lawson, the Chancellor of the Exchequer, is keen to promote direct ownership of shares for political reasons, so that the investor (and potential Tory voter) is more closely involved in the capitalist economy. This eloquently illustrates the ideological and political implications of promoting 'popular capitalism'. As with the promotion of small firms, encouraging mass share ownership represents a strategy for class restructuring in the UK in the 1980s.

Working for a wage: Wage labour and money incomes

Despite recent falls in the number of employees in employment and Mrs Thatcher's attempts to create an enterprise culture and popular capitalism, the vast majority of the UK population must work for a wage or depend upon the wages of others. There have been and still are great variations between industries and occupations in the ways in which people experience wage work, in their forms and levels of wage incomes, terms and conditions of employment, and the extent to which employees are subject to or exercise authority in the workplace.

The changing pattern of industrial employment.

We begin by summarising the main points about these labour market changes prior to 1979. Total employees in employment fell from a peak in 1966, to a low point in 1973, and then rose somewhat sporadically to another peak in 1979. Mining and manufacturing employment declined significantly and consistently after 1966; industries were differentiated by the rate at which employment shrank. In contrast, service employment grew, both in the public and private sectors, though within this very heterogeneous category there was great variation. Service sector expansion was associated with declining male and growing female employment and declining full-time and growing part-time employment. There was also growing low wage employment in sectors such as distribution, professional and scientific services (education, health) and miscellaneous services.

There are undoubtedly great, and changing, variations in wage levels within manufacturing and the services. However, as successive *New Earnings Surveys* reveal, in broad terms there had already been an important further shift towards a service-based economy prior to 1979, with a greater preponderance of poorly paid part-time jobs (typically taken by married women). In part, this was encouraged by state policies towards employers' national insurance contributions, taxation policies and the exclusion of part-time workers from basic 'fringe' benefits such as sickness benefit, holiday entitlement and pension rights. To some extent feminist demands for jobs that are more appropriate to the needs of people with child care responsibilities, as well as trades union demands for a shorter working week and less overtime, also accelerated the growth of part-time work.

Since 1979 the labour market tendencies established over the preceding years have been both reinforced and modified as a result of Thatcherite policies (Table 2.6). Between 1979 and 1983, as a direct result of government economic policies, there was a collapse of full-time employment in manufacturing. This was mainly a loss of relatively well-paid jobs, although in manufacturing industries such as clothing and footwear, manual workers are poorly paid. Service sector employment was, in aggregate, stable but with a further switch from full-time to low wage part-time work. Overall, the number of people in employment fell by almost 9 per cent in four years.

This aggregate decline was partially reversed in the next four years. Full-time male employment in manufacturing fell only marginally – a slowing down that reflected the scale of the preceding 'shake out'. Female full-time employment grew rather more. The major areas of growth were in the services, especially of part-time work for women. By 1987 almost one quarter of employees in employment worked part-time, whereas only one sixth had done so in 1979.

Table 2.6   Changes in employees in employment, 1979–87, thousands, seasonally adjusted

	1979	December of: 1983	1987
Total	22,670	20,670	21,474
Full-time	28,787	16,031	16,232
male	13,172	10,847	10,744
female	5,615	5,185	5,488
Part-time	3,883	4,639	5,242
male	n.a.	798	921
female	3,883	3,841	4,321
Service industries	13,328	13,337	14,672
Manufacturing industries	7,053	5,349	5,028
Other industries	2,289	1,984	1,774

Source: Training Commission, *Labour Market Quarterly Report*, Sheffield, July 1988

Service sector growth in part resulted from government policies to promote the City of London as a global financial centre. Almost one half of all employment growth since 1979 has been in financial services, not all of which have been full-time or well paid jobs, not least in the City itself. Much of the remaining service sector growth reflects the creation of a different sort of private sector service economy. Employment is characterised by a growth of part-time poorly paid jobs (facilitated by the dismantling of Wages Councils) concentrated in retailing, distribution, hotels and catering; the latter are linked to growing leisure and tourism industries. In addition, there has been revived growth in employment in personal services. The increased wealth of the new middle classes, based on two-income professional households, has led to demands for domestic cleaners, nannies, au pairs, and housekeepers, articulating new links between new middle and new working classes. This exemplifies the growing dichotomy within the service sector: some well-paid full-time jobs, but many more poorly paid ones, both part-time and full-time.

These labour market changes have had important repercussions on trades unions, with a great fall in union membership. Between 1979 and 1985 manufacturing employment fell by 13 per cent but trades union membership in manufacturing employment fell by 24 per cent. This was because job losses were concentrated in the heavily unionised 'old' manufacturing industries, such as shipbuilding, steel and engineering. 'New' manufacturing jobs were often in non-union plants as union membership was traded-off against higher, wages and enhanced fringe benefits. For example, 63 per cent of electronics plants in Scotland's

'Silicon Glen' and 86 per cent of high-tech health care companies in Scotland are non-unionised. Moreover, employment gains have been concentrated in non-union service industries. Furthermore, there has been an unprecedented legislative assault on trades unions by the Thatcher government. The unions have not, however, been passive objects in this changing pattern of labour demand and have, for example, actively competed with one another for sole negotiating rights in one-union plants. But these changes undoubtedly have posed great problems of organisation for them in attempts to protect jobs, wages and working conditions, and in politically representing their members' interests.

The changing pattern of occupations

There have been important changes in the occupational pattern over a long period. There were four main ones between 1971 and 1981: increased professional and managerial jobs, both for men and women; growth in routine clerical jobs, with a decline in male employment being more than offset by a growth in female employment; a decline in male jobs in manufacturing substantial losses of male jobs in unskilled labouring and in transport. The effects of these are clearly revealed in Table 2.7, which summarises the position in 1981. This is as near an approximation as it is possible to get to the start of Mrs Thatcher's period of office, using available statistics. The vast majority of employees – over 80 per cent – hold occupations that lack any significant degree of authority, though with important differences between men and women. Even so, there was considerable differentiation in the occupational structure of the wage-earning middle and working classes. Junior non-manual workers (mainly female) stood in a different position in the labour market to (mainly male) skilled manual workers, for example. By 1981 then, a strongly differentiated occupational pattern in terms of types and conditions of jobs had evolved, different in important ways from the equally strongly differentiated pattern of a decade earlier.

Incomes, rewards and deprivations

Before 1979 occupational differences in incomes tended to narrow, although they remained of considerable magnitude (as Table 2.8 shows). Male income differentials between occupational groups have expanded dramatically since 1979, however, in strong contrast to the preceding years. Over the period 1973–79, occupational groups which had a fall in real earnings were all towards the top of the incomes distribution. In sharp contrast, between 1979 and 1986 these groups received the largest increases; more generally, non-manual occupational groups received greater relative real earnings increases than did manual ones. This difference continued to widen between 1986 and 1987. This

Table 2.7   Persons economically active, by socio-economic group, 1981 (percentages)

Socio-economic group (SEG)	Men	Women	Total
1 Employers and managers in central and local government, industry, commerce etc. large establishments	5.5	2.1	4.1
2 Employers and managers in industry, commerce, etc. small establishments	8.7	4.3	7.0
3 Professional workers: self-employed	0.9	0.1	0.6
4 Professional workers: employees	4.5	0.9	3.1
5 Intermediate non-manual workers	7.3	14.4	10.1
6 Junior non-manual workers	9.5	37.3	20.3
7 Personal-service workers	1.1	12.2	5.4
8 Fore'men' and supervisors: manual	3.6	0.7	2.5
9 Skilled manual workers	26.3	4.0	17.6
10 Semi-skilled manual workers	13.6	10.4	12.3
11 Unskilled manual workers	5.8	6.7	6.2
12 Own account workers (other than professional)	5.3	1.8	4.0
13 Farmers: employers and managers	0.7	0.1	0.5
14 Farmers: own account	0.7	0.1	0.5
15 Agricultural workers	1.2	0.5	1.0
16 Members of armed forces	1.6	0.2	1.0
17 Inadequately described and not stated occupations	3.5	4.2	3.8
Total	99.8	100	100
Total number	15,527,000	9,879,000	25,406,000

Source: Census of Population (1981), Economic Activity in Great Britain, Table 17, HMSO

points to a growing differentiation between the middle and working classes and to persistent divisions within the working class in terms of wages. Despite more rapid growth in the 1980s, wages in many non-manual occupations (especially for women) remain far below those in manual occupations (especially for men). The main point, however, is that the overall distribution has widened significantly since 1979. In 1979 a worker in the top 10 per cent of the income distribution earned,

Table 2.8 Changes in earnings for occupational groups, 1973–87

	Av. wage, £ 1973	% change 1973–79	% change 1979–86	Av. wage, £ 1986
By gender				
Males – manual	157.1	5.0	5.7	174.4
– non-manual	190.0	1.0	22.4	244.9
Females – manual	82.6	20.5	8.0	107.5
– non-manual	104.2	14.9	21.7	145.7
Selected Occupational Groupings				
Professional, management & admin.	243.4	– 4.8	28.7	298.2
Managerial (exc. general management)	206.8	– 1.0	20.6	246.8
Clerical	142.9	2.6	16.7	171.0
Catering, cleaning and other personal services	123.6	5.7	8.7	142.0
Farming and fishing	117.1	4.0	6.4	129.5
Making and repairing (exc. metal and electrical)	166.9	– 0.8	7.0	177.2
Painting and assembling	157.1	3.2	3.2	167.4
Construction and mining	159.8	4.9	3.0	172.6
Transport and storage	154.9	7.1	4.0	172.4

Note: Average wage is calculated in real terms with respect to 1986 levels, and refers to gross weekly adult male earnings
Source: M. Adams, R. Maybury and W. Smith, 'Trends in the distribution of earnings, 1973–86', *Employment Gazette*, February 1988, pp. 75–82

on average, 2.33 times as much as one in the bottom 10 per cent; by 1987 this had increased to 3.0 times as much.

As income inequalities have grown so sharply in the 1980s, we will look in greater depth at those occupations associated with particularly high and low wages. The Royal Commission on the Distribution of Incomes and Wealth (1976) revealed that, in 1974–75, 65,000 individuals had annual incomes of £10,000 or more, representing about 0.3 per cent of those receiving employment income. High wage earners were concentrated in general management (55 per cent) and in professional and related occupations supporting management (including lawyers, company secretaries, accountants, marketing and advertising managers), administrative civil servants, local government officers and so on. Many of this group experienced a slight fall in income in the remainder of the 1970s, but these occupations, especially those in the private sector, generally experienced large wage increases in the 1980s. They remain those in which incomes are highest, often very high

Table 2.9 Remuneration of company executives and senior managers, 1988

Type of job	Average total money £	Full use of company car %	Percentage of holders of each type of job who receive the following							Bonus as % of recipients' avge. salary %
			Subsidised private telephone %	Help with housing %	Life assurance %	Free medical insurance %	Share option scheme %	Loans at low interest %	Bonus %	
Managing director	57,196	99.2	60.6	20.1	95.6	89.0	100.0	6.3	57.6	20.6
General manager	41,871	99.4	48.4	30.0	97.7	88.8	98.7	16.3	54.1	18.4
Financial exec.	30,773	88.1	38.5	12.6	95.3	82.9	80.8	7.2	49.2	14.3
Marketing exec.	26,978	91.9	37.8	11.8	94.7	79.0	66.7	6.8	48.0	12.4
Production exec.	26,060	85.2	44.0	9.3	93.5	81.3	71.8	2.6	51.0	13.2
Chief engineer	21,025	64.8	39.8	6.8	94.9	69.9	64.4	3.0	44.1	8.1
All jobs 1988	29,642	83.9	39.7	11.3	94.8	79.0	75.0	6.4	48.6	14.7
All jobs 1987	26,043	79.8	40.2	10.6	93.8	76.4	64.3	7.9	43.7	13.8

Figures for share option schemes are inflated because various types of scheme are in opertion and several executives benefit from more than one type.

Source: M. Dixon, 'Latest indicators of main executive perks', *Financial Times*, 5 October 1988

Table 2.10 The highest paid company directors in the United Kingdom, 1988

	Highest paid directors Earnings over £400,000	
Sir Ralph Halpern	Burton Group	1,359,000*
Christopher Heath	Baring Brothers	1,339,219
Lord Hanson	Hanson Trust	1,263,000*
+	Robert Fleming	1,238,000
+	Anglo Leasing	1,205,000
John Gunn	British & Commonwealth	988,647*
Robert Noonan	Marrier Estates	935,463
Sir John Nott	Lazard Brothers	816,731*
Richard Giordano	BOC Group	782,300*
Herve de Carmoy	Midland Bank	748,458
Robert Bauman	Beecham	693,474
'Tiny' Rowland	Lonrho	656,251
Michael Slade	Helical Bar	653,000
+	WCRS Group	622,000
George Davies	Next	561,152*
Maurice Saatchi	Saatchi & Saatchi	500,000*

Figures relate to most recent financial year. * Chairman; + Highest paid director.
Source: M. Skapinker, 'Burton's chief regains title of highest paid executive', *Financial Times*, 5 October 1988

indeed. On average, almost 15 per cent of their pay is in the form of profit-related bonuses rather than basic salary, as Table 2.9 shows. For the very highest earners in company boardrooms – who receive astronomical salaries, as is shown in Table 2.10 – the performance-related payments assume much greater significance. Increasingly, they are the key factor that enables boardroom base salaries to rise at around twice the rate of those of the workforce as a whole.

In contrast, selling, catering, and cleaning figure prominently among those occupations characterised by low incomes. These are precisely the sorts of jobs that expanded rapidly in the 1980s. These are industries characterised by a plethora of small, labour-intensive firms in competition with one another, with little unionisation and, at best, weak collective bargaining. This is a combination that is strongly associated with low wages. The Thatcherite emphases upon encouraging small firms, weakening trades unions, people 'pricing themselves into jobs' and creating a service economy are all integrally linked to the incidence and persistence of low pay. Together they form a potent recipe for the expansion of a low-wage, labour-intensive service economy.

Wages are only one form of monetary reward for work, however.

There are also other 'fringe benefits', very unevenly distributed between occupational groups. There were marked differences between occupational groups in entitlements to holidays with pay, sick pay and private pension schemes prior to 1979. Generally, manual workers had much less access to such benefits than did non-manual workers. Within the non-manual group, rights to these benefits increased with status and responsibility. In the 1980s, this gap widened. 'Fringe benefits' became an increasingly important way of distinguishing between employees. Many company executives and senior managers receive a wide range of such benefits: company cars or car allowances; subsidised lunches; subsidised private telephones; life assurance; free medical insurance (Table 2.10). It is noticeable that financial executives fare much better than production executives and engineers, a telling comment upon the priorities of the Thatcherite economy. For all such executives, however, 'fringe benefits' impinge on many aspects of their life-styles and the extent to which they remain 'on the fringe' is debatable. Whilst other non-manual workers received less in both the range and amount of such benefits, in general they remained in a more favourable position than manual workers.

Despite some slight reductions since 1945, a 'clear class gradient' remained in 1979 in terms of incomes and rewards.[6] After 1979, the class gradient becomes steeper, with sharper differences between occupational groupings of employees, a consequence of the political economy of Thatcherism.

Further differences between wage earners

Changing corporate strategies and government policies as to the composition of the workforce and forms of remuneration are widening income differences between occupational groupings in other ways. Such growing divisions reflect three related sorts of processes of labour market changes in the 1980s: the emergence of more sharply differentiated and multiply-segmented labour markets; the continued development of internal labour markets within big companies; a growing dichotomy between core and peripheral workers in the labour forces of big and small companies alike.

Companies are increasingly recognising the importance of constructing a committed core workforce by using a 'responsible autonomy' managerial strategy. An important mechanism in creating this commitment is to increase employee share ownership and to link pay to performance and profit. On average, in 1987–88 companies paid over 16 per cent more to 'above average' as compared to 'adequate' graduate employees within five years of recruiting them. These performance premiums varied widely between sectors, from 7 per cent in construction to 21 per cent in technical and scientific services. Companies are beginning to adopt profit-related wages across the whole range of their employees, not just senior managers and highly skilled employees in short supply. By the end of 1987, almost a hundred companies had registered schemes for profit-related pay with the Inland Revenue in response to provisions made in the 1987 Finance Act for tax relief on 50 per cent of profit-related pay. By early 1988 this had risen sharply to 430, covering 70,000 employees. Even so, as yet such schemes affect only a tiny minority of workers but they will become more influential if these rates of adoption continue.

This growth in performance and profit-related payments, often related to the introduction of decentralised wage bargaining, not only further differentiates between core and peripheral workers but also creates division *within* the former group. Moreover, such changes are also related to redefinition of working practices, intensification of work, increased demands for flexible working and so on. While providing a way of producing divisions within the bulk of the core workforce, performance-related payments have also enabled the gap between directors and senior managers and the rest of the workforce to grow. In addition, senior managers receive 'fringe benefits' denied to other employees. They sharply differentiate their recipients from workers who receive performance-related wage payments but are excluded from the lucrative world of fringe benefits.

The occupants of the core workforce fill more secure niches in the labour market than do those in the peripheral workforce. There is such great variety in the terms and conditions on which waged work is offered in this, often hidden, world of peripheral workers, that it is dangerous to generalise about it. The UK's growing army of part-timers, temporary workers, houseworkers and the self-employed – 'the so-called "flexible labour force"' – expanded by 1.15 million (16 per cent) between 1981 and 1985. Of this increase, 828,000 (72 per cent) was recorded between 1983 and 1985 and over 700,000 (60 per cent) was of temporary workers. These trends have since continued, though at a slower pace. There was an increase between 1984 and 1987 of 91,000 (7 per cent) temporary workers and of 133,000 (19 per cent) workers with second jobs, mainly as employees. These data must be treated as conservative estimates, as many workers may not declare second jobs and this shades into the 'black economy'. Whilst many women and fewer men did not want a permanent job, many others, especially men (almost 40 per cent), accepted temporary work of necessity rather than choice.

Casual and fixed-term contract workers differ in their personal characteristics and in the industries and occupations in which they are most concentrated. Casual workers are most prevalent in three industries: distribution, hotels and repairs: agriculture; other services. Fixed-contract workers are concentrated in other services and construction. In terms of occupations, 25 per cent of all casual workers had jobs in catering and cleaning. The remainder mostly work in sales or in professional posts in health, welfare and education. Contract workers are more evenly distributed but with a concentration in teaching. Thus the growth of a service-based economy in the 1980s has been closely linked to the growth of casual working, although casual employment has long been endemic in service industries such as retailing, catering, hotels, pubs and clubs. More surprising has been the re-emergence of casualised work in some branches of manufacturing, such as steel. Such particularly stark instances of the re-creation of casualised work revive memories of an earlier and harsher era.

Many companies have taken advantage of persistent high unemployment to recruit staff directly on a casual basis, often at very low wage rates. To some extent, they have been aided in this by legislative changes. The 1986 Wages Act removed about 500,000 workers below the age of 21 from the protection of Wages Councils, and confined the latter to setting a minimum hourly rate and single overtime rate. It removed casual workers' (along with new full-time employees') guaranteed access to premium rates on bank holidays. This increased the incentive to recruit young casual staff. As a direct result, there was an estimated 10 per cent increase in casual and temporary staff in the retailing sector over the Christmas 1987 period. Such staff were often paid little more than £2.00 per hour but this simply represents the seasonal expression of a more widespread practice of recruitment of cheap casual labour in retailing. More generally, in 1986 25 per cent of all casual workers were aged 16–19 years and a further 12.5 per cent were aged 20–24. Casual work is endemic among the young. For many it represents their only chance of waged employment in the UK of the 1980s.

Casualisation is not the only way in which divisions between core and peripheral workers, and within the peripheral workforce, have been re-drawn. Sub-contracting has expanded greatly. Manufacturing output rose by 35 per cent between 1979 and 1984 but services purchased by manufacturing companies increased by 56 per cent, indicating considerable growth in sub-contracting. Half of the increase in service sector employment between 1979 and 1985 resulted from increasing sub-contracting from manufacturing. A 1987 survey in the West Midlands revealed that 39 per cent of workplaces had experienced replacement of directly employed labour by contractors. Increasingly, sub-contracting is being institutionalised as a *planned* part of companies' production strategies, increasing competition between sub-contractors. As a result, wages and working conditions for those employed in such companies have deteriorated.

In branches of manufacturing such as clothing and service activities such as packing, homeworking has long been important but there is evidence that in the 1980s it has grown further. At the boundary homeworking shades into the 'black economy', though the latter is by no means confined to homeworking. Small-scale sub-contracting firms have made increasing use of 'off the cards' labour to cut costs and increase their flexibility in hiring and firing. There has also been some growth in 'informal' activities which provide services to those in formal employment. Electricians, joiners, painters and plumbers, themselves often already in formal employment or self employment, have found increasing scope for 'off the cards' work as other people engage in house improvement or maintenance. By definition, 'black' work is not recorded in official statistics so that it is impossible to estimate its precise extent. But it has undoubtedly grown in the 1980s.

Finally, the diverse forms of changing wage relations outlined above share one common feature; they refer to individuals and households finding waged work on some basis within the UK. For others, this has either proved impossible or, alternatively, better prospects and wages have been found by becoming temporary international migrant workers. For many professional workers, working abroad for a time has been and continues to be financially lucrative. Increasingly, however, they have been joined by construction workers or redundant skilled manual workers from chemical plants or steelworks. Such jobs abroad are usually offered on short fixed-term contracts. However, the high rates of pay – even after agents' fees have been deducted – make them attractive, especially to younger men able to earn wages that were formerly unimaginable in the UK. This, then, represents an individualised response to the reality or threat of unemployment but it is an escape route that is denied to the vast majority, as we show in the next section.

On the dole

A commitment to 'full employment' was central to the post-war settlement. Between 1944 and 1975 governments of both parties sought to achieve this objective, though by varying means. At times, its pursuit came into conflict with other policy objectives, such as maintaining a satisfactory balance-of-payments position. The long post-war boom meant that these conflicts between policy objectives could effectively be masked, however. For most of the period between 1945 and 1970, unemployment rates in the UK were less than 3 per cent with never more than 600,000 people registered as unemployed. Following a sharp increase to 900,000 in 1972, unemployment was falling in 1973–74 until there was a fundamental change in governments' views on the priority to be given to 'full employment'.

In 1975 it became clear that the choices between competing government policy options had become harder and could no longer be fudged. No longer could the cracks be papered over. The old Keynesian orthodoxy collapsed as international recession and deep structural weaknesses in the UK economy severely restricted the government's room for manoeuvre. The April 1975 Budget confirmed that government economic strategy now centred on restraining the growth of public expenditure, cuts in real wages for most workers, and rising unemployment as deliberate policy choices. The Budget statement correctly forecast that registered unemployment would rise to over one million for the first time in thirty years because of the policies it contained: thus was the commitment to 'full employment' jettisoned.

Unemployment fell somewhat in the final year of the Labour government, but it began to soar after the election of Mrs Thatcher's government in 1979, reaching well over 3 million. Unemployment became a much more widespread problem in the UK than in other major capitalist countries (Table 1.1). Registered unemployment began to decline in the mid-1980s from its earlier giddy heights, but the fall owes much to a series of 28 changes in the definition of unemployment. From 1982, for example, only those claiming unemployment benefit, as opposed to all those fit and able to work, were counted in the register. Even allowing for this downward massaging of the totals, registered unemployment remains at a very high level – around 2.3 million in May 1988. This considerably underestimates total unemployment. Even before the major change of definition in 1982, the Manpower Services Commission estimated that the actual number of unemployed exceeded the registered figure by 25 per cent. Moreover, long-term unemployment has grown sharply: by April 1988, over half a million people had been unemployed for three or more years.

Prior to 1979, the incidence of unemployment was unevenly distributed between members of social classes, occupational groups, ethnic minorities, age groups, men and women, and between residents of different areas. This sort of uneven distribution of unemployment, like unemployment itself, is endemic to capitalist societies. Some of these aspects of inequality are explored in later chapters; here we focus upon the unequal impact of unemployment upon members of different classes and how this has altered since 1979.

The marked class bias in the uneven incidence of unemployment has widened further in the 1980s. Manual workers (especially men) are more likely to be unemployed and less likely to secure another job because of a lack of vacancies than non-manual workers. Thus a growing proportion of the long-term unemployed is of manual workers, especially unskilled males, permanently surplus to labour demand (except for that created by temporary job schemes). This growing pool of long-term unemployed – part of an underclass, as some would see them – has become more or less solely dependent upon government welfare payments as a source of income.

This is but one aspect of class and occupational inequalities in the incidence of unemployment, however. There is also an increasing flow of people on and off the unemployed register. This involves some hundreds of thousands in any given month and is linked to the growth of casualisation, temporary contracts and sub-contracting. They occupy particularly precarious positions in the labour market, concentrated in specific occupations and industries. They form a large disadvantaged group within the working class, disproportionately susceptible to unemployment. As a result of the uneven incidence of long-term and short-term unemployment, 3 per cent of the labour force account for 70 per cent of unemployment weeks.

As they are disproportionately susceptible to unemployment, such groups are also disproportionately dependent upon state transfer payments for money incomes. There is a long history of state involvement with and, mostly inadequate, provision for the unemployed. It can be traced back to the New Poor Law of 1834 which created two of the most powerful realities within the working-class experience of welfare: the means test and the workhouse. Its abolition in 1948 was linked to the introduction of a national insurance scheme. This was to provide unemployment benefit and maintain working-class living standards in short periods of unemployment between jobs in a 'full employment' economy. In fact, means testing lingered on, for the new social security system involved two systems, each with its own level and method of distributing benefit. Payments as of right were provided to those who had bought a certain number of national insurance stamps; these could be in the form of retirement pensions or to replace earnings lost through sickness or unemployment. Many would be ineligible for such payments, however. To cater for them, a National Assistance Board (NAB) provided means-tested benefits. Because it believed that means-testing caused considerable non-take-up of benefits, the Labour government in the 1960s changed the name of the NAB to the Supplementary Benefits Commission (SBC). This was an attempt to dissociate the image of the institution from the Poor Law of the past and give the impression that it would in fact *supplement* other forms of benefit. In practice, supplementary benefit continues as an alternative for those who never were or have ceased to be eligible for unemployment benefit. Already by 1979 62 per cent of the unemployed in the UK were ineligible for unemployment benefit. This proportion has subsequently risen in parallel with youth and long-term unemployment.

The system of benefits, has assumed added significance for the incomes of the unemployed since 1979. As the cutting edge of Thatcherite policy is to encourage the market to undermine state welfare, recipients of unemployment benefit must, in some distinct way, be made worse off than those in work, and not just financially. They must be stigmatised in other ways too. Representing the unemployed as 'welfare scroungers' divides them from those in work whilst their low living-standards provide an incentive for those in work to remain there. In keeping with Mrs Thatcher's predilection for Victorian values, the legacy of the 1834 Poor Law lives on. In practice, this has led to a series of changes that have made the poor still poorer. In April 1981 earnings-related supplements for all short-term benefits (unemployment and sickness benefits, widows' and maternity allowances) were abolished. In addition, the statutory link between earnings and long-term

benefits, such as pensions, was abolished and these were only increased
in line with inflation. From July 1982 the Inland Revenue began to tax
all benefits, including unemployment and supplementary benefits. This
adversely affects those intermittently employed (as casual labour, for
example) though not those unemployed for the full tax year, as benefits
are less than personal allowances and tax thresholds. As a result of
these 1981–82 changes, benefits were cut by £2,200 million between
1979 and 1983 whilst the well-off and rich received £2,600 million in
tax cuts – a clear indication of Thatcherite priorities.

Furthermore, within the supplementary benefit system, there is
discrimination against the long-term unemployed. Long-term sick,
elderly or disabled claimants, receive a higher rate of benefit – but not
the long-term unemployed. They are regarded as less deserving cases,
unemployed from choice rather than necessity. This is certainly one of
the bleakest aspects of the attitudes of Thatcherite politicians and their
economic advisers in the 1980s.

Even so, despite the real squeeze on the value of unemployment
benefit, unemployment growth resulted in increased social security costs
as a proportion of public expenditure. This in turn helped increase
public expenditure as a proportion of GDP. Despite a decline from
1983–84, public expenditure in 1984–85 absorbed a greater percentage
of GDP than in 1979–80 – in strong contrast to the declared aims of
government economic policy. This was undoubtedly one reason for the
changes in the social security system, as proposed in 1985, replacing
supplementary benefit with income support. It lead to 1.4 million
claimants being better off but 1.7 million being worse off.

Because of the costs to public expenditure, and for other reasons, the
government has shown great interest in reducing registered unemployment by a plethora of temporary training and/or employment schemes.
It has been very successful in this: in 1985 they removed 570,000
people from the unemployment register; by 1986, this had risen to at
least 630,000. These schemes originated in the activities of the
Manpower Services Commission and the launch of the now defunct Job
Creation Programme in 1975. By the mid-1980s numerous schemes had
come and gone, with varying objectives.

Questions have been raised about the adequacy of the training on
offer and the provision of places relative to the numbers unemployed.
Despite claims by the Manpower Services Commission (now the
Employment Training Service) that quality of training was seen as a
crucial strategic issue, suspicions persist that the commitment to retrain-
ing the unemployed in new 'high-tech' skills remains a token one. For
example, the Community Programme, since its inception in 1982, has
been structured to provide part-time, poorly paid manual work. Like
similar schemes, it is more concerned to shuffle existing low-paid jobs
between a pool of unemployed, some of whom are at any one point in
time employed in this way: eight months after leaving, for example, 55

per cent of participants in Community Programme schemes were again unemployed. The main emphasis in government economic policy is on producing an expanding low wage, low productivity service economy, alongside a booming international financial services sector which can recruit key skilled employees on a global labour market if the need arises. While this remains so, there is little scope for large-scale, high quality (re)training programmes to provide highly skilled workers able to find well-paid secure jobs in manufacturing and services.

For the long-term unemployed, then, the future is one of dependency upon welfare payments, interspersed with spells on government temporary job schemes. In either case, they are 'clients of the welfare state' (or at least what is left of it), consigned to a future of minimal incomes. The long-term unemployed still bear the burdens of recession and are excluded from the benefits of renewed growth.

Although evidently aware of the political dangers of long-term unemployment, the government remains wide open to the charge that it is managing rather than resolving Britain's unemployment crisis. Governmental ambivalence reflects the actual gains as well as the potential danger that unemployment presents to it. For maintaining a 'managed' mass of unemployed – and the fear of those in employment that they might join it – provides a potent mechanism through which Thatcherite policies can be pursued. This deliberate creation of an 'underclass' of permanently unemployed, dependent upon state transfer payments in one form or another, is perhaps the most pernicious aspect of class restructuring in the UK in the 1980s.

In this chapter we have examined the way in which class relations have been redefined in various ways as part of the political-economy of Thatcherism and how this is reflected in the distribution and sources of income and wealth. At one end of this process is the 'underclass' of long-term unemployed, created and maintained by state policies. It is simultaneously managed by part of the new middle class and separated from the working class. Its existence provides a context in which there is intense competition in the labour market as mass unemployment encourages divisions within the working class. These extend far beyond a simple non-manual/manual divide and allow a redefinition of the divisions between classes. For example, managerial authority can be (re)asserted in the workplace whilst growing income inequalities provide a material basis of increasingly differentiated life-styles. Earning a wage now tends to be a much more precarious process than it once was; the trend is strongly away from full-time regular jobs with predictable wages. For many, it has involved a switch to no job at all, for others to precarious employment. The Thatcher government has encouraged these trends via its policies, informed by a view which was admirably summarised by Mr Norman Lamont, Financial Secretary to the Treasury in 1986. Mr Lamont asserted that the suggestion that employees need a guaranteed income to cope with household budgets rested on a 'misconception'. It is a misconception that the government has assiduously sought to eradicate via its policies and not without success. What must also be acknowledged is the political success of Thatcherism in blurring class boundaries whilst leaving the fundamental structures of power and property ownership in the UK, if anything, reinforced. The extension of private property ownership, via council house sales, privatisation, share option schemes and so on has above all else conveyed the image of a mass property-owning democracy. Yet in reality wealth has become increasingly unequally distributed.

Notes

1. J. Mack and S. Lansley, *Poor Britain*, (London: George Allen and Unwin, 1985), p. 183.
2. See J. Scott, *Capitalist Property and Financial Power*, (Brighton: Wheatsheaf Books, 1986).
3. J. Scott, op. cit, p. 94, emphasis added.
4. Scase (1982) points out that the petite bourgeoisie is a mixture of minor landlords, small capitalists, and the self-employed. They occupy different class positions and derive their incomes in different ways. J. Curran, R. Burrows, and M. Evandrou, *Small Business Owners and the Self-Employed in Britain: and Analysis of General Household Survey data* (London: Small Business Research Trust, 1987), stress that the self-employed are not just small business owners without, as yet, employees but are involved in the economy in different ways.
5. Reported by M. Skapinker, and N. Tait 'Worth taking the knocks' (*Financial Times*, 28 November 1987).
6. See R. Brown 'Work', in P. Abrams, and R. Brown (eds.), *UK Society: Work, Urbanism and Inequality* (London: Weidenfeld & Nicholson 1984) pp. 129–97. He summarises a wide variety of evidence on the pre-1979 patterns of rewards for and deprivations of work.

Further Reading

The distribution of income and wealth are discussed in N. Abercrombie and A. Warde, *Contemporary British Society* (Cambridge: Polity Press, 1988); Royal Commission on the Distribution of Income and Wealth, *Report No. 6* (London: HMSO, 1976); W.D. Rubinstein, *Men of Property* (London: Croom Helm, 1981) and P. Standsworth 'Elites and Privilege' in P. Abrams and R. Brown (eds.), *UK Society: Work, Urbanization and Inequality* (London: Weidenfeld & Nicholson, 1984) pp. 246–93.

D. Massey and A. Catalano. *Capital and Land: Landownership by Capital in Great Britain* (London: Edward Arnold, 1978) provide the best summary of land ownership and wealth. Although now dated, its importance as a source is a powerful testimony to the secrecy surrounding data on landownership. J. Scott, *Capitalist Property and Financial Power* (Brighton: Wheatsheaf Books, 1986) provides invaluable information on company ownership whilst R. Minns, *Pension Funds and British Capitalism* (London, 1980) examines aspects of institutional shareholding. R. Brown 'Work' and H. Wainwright 'Women and the Division of Labour' (pp. 129–197 and 198–245 respectively) in P. Abrams and R. Brown (eds.), op. cit., and S. Lonsdale, *Work and Inequality* (Harlow: Longman, 1985) discuss various aspects of employment, occupational and labour market changes. R. Hudson, 'Labour market changes and new forms of work in old industrial regions', *Society and Space* 7, (1989), 5–30 specifically discusses labour market changes in the 1980s. There is also much useful information on labour market changes in the Department of Employment's *Gazette* and the Training Commission's *Labour Market Quarterly Reports*, whilst the *New Earnings Surveys* contain a wealth of data on wages and related issues. The *Financial Times* is also a very useful source of information on many of the issues discussed in this chapter. Finally R. Hudson and A. Williams, *The United Kingdom* (London: Harper & Row, 1986) provide an overview of economic and employment changes and changes in government economic policy over the post-war period.

3
Divided by class II: consumption and life-styles

Introduction: class, consumption and life-styles

In 1957 Harold Macmillan (later Lord Stockton) remarked at a garden party in Bedford: 'Let us be frank about it. Most of our people have never had it so good'. This phrase, subtly modified, became a *leitmotif* for much of the post-war period. There has been a more or less steady increase in *average* per capita real disposable income and consumer spending (Fig 3.1). This, along with the growing number of two-income households, changes in work practices, shift patterns and increased leisure time and paid holidays, has helped change consumption norms, the division of domestic and waged labour, and household life-styles. In contrast, the relative decline in the UK's position in the international economic order in recent years has been reflected in newspaper headlines such as 'UK living standards fall in world league'.

As we have shown in chapter 2, however, incomes remained unequally distributed around this rising average trend before 1979. In the 1980s income inequalities between classes widened further. These changing inequalities are related to both stability and change in class structure: stability in the reinforced position of the landed aristocracy and industrial and financial bourgeoisie, change in the recomposition of both middle and working classes, and the emergence of an 'underclass' of permanently unemployed. In the 1980s the gap in living standards between those in employment and the unemployed has taken on an increased significance. These changes reflect the effects of economic restructuring and employment change, taxation policies and cuts in welfare benefits.

In a capitalist society, living conditions and standards fundamentally

£ 1985 prices

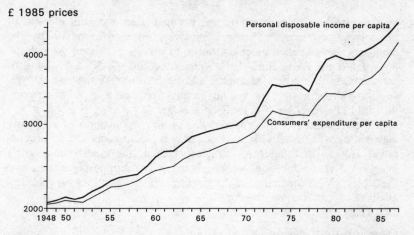

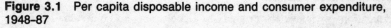

Figure 3.1 Per capita disposable income and consumer expenditure, 1948–87

Source: CSO, *Economic Trends*

depend upon money incomes and the capacity to buy goods and services in the market. Living standards are not reducible to monetary incomes, however, for there are important contributions – such as clean air, visual amenity, community, attachments to people and places – that cannot be bought and sold. The resurgence of 'green' and place-specific politics reflects this, as is illustrated vividly by the fierce battle amongst local pressure groups over the location of the rail link from London to the Channel Tunnel entrance in Kent. Nevertheless, in an economy organised around commodity production, purchasing power in the market is crucial. Not surprisingly, then, there were great variations in consumption patterns, living conditions and standards before 1979. Equally unsurprisingly, as successive *Family Expenditure Surveys* reveal, these have increased in the 1980s both directly because of widening income differentials and indirectly, as those on higher, more secure incomes have drawn more and more upon easily-available credit and 'plastic money' to boost further their spending power. Credit card debt rose from £674 million in 1983 to £964 million in 1985. By 1987, there were 13.1 million Visa cards and 11.4 million Access cards in circulation; in 1975 there had been 'only' 3.3 million and 3.1 million, respectively. Total consumer credit rose threefold from 1981 to reach £40 billion by mid-1988.

Growing differences in living standards are not just a product of widening income and credit inequalities in the 1980s, however. Divergent lifestyles also reflect a more general change in political philosophy, expressed in decreasing public sector service provision and a growing reliance upon the market in shaping the distribution of services. Partially removing the provision of educational and health services from the sphere of the market had been a central element of the post-war consensus. This was decisively reversed in the 1980s. The emphasis was switched more and more to private provision through the market. At the same time there were increasing costs at the point of consumption for those educational and health services that are, as yet, still provided through the public sector. For example, a prescription that in 1979 cost 20p, in 1988 cost 260p.

In the remainder of this chapter we examine the patterns of inequality between classes (usually defined in terms of socio-economic or occupational groups) in four crucial areas that shape the quality of people's everyday lives: education; health; housing; consumption patterns and life-styles. We conclude by examining class variations in political allegiances and voting patterns.

Class and education

Education provides a crucial link between an individual's family background and his/her own life chances and class position. Access to different amounts, levels and qualities of education reflect one's parents' social class. For most people, their formal education influences employment opportunities and class position, though for a few inherited wealth makes this relationship unimportant or irrelevant.

But how are these reciprocal links between generation, class and education to be understood? For some, the formal educational system is simply a mechanism for reproducing class structures. It constrains the places of individuals within them to those occupied by their parents, grandparents and so on down the generations. For others, it helps reproduce class structures but facilitates the movement of individuals within these. For a few, formal education offers a mechanism for progressively altering class structures themselves.

Increased state provision of educational services in the UK since the 1940s has been informed by the second of these views. No serious attempt was made, however, to abolish private fee-paying schools and the provision of education through the market for those able to purchase it. Likewise, no significant attempt has been made to abolish important qualitative differences between private and public sector provision of education. Nevertheless, state provision of and public expenditure on education was significantly increased at all levels from pre-school to higher education. This was intended to improve access to and equality of opportunity within the public sector. Equality of opportunity would provide a means to move towards a more meritocratic, even egalitarian, society. What in practice happened before 1979 is a rather different matter. In the 1980s Thatcherism has increasingly redefined 'meritocracy' in terms of ability to pay as 'merit' is rewarded through and reflected in the market for educational services.

One symptom of this is that the private sector, left substantially intact and *de facto* subsidised by the state (via tax relief on school fees) over the post-war period was the preserve of a small elite, began to expand in the 1980s. By the end of 1986, the Independent Schools Information Service claimed that independent schools had a 7 per cent share of the total school age population (compared to 2 per cent to 5 per cent before 1979) and no less than 17 per cent of the 16–18 year-old group. The numbers of pupils rose by a record 2.2 per cent in 1986, with a particularly sharp increase in pupils at the 'pre-preparatory' ages of two to seven. This was despite average fee increases that were well ahead of the rate of inflation. Typical annual charges then were £4,800 for older children boarding, £2,600 for older day pupils, £3,600 for preparatory boarders and £2,300 for preparatory day pupils. These figures in themselves are powerful evidence of the effects of class and income differentials in generating inequalities in access to such schools.

There is also strong evidence of recurrent class inequalities in access to and performance within state education at all levels. These inequalities existed prior to 1979 but have widened further in the 1980s. At pre-school level, the 1979 *General Household Survey* revealed that well over half the children of professionals, employers and managers attended playgroups or day nurseries. They were much more likely to do so than children whose parents were in semi-skilled or unskilled occupations. This gap has probably widened under Mrs Thatcher's government although the absence of comparable data in post-1979 *General Household Surveys* make a definitive judgement impossible.

This differential access by class in turn tends to reproduce and widen differences in performance. Comprehensive schools were introduced at secondary level to replace the division between grammar and secondary modern schools. Many comprehensives stream pupils by academic ability, however, which tends to reproduce class inequalities. In addition, a failure to invest in education has led to many split-site comprehensives, cobbled together from existing schools. As a result, several of the objects of comprehensive education have at best been partially attained in many schools.

Class inequalities have been magnified in two particularly important ways at secondary level. Firstly, there are enormous differences in the proportions of pupils staying on beyond minimum leaving age: 70 per cent of those whose parents are professionals, employers and managers compared to 27 per cent of those whose parents are manual workers. This is only the most striking manifestation of a more general process, however. Throughout the pupil's school career, there is a persistent class difference in survival and achievement rates. As parents' social class increases, the percentage of pupils without any formal educational qualifications decreases and the percentage with 'O' levels (or equivalent), 'A' levels and degrees rises. There is a marked division between those whose parents are in manual and non-manual occupations in the proportions who survive in and obtain formal qualifications from the educational system. This class divide has been maintained, even increased, in the 1980s as successive *General Household Surveys* reveal. It remains to be seen what effect changes in the organisation and management of schools will have on the existing class divide. In so far as they will lead to increasing differentiation between schools, as for example parent governors in middle-class areas articulate their demands more effectively than those in working-class areas, they are likely to reinforce class inequalities further.

Access to higher education shows a similar pattern of class inequality. The Robbins Report noted that children born in 1940–41 whose fathers had a professional background had a 33 times greater chance of entering higher education than those whose fathers were semi-skilled or unskilled manual workers. Although the situation has in some respects improved since then, with greatly expanded state provision, considerable inequalities remain. There are powerful pressures which militate against children from working-class families going on to higher education. For example, there are often material pressures to leave school before the sixth form to add to household incomes. For those who do stay on, there is often the problem of a working-class culture that is not tuned to the needs of children striving for academic success. It is expressed, for example, in the absence of their own rooms and peace and quiet for doing homework. Such an environment may mean that academic ability is not translated into examination results. The greatly expanded expenditure on sixth-form and further and higher education in the 1960s in practice largely benefited children of middle-class parents. Even the most direct attack on class inequalities in access to higher education, via the creation of an Open University, brought no radical change. The situation continues to be that children of middle-class origin have a greater chance of becoming university graduates than those from the working class.

Table 3.1 Social class of United Kingdom candidates accepted for Universities (percentages), 1979–84

Social class	Percentage accepted 1979	1984
Professional etc. occupations	19.8	22.1
Intermediate occupations	38.0	48.2
Skilled occupations, non-manual	21.1	10.1
Skilled occupations, manual	14.7	12.4
Partly skilled occupations	4.5	6.2
Unskilled occupations	0.9	2.1

Source: derived from UCCA statistics.

Class inequalities in access to universities have widened in the 1980s (Table 3.1). It is difficult to escape the conclusion that this reflects the effects of rising unemployment and the shrinking real value of student grants, which has pushed a higher percentage of maintenance costs onto students themselves or their parents. There have also been pressures on universities to cut admissions, with a consequently greater reliance upon formal educational qualifications in the form of 'A' level grades. The switch to student loans and an admissions system in which as Lord Chilver, the Chairman of the newly-founded University Funding Council, put it 'the student values education so highly that he or she is prepared to commit resources to it' can only widen class inequalities in access.[1] New proposals in 1989 for university funding (on a more direct per capita basis) may lead to marginal increases in admissions but will not affect the unequal social access.

In summary the educational system is riven with class inequalities. They condition who gets access to what sort of education and how well children from different social class backgrounds perform in attaining formal educational qualifications. Thereafter, the type of education they receive influences the occupations and industries that children enter into on leaving the formal educational system. In this way inequalities in access to and performance within the educational system both reflect and help reproduce class structures within the UK.

Undoubtedly, access to 'top jobs' in UK society is closely constrained by class and educational background. Class structure and education are mutually reinforcing. The ruling elites (Church, armed forces, judiciary, civil service, parliament, industry and business) are overwhelmingly drawn from the products of a very few public schools and universities, predominantly Oxbridge. They continue to play a pre-eminent role in elite recruitment. Indeed, an Oxbridge education has become more common amongst most elites over the course of the twentieth century.

The link between a select few public schools and the Oxbridge Universities is particularly important in this respect. Public schools educate a small (though growing) minority of children in the UK but have usually provided 60 to 80 per cent of those holding these elite positions. In some instances, there would seem to have been some decline in their importance. For example, in 1939 84 per cent of under-secretaries and higher grades in the Civil Service had attended public schools, compared to just over 60 per cent in 1970. Whereas between 1918 and 1974 75 per cent or more of Conservative MPs attended public schools, by 1983 this had fallen to 63 per cent. This change is in fact symptomatic of the changing class basis of the Conservative Party, which Thatcherism both grew out of and reflects. In other instances, though, it would seem that the role of the public schools has remained enormously influential and, sometimes, has increased. For example, in 1939 64 per cent of army officers of the rank of major-general or above had attended public schools compared to 86 per cent in 1970.

Educational background and shared experiences have also been important in the social construction of industrial and financial elites in the UK. The City of London has constantly sought to erect *non*-economic barriers to entry by establishing exclusive associations. These gradually assumed a distinctive social character based upon the most prestigious public schools. In some respects, reform of the City via deregulation and the 'Big-Bang' in 1986 can be seen as an attempt to shake up this cosy network of 'old school tie' linkages in the City.

More generally, there has been a broader trend towards the growing significance of a public school and Oxbridge education amongst directors of both industrial and financial companies. For example, in 1906 about 37 per cent of finance directors attended both a public school and Oxbridge whereas in 1970 52 per cent did so. This re-emphasises the very powerful and long established connection between the educational system and the ruling elites at the pinnacle of the UK class structure.

Channelling products of select public schools and Oxbridge to key positions of control and power in the UK society is one aspect of a more general process whereby occupational opportunities are differentially allocated on the basis of educational and class backgrounds. The small trickle of children of working-class backgrounds, educated in state schools, who graduate through Oxbridge to positions of decisive power serves in practice to legitimate a profoundly unequal system. It creates the illusion that anyone from the working class can transcend his or her class origins. People in professional and supervisory non-manual occupations tend to possess higher educational qualifications than junior non-manual workers. Skilled manual workers, especially younger ones, tend to possess those educational qualifications that can be obtained in schools and colleges. Non-skilled manual workers of all ages possess few formal qualifications.

These differentials have tended to widen in the 1980s, as successive *General Household Surveys* show, with growing unemployment being heavily concentrated amongst the formally unqualified. Many young people leaving school, generally those least well qualified, have been unable to find waged employment. A study by the Manpower Services Commission in the late 1970s revealed that over 50 per cent of unemployed young people had left school without any qualifications while most of the remainder had poor CSE grades. One response to this has been the creation by the state of a variety of temporary employment/training schemes for young people; such as YTS and YOP. By 1983–84 25 per cent of all 16 year-old school-leavers were engaged in such schemes. Access to these schemes often depends upon the same criteria as are used in recruitment to permanent jobs: those with some formal educational qualifications are taken into such schemes, those with poorer or no qualifications are not.

Educational qualifications continue to be a key to the transition from school to work and from school to youth training schemes as well as into employment or unemployment. In addition, affluent upper and middle-class parents can buy access to additional courses for their children to boost their competitiveness in the labour market. In the 1980s this is more likely to involve enrolment in a Berlitz language school or a prestigious secretarial course than a spell in Swiss finishing schools.

Differential access to education both reflects and reproduces class inequalities. In the immediate post-war period, most men went into an occupation that was the same as, or similar to, that of their father. Subsequently, there was some alteration in this pattern, although the working class remains largely self-recruited. A limited amount of long-range mobility via Oxbridge offered an important avenue for a small number of individuals from the working and lower-middle classes. For most, however, opportunities for mobility between classes have been more restricted. Perhaps the most significant change has been the growth of the service class. Only about 25 per cent of the service class (approximately defined as professionals, managers and employers) has been self-recruited and indeed it was recruited from all other classes in roughly similar proportions.

Many commentators would argue that the main reason for these changes lay in the expansion of and improved access to the educational system over the last forty years or so. But in fact class inequalities in opportunity in schools have been remarkably stable. Tawney's comment in 1931 that 'the hereditary curse upon English education is its organisation along class lines' remains as valid now as then. Others argue that changes in educational provision since 1944 have not represented a radical attack on the class structure of the UK. They have merely facilitated changing patterns of service class recruitment. This suggests that patterns of occupational change have been more important in producing mobility than has the educational system. Educational changes helped meet the changing labour demands of capitalist production in the UK as the growth sectors of the economy and government economic policies have altered. Changes in schools in the 1980s – such as a core curriculum, the increasing emphasis upon inculcating the enterprise culture in school children, and initiatives such as TVEI – are part of a policy to restructure state educational provision in schools to bring it more into line with the needs of the Thatcherite political project.

For many years it was argued that equality of opportunity should be a central educational goal but this goal is unattainable without first achieving a greater degree of equality in society itself. Equality of opportunity can no longer be seen as the principal mechanism through which to move to a more meritocratic society, let alone an egalitarian one. In an era in which society is becoming more unequal and government policies strongly encourage this tendency, abandoning even the goal of equality of opportunity, class divisions in access to and performance within the educational system can only widen.

Class, health and health care

Few would deny that good health is important to everyone, yet there are persistent class differences in health conditions, in the incidence of different diseases and in mortality rates. Such evidence is certainly not new. Much of it was brought together in the politically controversial 'Black Report', which the Conservative government attempted to suppress. The Black Report revealed marked class inequalities in health conditions, perhaps most dramatically in differential death rates. It is worth quoting the Report (pp. 355–60) on this point:

. . . at birth and in the first month of life, twice as many babies of unskilled manual parents (Class V) die as do babies of professional class parents (Class 1) and in the next eleven months four times as many girls and five times as many boys. A class gradient can be observed for most causes of death . . . if the mortality rate of Class I had applied to classes IV (semi-skilled manual) and V during 1970–2, 74,000 lives of people under 75 would not have been lost.

The differential class experience of ill-health and premature death continues throughout life. Moreover, class differences rose from the 1950s to the 1970s. The Black Report concluded that possibly its single most important general finding is the lack of improvement, and indeed in some respects the deterioration, in the health experience of semi-skilled and unskilled workers and their families relative to professionals during the 1960s and 1970s.

Recent evidence suggests that such differences have, at a minimum, persisted or even widened during the 1980s. For example, the 1987 Health and Life-style Survey revealed marked inequalities in the experience of ill-health and class differences in the incidence of disease. It considered the influence of social class inequalities on health as the most salient finding in the survey. In some respects the health of the lower occupational classes has deteriorated against a backdrop of general improvement in the population. Managers and executives may be more prone to stress-related ulcers and cardiac complaints but middle-aged men in the lowest income groups are three times more likely than those with the highest incomes to report frequent illness in the mid-1980s. One expression of this is the disproportionate number of older applicants for the Job Release Scheme who are low-paid, semi-skilled and unskilled workers.

This relates to a broader point: the growing significance of increased unemployment in widening health inequalities in the 1980s. The unemployed are more likely to suffer from ill-health than those of the same age who are in employment. Detailed longitudinal studies reveal evidence of increased ill-health associated with the threat of redundancy, redundancy itself and subsequent unemployment.[2] As well as detrimentally affecting those who become unemployed, this increases pressures on the budget of the National Health Service at a time when it is already under considerable strain.

There is undoubtedly a growing divide between the health conditions of those in and out of work and, more generally, growing class inequalities in health conditions in the 1980s. Why should such inequalities exist – and why should they have widened recently? In so far as they reflect more hazardous working conditions associated with some occupations, then labour market changes would lead one to expect a narrowing of differences. On the other hand, persistent and widening differences in incomes impose differential constraints on living conditions in terms, for example, of housing or consumption patterns, nutrition and environmental conditions; these generate widening inequalities in health conditions.

This raises broader issues about government policies towards health inequalities and the determinants of health status to which we return below. First, however, we focus upon the more specific issue of class differences in access to health care. This must be seen in the context of the creation and evolution of the National Health Service (NHS). The original goal of the NHS was to guarantee equality of access to health care, irrespective of income or class position. Prior to the NHS, there was a diverse system of health care provision, strongly class-biased, with access to facilities determined by capacity to pay. The NHS inherited those facilities. From the outset it has been characterised by tensions between the need for public investment to modernise inherited facilities and build new ones, and pressures to limit public expenditure. Nevertheless, between 1948 and 1979 public expenditure on health care increased enormously, if unevenly and intermittently, but without removing class inequalities in access to care. Class inequalities in access are an integral part of public sector health care and health care is regressively allocated; those in greatest need receive least. The Black Report spelled out the reasons for this. The relatively educated, affluent middle classes are able to influence the organisation of health care services within the NHS to meet their own perceived needs. Class differences in access to NHS health care reflect a 'social inverse care law', with the middle class in a more favoured position than the working class, who are consequently less able to use its services effectively. The reduction in NHS provision relative to growing needs in the 1980s has exacerbated this situation and reinforced the social inverse care law.

Differential access to care within the NHS is only one facet of class inequalities, however. Private sector provision was not abolished with the creation of the NHS – indeed, in important ways the NHS presupposed a continuing private sector. The option of private sector health care has remained for those who can afford it. Furthermore, in the last decade there has been a considerable expansion of private sector provision. In the early 1970s there were about 4,500 (out of 36,000) beds in private hospitals and nursing homes for acute cases, with about another 4,500 private beds in NHS hospitals. Most of the private institutions were non-profit-making charities and trusts, such as Nuffield. From 1977 private sector developments were influenced by the expectation that the Labour government would eliminate pay beds in NHS hospitals. This led to rapid growth in the provision of private beds for acute care, especially around London: by 1979, there were around 6,600.

Private health care continued to expand in the 1980s. Acute beds in private hospitals increased from 6,600 in 1979 to over 10,000 in 1985; the number of hospitals rose from 149 to 201. This growth was concentrated in the 'for profit' sector which increased from 61 to 106 hospitals and from 1,900 to 4,400 beds, in response to very high rates of return. In 1981, these were estimated at 15–30 per cent, on a turnover of £330 million. This led to increasing investment by multi-national capital in health care provision in the UK. Companies such as American Medical International (with 12 hospitals and 1,200 beds), Hospital Corporation of America, Humana, National Medical Enterprise and St Martin's Property Investment (owned by the Kuwaiti Investment Office) expanded their activities. It was a very selective investment, avoiding areas of medical care where the need for investment was high and/or profitability was low, and was concentrated around the location of greatest purchasing power, London.

As well as this growth in acute care, there has been an increase in private sector sheltered and nursing homes for the elderly, a reflection of greater longevity among those able to afford such facilities. These doubled to 5,100 between 1981 and 1984. They are projected to go on rising as the population ages and as the number of elderly in long-term care outside the NHS rises at 6,000–7,000 a year for the foreseeable future.

There undoubtedly has been some selective widening of access to private medical care through perks such as BUPA membership for senior managers (Table 2.9). By 1985 30 per cent of medical insurance policies were wholly paid by employers and a further 15 per cent were partly paid. State policies (via tax reliefs, hidden subsidies to cut private sector costs and so on) have also helped in this tightly-defined broadening of access. Despite such tinkerings at the margins, access to private health care remains very strongly class biased, powerfully rationed by the capacity to pay. A slightly larger minority of people now have access to private sector care whilst standards of provision have declined for the vast majority reliant on the NHS because of government expenditure restrictions. The gap between the privileged few and the rest of the population has increased.

The policies of successive Thatcher governments have exacerbated the class inequalities summarised as the social inverse care law. The Secretary of State for Social Services, Patrick Jenkin, summarily dismissed the recommendations of the Black Report for reducing inequalities in health care; he stated that 'I must make it clear that additional expenditure on the scale which could result from the report's recommendations - the amount involved would be upwards of £2 billion a year – is quite unrealistic in present or any foreseeable economic circumstances . . .'

This sort of stance could perhaps be defended in the context of a deep national economic crisis (albeit one of the government's own making). Subsequent attitudes towards expenditure on the NHS cannot be justified in the same way. Although NHS expenditure has subsequently been increased, there is widespread agreement that it has not matched the growth in needs for medical care. It became crystal clear in 1988, when the government made clear its preference for further tax cuts for the wealthy (on a scale not dissimilar to the £2 billion figure mentioned by Mr Jenkin) and a £15 billion repayment of the National Debt rather than boosting NHS funding. Mrs Thatcher's administration was increasingly regarding the NHS as a rump organisation to provide minimal medical provision for the unemployed and poor. The structural inequalities within the system that generate the social inverse care law are being deepened by a government that displays no commitment to the equitable provision of health care. Moreover, the NHS is a rump organisation within which privatisation and sub-contracting are being encouraged. The original goals of the NHS have clearly been rejected. No longer can it credibly be maintained that there is equal access for all to health care in the UK. This is no longer a goal on the government's political agenda.

There is, however, considerable confusion amongst government ministers as to whether there are class differences in health conditions and access to health care. For example, in March 1981, Patrick Jenkin, Secretary of State for Social Services claimed that there was evidence to refute the claim that the working class suffered poorer access to health care. Other government ministers, notably Mrs Edwina Currie, have subsequently conceded that the working classes do suffer from poorer health; while denying that this has anything to do with levels of NHS provision and class differences in access to medical care. Headlines such as 'Hospitals cuts axe 3,000 beds' (*Financial Times*, 8 March 1988) are not significant for Mrs Currie whereas they actually represent a widening of inequalities in access to care and health conditions. Rather than being a product of the social inverse care law, to Mrs Currie the poorer health of the working classes is a function of ignorance and a predilection for unhealthy foods such as fish and chips and sugary tea. As such, it is to be tackled by individuals changing their diets and life-styles rather than by more appropriate government provision to narrow class differences in access to care. To some extent people *could* change to a healthier diet and life-style, but simply to blame the poor for their particular choice of cheap foods is to ignore the social processes that led to low incomes and poverty in the first place. The problem of class differences in health conditions goes beyond class inequalities in access to health care, important though these are, and lies outside the specific area of health care. A complex of social and economic factors affect health and all favour the better off. Consequently, reducing inequalities in health crucially depends on measures to reduce differences in material standards of living at work, in the home and in everyday community life. In particular, tackling class inequalities implies the general need for an anti-poverty strategy. This raises the question of the extent to which an attack on class inequalities in health conditions and care in the UK is possible. It is clearly incompatible with the existing pattern of class relations in the UK and with the government's attitude towards privatised provision of health care through the market, the supreme allocator of resources.

Class, tenure and housing

Relations between class, incomes and housing are complicated. In general, those with higher incomes can afford to buy better quality dwellings in more desirable surroundings whilst many of the less affluent rent council housing. Some have suggested that tenure groupings represent 'housing classes', others that owner occupation generates specific economic interests which are different from those of owners and non-owners of capital. Yet others have been, correctly, critical of such views.[3] For location in the same tenure category can conceal enormous differences in housing experiences: that is, there are owner-occupiers and owner-occupiers, tenants and tenants. Class interests are not coincident with tenure but tenure groupings do not replace class interests as a basis for social organisation and political practice. What is undeniably true is that homes represent a source of wealth for those who can afford to purchase a house (or houses) and for private landlords houses are a source of rental income.

There have been, over a long period, major changes in housing in the UK. Around 1900 90 per cent of households rented their dwelling from a private landlord. The remaining 10 per cent were owner-occupiers. The inter-war growth of owner occupation and the beginnings of local authority provision resulted in a rather different tenure pattern in 1947; 60 per cent privately rented; 26 per cent owner occupied; 13 per cent public sector rented. Since then, private renting has declined and owner occupation has increased. Public sector renting increased after 1947 but has fallen in latter years, especially since 1979. By 1985 only 11 per cent of dwellings were privately rented, 27 per cent publicly rented and 62 per cent were owner-occupied.

Changing tenure patterns reflect the interacting effects of government policies towards housing, the actions of construction companies, private landlords, building societies and related agencies, and rising average real incomes. The social class composition of each tenure group has also altered, but there is still a strong class differentiation in tenure. The *1981 Census of Population* revealed that over 80 per cent of professionals, employers and managers were owner-occupiers while over 50 per cent of unskilled manual workers rented from a local authority. Moreover, there is a very marked class differentiation in second (and third) home ownership, which is also increasingly located abroad.

The benefits of wealth that owner occupation both confers and reflects also has a class basis. Undoubtedly because of owner-occupation inter-generational transfers of wealth will become increasingly important. Relationships between tenure, occupation and class have been further complicated, arguably deliberately, since 1979 as part of a more general Thatcherite strategy of promoting the virtues of Victorian self-help, allied to the promotion of late-twentieth century popular capitalism. Nevertheless, considerable class differences in tenure patterns remain. By 1985, for example, 87 per cent of professionals, employers and managers were owner-occupiers, as were 33 per cent of *unskilled* manual workers; but 58 per cent of unskilled manual workers rented from local authorities (LAs) as compared to only 4 per cent of the professionals.

Differences between furnished and unfurnished privately-rented accommodation also interact with class, age and length of stay to produce markedly different groups of tenants. There are diverse groups of short-stay tenants including students, newly married couples, single person households and people who move in the course of their employment. For them, short-stay furnished lets are convenient, easy to enter and leave. In contrast, the unfurnished sector continues to be the domain of the longer stay, more elderly and low income households as the 1987 *General Household Survey* shows. Such people are effectively trapped in the privately rented sector, being excluded from alternative tenures. Often they inhabit poor quality dwellings. But within the sector there are also very high quality dwellings in prestige locations, rented by the extremely affluent, members of the bourgeoisie and other people of property.

Mrs Thatcher's government viewed the decline of the privately rented sector with concern and tried to create more attractive economics of landlordism via the 1980 Housing Act. It created new short term (1 to 5 year) tenancies, after which landlords were assured of vacant possession. Some dismiss the changes as essentially cosmetic. This seems a reasonable judgement as privately rented tenancies fell from 13 per cent in 1980 to 11 per cent in 1985. As a result, fearing a permanent divide between owner-occupiers and the remaining local authority tenants, the government announced plans in 1987 to allow local authorities to subsidise construction of dwellings for private renting by housing associations and similar organisations.

Once again, the government acknowledges a need for selective intervention despite its general ideological predilection for market solutions.

The extreme degree of social polarisation within the privately rented sector is absent within what remains of local authority housing. In the late 1940s public sector housing was seen as providing decent quality general needs housing for a wide social spectrum and a majority of the population. Public sector provision via local authorities and new town development corporations (which transferred their residual housing stock to Local Authorities in the 1970s) subsequently increased, then later declined. Moreover, such housing increasingly became regarded as, at least, a second best tenure for those unable to afford owner occupation. One particularly visible manifestation of this second best character appeared in the later 1950s and 1960s. Local authorities, faced with pressure to cut expenditure, switched to supposedly cheaper, system-built high rise blocks to rehouse people from slum clearance schemes. This unpopular building form stigmatised council housing even further. Neither Conservative nor Labour governments in the 1970s subsequently displayed much enthusiasm for providing good quality Local Authority housing, placing increasing emphasis on housing associations.

The most serious attack on local authority provision came after the 1979 general election. It came in three forms: first, via greatly increased sales of council houses (which we consider below); secondly, via very severe cuts in public expenditure on housing which meant the virtual collapse of council house building, which fell from 100,000 a year in the late 1970s to 20,000 in 1986. This has reinforced the role of the residual stock as a low quality 'sink' for those unable to afford owner-occupation. Furthermore, public expenditure restrictions resulted in 84 per cent of LA houses, in England alone, requiring repairs averaging £4,900 each in 1985; thirdly, since 1987, by giving tenants the right to opt out of local authority control and transfer their tenancies to a housing association or similar landlord. They are encouraged to do so by the fall in the quality of their dwellings via non-repairs because of expenditure restraints.

Changes in the composition and size of the LA stock have had considerable implications for the class composition of LA tenants. Evidence from the *General Household Surveys* of the 1970s suggests that the local authority sector was increasingly housing the poorer households. The evidence from the 1980s points to a continuation of this trend as a deliberate result of Thatcherite policies to reduce council stocks to a residual ghetto for the poor and unemployed.

This, however, does not tell the full tale. There are still differences in quality within the remaining LA stock. Housing managers and officials continue to determine the rules of access and allocate households to dwellings in a situation where need has generally outstripped supply. Local Authorities have great discretion in deciding what constitutes housing need and there is considerable variation in the criteria they adopt for this. A household is allocated points in relation to these criteria (such as length of residence and household size). These determine its position in the waiting list. This determines whether or not it gets a dwelling. However, the *quality* of housing allocated depends upon housing managers' assessments of tenants: the better the grading, the better the accommodation. This is especially significant in relation to transfers within a local authority's housing stock.

The meshing of allocation and transfer rules with the physical attributes of particular types of council houses produces a mosaic of different types of council housing areas. At one extreme, are the better quality small-to-medium sized houses, especially the general needs dwellings of the 1940s and 1950s. These are allocated to the respectable working class, typically stable white families with heads in full-time semi-skilled or skilled manual or clerical non-manual jobs. The stock of such houses is now much reduced through the selective selling-off of houses in the 1980s, so that council tenants and owner-occupiers often inhabit formerly identical dwellings next to one another. At the other extreme are the 'difficult-to-let, difficult-to-live-in, and difficult-to-get-out-of' estates.[4] Often, but not exclusively, these are 1960s system-built blocks, 'sink estates' in which 'problem families' are deliberately concentrated. The implications of social segregation within the public sector stock have become more serious since 1979 because of broader changes in labour markets and housing provision. We have already travelled a long way down the road to a situation where state housing has become stigmatised welfare housing associated with the unemployed, low paid, blacks and other minority groups.

Owner-occupation has grown considerably in the United Kingdom over the post-war period. Owner-occupiers tend to have higher incomes and more wealth (often precisely because of owner-occupation) than tenants. By the late 1970s 90 per cent of professionals and 80 per cent of employers and managers were owner-occupiers – but so too were many people from other occupational groups. The profile of owner-occupying households reflects the rules of access to this tenure. These rules are structured by the interaction of state policies with those of agencies providing credit to finance owner-occupation.

Given the choice, most people would opt for owner-occupation. But this is not the point. Politicians and bureaucrats have created conditions which make this choice all but inevitable. State policies have aimed to make owner-occupation a financially attractive proposition whilst house price escalation, especially in the South East, has further enhanced this. Since owner-occupation, for most people, necessitates borrowing money, the lending policies of the main credit agents – building societies, banks, insurance companies and local authorities – are vital. Despite the growing share of mortgage business taken by the banks and insurance companies, reducing the building societies 'share' of new mortgages to 55 per cent in 1987 from 85 per cent in 1984, building societies remain the main source of credit for house purchase.

The main determinants of whether a mortgage is granted are level of income, type of job and form of employment contract. Consequently, building societies favour non-manual salaried workers, though in the 1970s more unionised, especially skilled, manual workers became seen as credit-worthy as they achieved better working conditions and more secure employment contracts. By the end of the 1970s absolutely more, though relatively less, manual heads of households were receiving mortgages than were non-manual ones. This trend has continued in the 1980s with increasing council house sales boosting manual mortgagees whilst non-manual purchasers turned increasingly to banks and insurance companies.

Local authority mortgage schemes evolved to complement those of building societies, providing finance for lower income purchasers of cheaper, older properties. However, the poorest householders seeking the cheapest houses have difficulty in getting local authority mortgages. For them, the fringe banks and finance companies act as lenders of last resort, providing loans at punitive interest rates.

The combined effect of state policies and differential access to credit has been a regressive form of financing owner-occupation. Public subsidies in the form of income tax and capital gains tax relief have helped owner-occupiers who, on average, have higher incomes than tenants. Furthermore, within the owner-occupied sector, the richer households have gained most. Overall, the system of housing finance has given most to those who need it least; and it has given most since 1979. By the start of the 1980s owner-occupiers benefited by over £2,000 million a year, a vast subsidy to the better off. Thatcherite policies to increase council rents while raising the upper limits on mortgages qualifying for tax relief have since further increased the differential subsidy to the better off. By 1987, for example, 800,000 high earners escaped paying £270 million in tax above the standard rate because of mortgage tax relief, while total tax relief on mortgages was over £4,500 million.

As owner-occupation has increased, so too has diversity of owner-occupiers. There is a world of difference between the housing experiences of the landed aristocracy living in grand mansions, the residents of a suburban Bellway three-bedroomed semi and those in old, run-down inner housing. All may be owner-occupiers but they live in social worlds that are, literally, classes apart. This takes on added significance in the context of the greatly increased sales of council houses to sitting tenants after 1979 (over one million to 1987). This has increased the divide between the remaining council tenants and owner-occupiers *and* exacerbated divisions between owner-occupying groups. Increased, but selective, purchases by sitting council tenants reflected the financial advantages of owner-occupation – with houses generally sold at two-thirds of market price – and the perceived disadvantages of the authoritarian managerial practices of LAs as landlords. This provided space for proposals for tenants to opt out of LA control. More generally, it helped discredit the statist conception of socialism, that emerged in the late 1940s, and provided opportunities for market solutions, reinforcing the acceptance of aspects of Thatcherism amongst key sections of former Labour voters.

Even so, the Thatcher government recognises the political and social dangers of polarising housing provision around a private market for owner occupiers and a rump public sector for an underclass of the unemployed and poor. It is in this context that the seemingly paradoxical recent government attempt to revive the privately rented sector (using public expenditure) must be understood. For it is difficult to encourage the private rented sector in a market biased towards owner-occupation. Widespread owner-occupation confers powerful privileges on both old established and recently converted Conservative voters. Politically, it would be very damaging to tamper with these privileges. In these circumstances, the pill of public subsidy to private landlords was easier to swallow than the politically dangerous admission that market-led solutions to housing provision are iniquitous and divisive.

Class, consumption and lifestyles: further comments

Consumption patterns remain markedly unequal between classes, both inside and outside the home. These differences can be summarised as follows. Firstly, those in households headed by people in middle-class or white-collar occupations consume considerably more than those in manual employment. Secondly, expenditure on food and alcohol varies least between households and that on consumer durables and services varies most. Thirdly, the unemployed and economically inactive are relatively deprived, especially with respect to services and consumer durables. Spending on anything other than the necessities of food and shelter declines with the absence of a job. Fourthly, non-manual workers are most distinct in the extent to which they purchase consumer durables and services.

There are, then, important class differences in the ownership of consumer durables and domestic 'labour-saving' devices. These have, however, partially altered in the 1980s. In some cases, for example, there was almost universal household possession in 1979: 92 per cent of households possessed a refrigerator, 97 per cent had a television set. In other cases, there has been considerable growth in ownership in the 1980s (Table 3.2). In this sense, the Thatcher years can be said to have witnessed decreasing class differences. But substantial minorities, concentrated among the poor and unemployed, still lack central heating, deep freezers, telephones and washing machines (Table 3.3). For some, the lack of consumer durables is a matter of choice but for many others it is a matter of necessity so that class differences are perpetuated.

Table 3.2 Household ownership of selected consumer durables 1979–87

	% owning	
	1979	1987
Home computer	–	18
Video recorder	–	46
Deep freezer	40	74
Washing machine	74	83
Tumble drier	19	39
Dishwasher	3	8
Telephone	67	83
Microwave	–	30
Central heating	55	73
Car/van – one	44	44
– more than one	13	19
in total	47	63

Source: Office of Population, Censuses and Surveys, 1988

Table 3.3 Households with durable goods, 1985 (percentages)

	Economic status of head of household		
	Working	Unemployed	Economically inactive
Refrigerator	97	92	93
Deep freezer	78	55	49
Washing machine	91	77	68
Tumble drier	43	28	18
Dishwasher	9	1	2
Telephone	89	55	75
TV			
colour	92	76	80
black and white	7	19	17
Video recorder	45	30	10
Home computer	20	10	2

Source: Central Statistical Office, *Social Trends*, HMSO, 1988, p. 108

Furthermore, these data reveal nothing about quality; for example, of the differences between an old black and white and a new colour television set, or a brand new washing machine and one that is twenty years-old. Such qualitative differences reflect income differentials and are class-related. The uneven growth in possession of these consumer durables reflects the interacting effects of two things. One is rising real incomes and booming credit for those in work (especially in households where married women work for a wage). The other is falling real prices, coupled with a second-hand market for those unable to afford the latest 'state-of-the art' technology as a result of the fact that others can.

Ownership of new 'high-tech' and generally more expensive consumer durables (home computers; microwave ovens; videos) is much more restricted. Others – notably dishwashers – are 'older tech' but remain more expensive and little adopted. Price is a strong deterrent and ownership of these consumer durables remains heavily concentrated among the more affluent, often two-income middle-class households. As their price falls in real terms, they will doubtless diffuse across a wider spectrum of social classes but to date there has been an increasing class differentiation in their ownership.

Overall, then, in the 1980s there has been a reduction in class inequalities of possession of several consumer durables that can have an important effect on the quality of people's daily lives but in other respects new class divisions have opened up. The pattern is a complicated and shifting one but, to some extent, it reinforces the tendency towards a convergence across classes on an increasingly privatised life-style.

Another important aspect of life-styles centres on mobility. One indicator of this, albeit an imperfect one, is household ownership of or access to a private car. In 1979, 44 per cent of households owned a car; 13 per cent had more than one. There were considerable class differences in household car ownership and in the quality of vehicles owned. For example, in 1979, 70 per cent of households headed by employers, managers or professionals had at least one car but only 9 per cent of those headed by unskilled manual workers had a car. By 1987 this pattern had altered little, the most significant change being the increase (to 19 per cent) of two plus car households, reflecting the redistribution of income to the affluent middle classes. This is a sharp reminder of how class differences in living standards have deliberately been increased as a consequence of income polarisation since 1979.

It is important not to confuse car ownership per household with personal mobility, however. This is especially so in one-car households. In these, for much of the time, all but one household member are in the same position as people in no-car households. This produces sharp age and gender differences in mobility, with public transport cut-backs in the 1980s exacerbating already well-known problems.

Differences in mobility are connected to those in leisure, recreation and holidaying behaviour. Although 70–80 per cent of all leisure activities are home based, many forms of non-home-based recreation and leisure require access to a car. For example, the most popular recreational activity revealed by the *1986 National Survey of Countryside Recreation* was going for a drive, outing or picnic in the countryside. In all, 54 per cent of people aged 12 or over undertook such activities, with strong class differences being reflected in car

Table 3.4   Expenditure on selected leisure items in 1985 by gross normal weekly income of household

	Up to £100	Over £100 up to 150	Over £200 up to 250	Over £300	All house-holds
Average weekly household expenditure on selected items: £s spent					
Alcoholic drink consumed away from home	1.68	3.72	6.28	11.35	5.76
Meals consumed out	1.01	1.99	3.45	7.98	3.55
Books, newspapers, magazines etc.	1.48	2.17	2.81	4.15	2.58
Television, radio & musical instruments	2.04	3.29	4.65	6.59	4.20
Holidays	1.13	2.70	4.24	12.35	4.98
Cinema admissions	0.03	0.05	0.11	0.17	0.09
Theatre, concert etc. admissions	0.04	0.16	0.26	0.55	0.23
Subscription & admission charges to participant sports	0.11	0.34	0.48	1.55	0.61
Admission to spectator sports	0.02	0.08	0.15	0.23	0.11
Sports goods (exc. clothes)	0.03	0.07	0.24	0.85	0.31
Total weekly expenditure leisure	8.64	16.12	26.27	52.70	26.08
Expenditure on above as % of total	12.3	12.9	15.0	18.1	16.1

Source: Central Statistical Office, *Social Trends*, HMSO, 1988, Table 10.18

ownership. As social class fell, such trip making declined markedly. Holiday making, both in the UK and abroad, has also become increasingly linked to car ownership and thus reveals strong class differentiation.

There are some definite relationships between class, income and expenditure on different kinds of leisure activities (Table 3.4). As income rises, so too does expenditure on a range of leisure activities and items, both in absolute and relative terms. In almost all areas of leisure the more affluent professional and managerial classes quantitatively do more and qualitatively do better than any other class. These differences in leisure expenditures and activities are indicative of significant differences in life-styles. For example, not only does spending on books, newspapers and magazines vary but there are also big differences in what is purchased. For instance, statistically speaking, unskilled and semi-skilled manual workers and their families read neither *The Times* nor *Financial Times*. Although mass ownership of a television set exercises a homogenising effect on the views that different classes receive of the world, in other respects they receive quite distinct images by virtue of the other media channels through which they choose to get information.

The greatest differences between income groups, however, are in expenditure on alcoholic drinks and meals consumed outside the home, and on holidays. The middle classes and more affluent strata of the working class can spend more on food and drink outside the home because they can afford the costs of so doing. The more heavily home-based television and video life-styles of many of the less affluent working class and unemployed are less a matter of choice than of necessity.

These class differences are even sharper in relation to holiday making. Since the early 1960s, there has been little variation in the percentage of adults taking an annual holiday – around 55 per cent. Thus those not taking a holiday are spread over all social classes but most of those who do not take a holiday cannot afford to do so. For those who can and do choose to take a holiday, expenditure, frequency and location vary with class and disposable income. There are considerable differences in the holidaying experiences of those who, in August, can afford to take week in Torquay as opposed to two weeks in Torremolinos or three weeks in Thailand. The latter may also have a couple of weeks in Tangier in the spring, another two weeks skiing in Cortina d'Ampezzo in winter, and week-ends in a country cottage somewhere in rural England in the intervening months. Once again, the considerable redistribution of income to the already affluent has exacerbated existing tendencies and helped sharpen class differences.

How then might we summarise the many class differences in living conditions and life-styles? At the risk of some over-simplification, we can recognise five broad groups in the UK in the 1980s. First there are the small minority of the solidly Conservative upper class, the landed aristocrats and the major industrial and financial capitalists. They are those who own considerable amounts of property in all forms and lead life-styles that are beyond the imagination of the vast majority of the population. Secondly, the predominantly Conservative middle class, owner-occupiers with building society or bank mortgages, cars and a clutch of consumer durables. They lead mobile life-styles, actively participating in a variety of leisure activities and holidaying at home and abroad. Thirdly, the affluent working class of skilled manual and intermediate non-manual workers, many of whom are now owner-occupiers as a result of the selling-off of council houses, and share owners as a result of selling-off nationalised industries; not infrequently they have been converted to Thatcherism as a result. Often they possess a car and a range of household consumer durables and take an annual package holiday in Spain. Fourthly, the rump of the semi-skilled and unskilled manual working class, mainly voting Labour and living in housing rented from a Local Authority, sometimes with a car and few consumer durables, but with many unable to afford an annual holiday, particularly a foreign one. Finally, the underclass of unemployed, many not bothering to vote, subsisting, on state welfare payments in poor quality dwellings on 'sink' council estates. They live on or below the boundaries of poverty in conditions of squalor that are beyond the imagination of the affluent upper and middle classes. Although these class stereotypes are over-simplifications, they do indicate the degree to which life-styles and living conditions in the UK have become both differently and more deeply divided along class lines in the 1980s.

Class and politics

Rather than take a broad view of 'politics and power', which in a sense permeates all aspects of inequality in the UK in the 1980s, we focus here on class and electoral and party politics. In particular, since the class composition of those elected to Parliament and of those in state employment was considered in chapter 2, we examine which classes vote for which parties.

The election of Mrs Thatcher's first government in 1979 both reflected and enabled momentous political changes. It registered a change in the relationship between class and politics, as expressed through the electoral process. The links between politics and class have been, and remain, complicated ones, however. Classes are the object of party competition, something in a way 'produced' by parties, as well as something pre-given. Classes *are* pre-given, in two senses. The relations of production are what they are at any given moment, while classes have a form and a content given to them by previous conflicts and struggles. But classes are constantly being 'reproduced' in new ways, both materially and ideologically, by policies and campaigns aimed at defining people in particular class terms.

For much of the population, party political choices are at best connected to class interests only in a loose sense. Undoubtedly, in general terms the Conservative Party represents the interests of capital against labour while the Labour Party was formed to defend the interests of labour against capital. Although political parties clearly express class interests, the ways in which they do so are complicated. Political parties formulate programmes for, and develop links with, numerous elements in society outside the class whose interests fundamentally inspire them. The significance of this is revealed by examining the basis of class support for Thatcherism, how this was constructed and how it has been maintained.

This in turn requires a brief consideration of the links between party politics, voting and class in the UK in the post-war period. It seems reasonable to infer that the political loyalties of the owners and controllers of capital will have remained firmly with the Conservative Party. By 1986, for example, over 90 per cent of the political donations of £2.25 million made by British public companies was to support the activities of the Conservative Party; over £500,000 was given by only ten companies. What, though, of those who depend upon being able to earn a wage as their source of income, whether 'middle' or 'working' class? There was a reasonably strong relationship between party political support, voting and class over the period from 1945 until the late 1950s or mid-1960s, depending on one's interpretation of the electoral data. Manual workers tended to vote for the Labour Party, non-manual workers for the Conservative Party; in both cases about two-thirds of each group voted for 'its' party. In this sense, there was a class cleavage in voting patterns. Even so, there was also considerable 'cross class' voting in this period. Between 25 and 30 per cent of manual workers voted Conservative while 25 per cent of non-manual workers voted Labour.

How, then, in the period to the late 1950s-mid-1960s were the programmes of the two major political parties constructed so as to both define 'core' classes of support and at the same time attract cross-class support? In part, the origins of this cross-class voting lie in the character of the political parties and the considerable consensus on economic and social policy that emerged after 1945. It soon became clear that the post-war Labour government was committed to reforming rather than replacing capitalism and that succeeding Conservative governments accepted the goals of 'full employment' and the creation of a welfare state. Moreover, it seemed that Butskellite economic policies offered a route to more-or-less full employment and generally rising living standards, especially in the 1950s. Thus white-collar support for the Labour Party to some extent reflected the growth of the welfare state and, more generally, of social mobility as people moved into non-manual jobs but retained Labour Party affiliations and sympathies acquired through socialisation in their parents' working-class culture. Conversely, working-class Conservative voting was associated either with a deferential culture, in which manual workers knew and accepted their place in the social order, or, conversely, with middle-class aspiration. More generally, the Conservatives projected themselves as the 'one nation' party. This emphasis on the precedence of shared national identity over class differences linked to strands that run deeply through Conservative politics, such as respect for law and order. Then as now this resonates powerfully with many working-class voters, sometimes tinged with racist overtones. Although indubitably an over-simplified view of the links between class and party politics, it nevertheless helps identify some important points about them.

From the late 1950s, however, the links between party support and class began to alter. This process is referred to as dealignment, although the alignment between class and party was always far from perfect. Thus there are two separate, analytically distinct, though in practice related, elements. Partisan dealignment involved decreasing support for both major parties and growing support for other parties and/or growing abstention in general elections. It began with the resurgence in the Liberal vote in the late 1950s and developed further with the growing

Table 3.5 Voting by occupational class (in percentages)

	Conserva-tive	Labour	Alliance	Nationalist	Other/ Non-voting
1979					
Professional	42.9	18.0	17.1	1.7	20.3
Administrative/ Managerial	50.0	13.0	10.2	1.3	25.6
Routine Non-Manual	39.5	19.9	14.7	1.7	24.3
Skilled	27.1	36.8	8.2	1.7	26.2
Semi-skilled	23.8	44.7	8.6	1.4	21.6
Unskilled	17.2	43.8	9.3	1.8	27.8
1983					
Professional	42.8	11.2	23.4	1.0	21.5
Administrative/ Managerial	48.8	9.7	18.9	0.6	22.0
Routine Non-Manual	37.5	17.0	17.4	1.0	22.0
Skilled	31.0	31.7	24.6	1.6	33.3
Semi-skilled	20.9	27.8	19.8	1.6	29.8
Unskilled	15.9	31.7	16.5	1.3	34.5
1987					
Professional	40.4	16.1	27.6	0.9	14.9
Administrative/ Managerial	49.7	10.0	18.8	0.8	20.7
Routine Non-Manual	36.1	20.2	17.4	1.5	24.8
Skilled	27.0	26.2	16.9	1.6	28.3
Semi-skilled	21.7	40.6	15.3	0.9	21.5
Unskilled	17.8	32.5	13.2	1.6	34.9

Source: R.J. Johnston, C.J. Pattie and J.G. Allsop, *A Nation Dividing?* (London: Longman 1988)

support for nationalist parties in Scotland and Wales and with the increasing complexities of party politics in Northern Ireland. It took a new twist with the emergence of the SDP, the formation of the Liberal-SDP Alliance and its transformation into the Social and Liberal Democratic Party, alongside a rump SDP. These partisan dealignments in the middle ground of party politics in the 1980s have been particularly important in enabling Mrs Thatcher to retain power.

Class dealignment refers to the declining probability that any individual will vote for the party associated with his or her social class. Between 1964 and 1974 there was increasing white-collar support for the Labour Party, from people employed in the public sector, especially in welfare services. There were, however, no perceptible changes in working-class voting patterns in this period. In contrast, after 1974 there was a steady decline in the percentage of manual workers, especially skilled manual workers, who voted Labour. The chief beneficiaries of this in the 1979 general election were the Conservatives (Table 3.5). This was undoubtedly crucial in bringing about the election of Mrs Thatcher's government.

Why then, should there have been this selective switch in working-class support to the politics of the 'new right' in 1979? To some extent, it clearly reflected the experiences of the preceding years of Labour governments, wracked by economic crises. Simultaneously, people experienced mounting unemployment and increasing inflation. This was a combination that orthodox Keynesianism believed impossible, so that the credibility of economic policies based upon it was eroded. To some considerable extent it also reflected the impact of the public sector strikes during the 1978–79 'winter of discontent'. These clearly revealed that the Labour government could no longer restrain working-class militancy via its close links with senior trades union leaders. The Conservative election campaign was skilfully constructed to emphasise the failings of Labour's policies. It promised to restore prosperity by dealing firmly with the trades unions, reducing inflation and encouraging job creation in an enterprise economy. It was a campaign that was particularly successful in attracting working-class support to Mrs Thatcher's brand of post-consensus Conservatism.

Such an interpretation is fine in as far as it goes. However, the creation of a substantial, but selective, basis of working-class support for the politics of Thatcherism needs to be set in a broader context. From around the end of the 1950s, it increasingly became apparent that the class compromises of the post-war consensus were incompatible with capital accumulation and economic growth in the UK. Changing patterns of employment and occupations also weakened both major parties' hold on 'their' respective segments of the labour force. The middle classes were affected in contradictory ways by several changes. First, by the necessity for white-collar workers to unionise, the continuing dequalification of various traditionally middle-class occupations, the encroachment of the working class on formerly middle-class preserves (such as access to grammar school education) and, especially in the 1970s, the effect of inflation. Such changes tended to polarise the middle classes, partly towards the Labour movement, partly towards anti-union and authoritarian positions. Thus many of the middle class remained attached to or were converted to Thatcherite neo-conservatism while minorities expressed support for the programmes of the Labour and Liberal parties in 1979 (Table 3.5).

By the 1970s the former bases of working-class political culture were under severe strain. The working class experienced the full impacts of de-industrialisation as the failures of consensus politics to promote economic modernisation and an internationally-competitive manufacturing sector were revealed in collapsing manual employment and soaring unemployment. This both weakened working-class faith in Labourism and loosened the bonds of a working-class culture constructed around a particular pattern of industries and employment. For some, it is this reduction in the extent of the traditional working class of manual workers, rather than class dealignment, which underlies the declining electoral fortunes of Labour. As Leys[5] (emphasis in original) remarks, with sharp insight:

The loosening of the bonds of the old working class culture provided an opportunity to redefine the 'classness' of the workers most affected by these changes. The working class did not 'whither away'. It began to break out of its traditional mould and became susceptible of being 'formed' again in new ways. The radical right . . . realised this. The electoral victory of Thatcherism demonstrated the enormous importance of their perception that a fresh opportunity had arisen to create a new kind of 'conservative working man'. It was a struggle – not necessarily permanent, but a victory all the same – in the struggle between classes, *about* classes.

In the 1970s, then, the emphasis shifted from the maintenance of established class allegiances to the redefinition of classes and the articulation of new grounds for party allegiance. This move was initiated by the Conservative Party, which proved to be infinitely more adept and effective than the Labour Party in seizing the initiative and taking advantage of the changes.

This redefinition of the terrain was partly in response to the emergence of new social movements that began to spring up, or to become re-invigorated, from the 1960's. These cut across conventional party lines, each concentrating on one issue or set of themes. These included equality for women, equality for blacks, preservation of the environment, nuclear disarmament and the creation of global peace. Although these issues cut across party and class boundaries, the people involved in the movements are far from being a cross-section of British society. The most prominent group is the so-called 'new middle class' – professional and technical-scientific workers, highly educated and, often, in state employment, along with housewives and students.

The key point about the emergence of these groups is vis à vis the rise of the new right is that they are protest movements, challenging the parameters of established party politics and state policies. From this standpoint, the emergence of new and radical political forces in Britain may be seen as the collapsing hegemony of the dominant class, which had either to be reconstructed or succumb to the pressure of opposing social forces. The 'Thatcherite' themes of family, law-and-order, racism, 'hard work' and the like appealed to popular reactions *against* these new movements, in language which tapped a large reservoir of traditional sentiment among ordinary people. By contrast, the Labour Party's emphasis throughout the 1970s was almost wholly on the economic issues of immediate concern to the workers as workers (with a strong bias towards male workers), and only very secondarily on issues such as personal security, racial or sexual emancipation or the environment. In short, the Labour Party did not respond as positively to these new movements as the Conservative Party responded negatively. In fact, in different ways the Liberal Party (via its version of community politics) and the National Front (via racism) responded more strongly to these shifts than did Labour. While the former in particular helped split the non-Conservative vote, the crucial point is that the political programme of the new right was constructed to redefine its class basis of support on a range of non-economic and seemingly non-class issues.

This not only helps explain why Mrs Thatcher's government was first elected in 1979, but also why it was subsequently re-elected in 1983 and 1987 and has succeeded in maintaining broadly the same pattern of class support (see Table 3.5). While the process of class dealignment may have halted, there is no evidence of a realignment onto the old model of the 1950s. Rather a new and more complicated pattern of links between class and party political allegiance has been established, though not necessarily permanently. Despite what in many ways is an appalling economic record after 1979, the Conservative Party has, by and large, retained the support of the working class at the same level as in 1979. This reflects a combination of factors.

First, the uneven and divisive distributive effects of Thatcherite economic policies within the working class. For example, this is seen in their promoting the virtues of private ownership of houses to former council tenants and of shares to workers in newly-privatised industries. Secondly, there are many strands of Thatcherite politics that are only tangentially related to national economic performance. Thirdly, one can add the (perhaps) fortuitous effects of events such as the Falklands/Malvinas War in whipping up nationalist sentiment, or the 1984–85 miners' strike in mobilising opinion against the trades unions and for the maintenance of law and order. Fourthly, there was the split in the opposition vote between the Alliance (then the SLD and SDP) and Labour. Fifthly, there were the divisions within these parties which make them (and some of their leaders) appear as distinctly non-credible alternative governments.

There has been some switch of professional support to both the centre parties and Labour, especially in 1987 (despite the material benefits accruing to them from changes in taxation and so on), mainly in response to the authoritarian turn of Thatcherite policies. To a lesser extent, there has also been a parallel switch in support from clerical and related workers. But the manual working-class converts of 1979 have, as it were, held firm to Thatcherism in the critical moments of 1983 and 1987, despite some wavering in the intervening years. This, coupled above all with the increasingly uneven geographical concentration of votes for Conservative and Labour, the lack of a parallel concentration in those for the SLD and SDP and the first-past-the-post electoral system, have combined to return Mrs Thatcher to power with vast parliamentary majorities despite winning a minority of votes nationally.

Notes

1. Quoted in the *Times Higher Educational Supplement*, 14 October 1988.
2. A good example of such a longitudinal study is N. Beale and S. Nethercott, 'Job loss and family morbidity: a study of a factory closure', *Journal of the Royal College of Practitioners*, 35 (1985) pp. 510–14.
3. These three positions are exemplified by, in order: J. Rex and R. Moore, *Race, Community and Conflict: A Study of Sparkbrook* (Oxford, 1967); P. Saunders, *Urban Politics* (London, 1979); B. Elliott, (1984) 'Cities in the Eighties: the Growth of Inequality', in P. Abrams and R. Brown (eds), op. cit, pp. 21–57.
4. The phrase is Taylor's. See P. Taylor, 'Difficult to-let', 'Difficult to live in', and sometimes 'Difficult to get out of', *Environment and Planning, A*, 11, (1979), pp. 1305–1320.
5. C. Leys, *Politics in Britain* (London: Verso, 1986).

Further Reading

A.H. Halsey, A.F. Heath and J.M. Ridge, *Origins and Destinations: Family Class and Education in Modern Britain* (Oxford: Clarendon Press, 1980) and R. Burgess, 'Patterns and processes of education in the United Kingdom', in P. Abrams and R. Brown (eds), op. cit. (1984) pp. 58–129, provide comprehensive coverage of class inequalities in education. P. Stansworth, 'Elites and Privilege', in P. Abrams and R. Brown (eds) op. cit, pp. 246–93, analyses the links between education and the composition of elite groups. T, Blackstone, 'Education', in N. Bosanquet and P. Townsend (eds), *Labour and Equality* (London: Heinemann, 1980) pp. 226–43, examines the relationships between educational policy, equality of opportunity and social inequality.

The best commentary on class inequalities in health care and conditions is P. Townsend and N. Davidson, *Inequalities in Health* (Harmondsworth: Penguin, 1982). More recent data for the 1980s are given by the Health Promotion Foundation Trust's *Health and Lifestyle Survey*, available through the ESRC Data Archive (Essex University, 1987) and the Health Educational Council's *The Health Divide: Inequalities in Health in the 1980s* (London, 1987). D.R. Phillips, 'Public attitudes to general practitioner services: a reflection of the inverse care law in intra-urban primary health care?', *Environment and Planning A*, 11 (1979) pp. 815–24 discusses the 'social inverse care law'. The expansion of private sector health care has been carefully analysed in a series of publications by J. Mohan, for example, 'Restructuring, privatisation and the geography of health provision in England, 1983–87', *Transactions of the Institute of British Geographers*, 13 no. 4 (1988) pp. 449–65.

For a good general introduction to housing, see J.R. Short, *Housing in Britain: the post-War Experience* (London: Methuen, 1982). Class inequalities in consumption and life-styles are discussed in N. Abercrombie and A. Warde, op. cit. R. Pahl, *Divisions of Labour* (Oxford: Blackwell, 1984) provides interesting evidence of changing life-styles.

The changing class composition of party political support is considered in R.J. Johnston, C.J. Pattie and G.J. Allsop, *A Nation Dividing?* (London: Longman, 1988).

4
Divided by gender

Introduction: the UK as a patriarchial society

The United Kingdom is a patriarchial society and this constitutes one of the major cleavages in British society. While there are a variety of definitions of patriarchy these all centre on the notions of male domination and female subordination. In other words patriarchy is a system of social relationships through which men exploit women.

How is patriarchy constituted? Reproduction is not the distinctive element for, apart from child-bearing, almost all the tasks assigned to women either in or outside of the home could be done by men. Patriarchy also does not constitute a set of specific and absolute relationships; the form of these varies between societies. However, certain general tendencies are common to all capitalist societies; these centre on domestic work, paid work, the state and male violence and sexuality.[1]

Gender inequality is shaped by and helps shape a number of features of capitalism in the UK. Of central importance is the role of women in domestic labour. This contributes to the reproduction of labour power, both via child-bearing and replenishing tired husbands and working children. This work is not formally paid even though it is essential to the reproduction of labour. The lack of formal payment is important in that it weakens considerably the independence of women, leastways within family units.

Also of importance are patriarchial relations in the work place. The need to double-up the role of wife and mother with that of a paid employee weakens the position of women in the labour force. However, the position of women is also weakened by patriarchial relationships in the work place. In particular, women's access to paid work is socially controlled: there is restrictive entry to some occupations and there are many forms of informal discrimination in recruitment, promotion and redundancies. There are no simple outcomes from the dual roles that women occupy in domestic and paid labour; instead there are tensions between the two roles. This tension and its implications for the gender division of labour is a central theme of this chapter.

There are other important elements of patriarchy in the UK. The state is both capitalist and patriarchial, and this is evident in its attitude to women's role in the reproduction of labour power. Considerable material and ideological support are provided for the form of the household in which women provide unpaid domestic service for males – that is the family. This affects many aspects of society including the type of housing constructed (most council housing has been designed for families), as well as the income, leisure and levels of consumption available to women.

Gender inequalities have long roots in UK society. They were considerably influenced by developments in Victorian times when there was a growing differentiation between women's roles in the work place and in the home. To some extent these gender divisions have been lessened in the post-1945 period. This is partly the outcome of structural changes in the economy leading to increasing participation by women in the paid labour force. However, women have also become better organised in pressing their demands for societal reforms. One expression of this is the growth of women's political movements. This has contributed to the enactment of formal legislation to improve women's position, notably the Equal Pay Act of 1970 and the Sex Discrimination Act of 1975. The feminist movement has also led to some changes in attitudes to women's rights and needs, although the persistence of male chauvinism should not be underestimated.

One of the most interesting questions about the 1980s is how gender inequalities have changed under the UK's first woman Prime Minister. It will be argued in this chapter that Mrs Thatcher's emphasis on individualism, market forces and 'the family' have done little to advance the causes of women; in some respects it may have harmed them. Mrs Thatcher's government has sought to increase the ideological weight attached to the family through promotion of the idea of 'traditional' or even 'Victorian' family values. This has unstated implications for the role of women within such families.

It is of course true that the state has provided a number of supports for the family throughout the post-1945 period. Amongst these are legal supports such as the denial of child custody to lesbian mothers in cases of civil dispute, and the provision of tax advantages. Furthermore, given the profound inequalities which exist in income distribution, the wages received by some families are insufficient to support all their members. Therefore, a system has evolved whereby the state makes a series of supplementary income payments to families, including child benefit allowances (although these have been frozen in monetary terms since 1986). What is in question is whether the ideological posturing and the actual policies of Mrs Thatcher's governments have deepened, lessened or simply left unmodified these inequalities.

Patriarchy is constituted of more than just a series of state policies and divisions of labour. Male violence also helps to sustain patriarchy. A study of family violence in Edinburgh and Glasgow confirms the extent of this: three-quarters of all attacks were against wives.[2] This strongly contrasts with the highly idealised view of the family and family ideology in patriarchial society. Yet that ideology is very strong and, for example, it influences the educational opportunities open to women. Girls are usually thought to have 'dual careers' while boys have 'careers'. Indeed the family is one of the prime agencies for socialising children into sexually differentiated roles.

None of these relationships individually constitutes an adequate explanation of gender-related inequalities in the UK. Instead they have to be viewed as an interrelated set, which form something of a vicious circle from which it is difficult for women to escape. The outcome is not a single model of gender inequality for all men and women, for there are many contradictions between the different elements.

Gender inequality also interacts with other sources of inequality, including class and race. Patriarchy has varying meanings amongst different racial groups, not least because the family can be *relatively* less important as a locale of exploitation for black women. One reason for this is that at times the family has been important as a bastion of resistance to racism and has therefore seemed to be less of a place of oppression. This is not to say that black women do not suffer from gender inequalities, but that their experiences may be different from those of white women.

The lives of women are also affected differently by patriarchy, depending on their social class. Educational opportunities, the availability of assistance with domestic chores and discrimination in the work place affect working-class and middle-class women differently. This is not to say that gender inequalities do not exist within particular classes but the experiences which working-class and middle-class women have of inequality are different.

There has been a tendency in traditional class analyses to ignore issues of gender. Married women are seen as being marginal to the occupational structure of society and their class position is determined by that of the bread-winning (male) household head. In other words, the household rather than the individual is seen as the unit of analysis. Even where women have jobs outside the home there is considered to be no conceptual problem, for the labour market participation of married women is seen as being intermittent and limited and to be conditioned by the class context in which it occurs.[3]

Such a view is problematic if only because it ignores the unpaid labour provided by women in the household. However it is also unsatisfactory in that it does not take into account the fact that married women are taking shorter career breaks for child-bearing and are developing longer careers. Many such women have been or are active participants in the paid labour force.

This does not mean that women's class positions can be interpreted simply from their occupational experiences; instead there is a need to take into account patriarchially-conditioned inequalities. Patriarchy and class in reality are interdependent. Patriarchy and class are shaped by and help to shape women's specific participation in the labour force. This is the focus of the following section.

Men and Women in the Paid Labour Force

Married women's participation in the paid labour force is conditioned by their role in the household. Since 1950 there has been a sharp increase in their participation rates. This is partly a result of state action to subsidise at least part of the costs of reproduction via increased schooling and caring provision. Nevertheless, the employment experience of most women is different from men's in that many have interrupted careers, either through child bearing and rearing or through giving up their jobs to look after elderly dependants.

Women's and especially married women's participation in paid work does play an important role in the UK economy. In particular it contributes to reducing the overall value of labour power. Married women are often paid low wages and this helps to undermine wage levels generally. In addition the very existence of this reserve of cheap labour has helped to shape the overall development of the economy. The division of labour presupposes the existence of different types of labour power with different degrees of skill and training. This is illustrated by assembly work. There is no inherent need for assembly tasks to be labour intensive but the availability of cheap female labour helps to condition this.

The position of single women in the economy is somewhat different. While they are young there is an implicit assumption that they are living at home and that therefore their parents will continue to subsidise their maintenance and other costs. This is a tendency which Mrs Thatcher's government has sought to reinforce through changes in the social security system, especially the withdrawal of most benefits from 16–18 year-olds. Later in their life-cycle, there is an assumption that their low wages are supplemented by the notional 'family' wage paid to men; this is supposed to cover all the members of the family. There are, of course, many women who have access to neither a family wage nor subsidised accommodation in a parental home. Unless they are one of the minority of women in relatively well-paid jobs, the result may be that they are depressed into poverty.

What is indisputable is that over time women have come to occupy an increasingly important role in the labour force. This is certainly not a creation of the twentieth century. Even in 1901 women formed one quarter of the paid labour force. According to the *General Household Survey*, by 1984 that proportion had increased to 41 per cent, of whom married women represented 27 per cent and non-married women 14 per cent. The changing role of married women is particularly striking. Whereas in 1911 only 10 per cent worked outside the home, this had increased to 22 per cent by 1951. By this stage the strategic requirements of two world wars had already led to greater experience of married women in the workforce. Thereafter, acute labour shortages during the 1950s and 1960s led to a rapid increase in their participation and, by 1985, one half had paid jobs. The proportion of working single women also increased to 68 per cent. As a result the share of jobs held by men had fallen to 59 per cent by 1985.

There is still inequality amongst women in their access to paid work. Age or, more precisely, the existence of dependent children is critical in this. In the early twentieth century working women were almost exclusively young and single. Hence there were high participation rates amongst the 15–27 group but very low rates in all other age groups. This changed in the 1960s. With married women returning to work after child-bearing and rearing, there were double peaks in the age-related participation rates. Even this pattern is undergoing change as there is an increasing tendency for women to return to work between births.

Despite these tendencies, the domestic roles of women, and in particular whether they have young children to care for, are still the key to their labour force participation. According to the General Household Survey for 1985 75 per cent of women with no dependent children, compared to 51 per cent of those with children and 36 per cent of those with children aged under 5 were in paid jobs. In addition, married women are twice as likely as non-married women to be in part-time jobs. Changes in the structure of demand for labour, increasing male unemployment and growth in women's aspirations and expectations have all contributed to these labour market changes.

During the Thatcher years women have continued to make some occupational gains, leastways in terms of activity rates. The proportion of all women in paid jobs or seeking work increased from 64 per cent to 66 per cent between 1979 and 1985 (Table 4.1). However, in reality the position of women has worsened in many respects. First, the rate of increase in the participation rate has been slower than in the preceding period, 1973–79, when it rose from 60 per cent to 64 per cent. Secondly, the proportion of women working full-time has actually fallen during the period 1979–85 from 34 to 33 per cent. Thirdly, women's unemployment rates have increased sharply so that the proportion in work as opposed to the economically active (in or seeking work) has actually fallen.

Increased female participation rates do not equate in any simple way with greater labour market equality. Women only have easy access to a few segments of the labour market. In 1980 30 per cent of women were in clerical jobs, a further 10 per cent were in semi-skilled factory

Table 4.1 Women's economic activities, 1973–85

Women aged 16–59		Great Britain		
Marital status and economic activity	1973	1979	1983	1985
		(percentages)		
Single				
Working full-time	72	63	53	53
Working part-time	3	4	5	13
All working	76	67	58	66
Unemployed	3	6	13	12
Base = 100%				
Widowed, divorced, or separated				
Working full-time	41	36	28	32
Working part-time	21	22	21	24
All working	63	59	49	56
Unemployed	3	5	8	8
Base = 100%				
Married				
Working full-time	25	26	25	27
Working part-time	28	33	31	32
All working	54	60	57	59
Unemployed	1	2	4	4
Base = 100%				
Total				
Working full-time	34	34	31	33
Working part-time	23	26	25	27
All working	58	61	56	60
Unemployed	2	3	6	6
Base = 100%				

Source: *General Household Survey*, OPCS, 1987

jobs and 11 per cent were in semi-skilled domestic work. This emphasises the importance of structural change in the economy (shifts from manufacturing to services and within these sectors) in increasing participation rates. Yet while women provided more than three-quarters of the clerical workforce and of catering staff, they only constituted 8 per cent of managers. This confirms the high degree of occupational segregation by gender in the labour force.

One particular feature of occupational segregation has already been noted, that is, the disproportionate number of women in part-time jobs. Part-time working started to become widespread towards the end of the Second World War but never exceeded 7 per cent at that time. Subsequently the number of part-time jobs has increased sharply and the vast majority of these are filled by women. Only 2 per cent of all men of working age compared to 3 per cent of non-married women and 14 per cent of married women had part-time jobs in 1985. Almost nine out of every ten part-time jobs were filled by women. For some women this may reflect a conscious life-style choice, while for many married women part-time work allows them to return to employment while still retaining some flexibility to look after their children. But for many women part-time jobs may be the only work which is available. In passing it can be noted that single mothers are least likely to be working part-time, as the system of state benefits and taxation makes full-time work the only viable option for this group.

Not only do women predominate in part-time work but they are also concentrated in a few occupations. Eighty-five per cent are in the service sector and two-thirds of these are in just four types of jobs: catering, cleaning, hairdressing and clerical work. Within manufacturing, women are similarly concentrated in low paid and low skilled part-time jobs. This underlines an important point: part-time work is more than a facet of occupational segregation, it is central to it. It is extremely rare to find a woman working part-time doing the same job as a man.

With the decline in manufacturing, the number of part-time jobs available to women in this sector fell by 52,000 between 1980–85. But the number in part-time service jobs increased by some 600,000 in the same period. In consequence women are becoming more concentrated in non-unionised and low paid work. Even more worrying is that the return of married women to the work force after a period of child-rearing often involves downward occupational mobility compared with the jobs which they held previously. For example, many school-teachers return to low skilled cleaning or catering jobs.

Improvements in maternity benefits have helped women in some respects. In particular the 1975 Employment Protection Act made it illegal to dismiss women because they were pregnant. It also established the right to maternity leave and to return to a job within 29 weeks of giving birth. However, the Conservative government's 1980 Employment Act actually weakened these rights. Firms with less than six employees were exempted from granting women the right to return to work after having babies. This Act was not primarily conceived as an overt measure to reverse previous positive discrimination in favour of women. Instead it was mainly a measure to promote small firm growth. However, yet again the economic philosophy of the government – in this instance the promotion of small firms and deregulation – had deepened inequalities in the UK.

It is not only skill content and pay which vary between part-time and full-time jobs. Full-time posts are also likely to have more opportunities for earning overtime and bonuses. They are also more likely to have a whole series of fringe benefits attached to them such as sick pay, maternity leave or holiday pay. For those on low incomes these are more than fringe luxuries: they represent the difference between bare existence and some comfort, and between security and insecurity. This is underlined by another feature of part-time jobs, the fact that the number of hours available may fluctuate strongly from week to week and from year to year. Many employers use part-time workers as a flexible buffer to absorb changes in their volume of business and to protect full-time workers from the consequences of these. Instead, the consequences are carried by their part-time – and largely female – staff.

Homeworking is another area in which there is occupational segregation between men and women. There are no precise estimates of how many homeworkers there are in the UK but the TUC considers that the total is approximately 250,000. The majority are women and many work in or on the edges of the black economy. Homeworkers are in fact a very diverse group. At one extreme are the professionals, some of whom are teleworkers using computers or advanced telecommunications in well-paid sub-contracting work. For them homeworking offers the advantages of flexibility and a comfortable working environment, although there may also be difficulties of social isolation. Both men and women can be found in such jobs, many of which may be in computing or publishing. At the other extreme are an estimated 130,000 child minders working from their own or other people's homes, often on a part-time and seasonal basis, so as to fit in with school hours and terms.

There are also large numbers of homeworkers in manufacturing, especially in the clothing sector. According to a 1988 report by Birmingham City Council, *Homeworking in Birmingham*, there may be as many as 5,000 such workers in that area alone. Amongst the many case studies is Saroj:

Saroj's workplace is her home. She is usually to be found in the front room of the run-down terraced house in Handsworth, Birmingham. Small, dark and dusty, the room is filled with clothing material, an old sewing machine, a portable TV for Saroj's two and a half year-old son to watch all day, and a budgie in a cage.

Working as a seamstress Saroj sews pockets onto trousers, for which she gets paid 90p a pair. She works an average of 56 hours a week for which she earns between £20 and £25.

All she knows about her employer is that he runs a small clothes manufacturing company at the cheaper end of the fashion market and that he employs about 30 other homeworkers.

She is startling testimony that the world of sweat shops still persists in many British cities and has grown in the 1980s; it is a world mostly inhabited by women.

Table 4.2   British Rail workforce in 1984 (excluding corporate headquarters)

	Total	Men	Women
All workers	149,517	140,530	8,987
Comprising:			
Senior managers	591	589	2
Managers	8,037	7,868	169
Clerical	17,489	11,913	5,576
Drivers	21,506	21,499	7
Guards	11,072	11,008	64
Signalmen	6,708	6,671	37
Track repair	20,201	20,201	–
Workshop	18,642	18,595	47

Source: *Financial Times*, 25 June 1986

Occupational segregation

British labour markets are characterised by pronounced occupational segregation by gender. This is evident in homeworking, part-time jobs, manual and non-manual employment and between particular sectors. For example over one half of all men in the 1970s were in occupations in which they outnumbered women by a ratio of at least 9 to 1. There is both vertical and horizontal occupational segregation between men and women. Not only are they segregated into different occupations but they also have different prospects for promotion within these.

British Rail provides examples of both processes (Table 4.2). In 1984 it employed only 8,987 women compared to 140,530 men, that is less than 7 per cent of the total. Moreover women were disproportionately concentrated in lower grade jobs. Well over one half were in clerical jobs and only two had reached the grade of senior manager, compared to 589 men. The same pattern is evident in the civil service where in 1987 women constituted 76 per cent of administrative assistants but less than 10 per cent of higher grade employees (Table 4.3). While some progress had been made between 1982 and 1987 in breaking down occupational segregation in the middle rank posts in the civil service, the higher echelons continue to be largely male preserves.

Occupational segregation is the outcome of several linked processes. Women are excluded by law from some jobs such as on North Sea oil rigs and in underground mines. But social processes of exclusion are far more important than legal ones. The most important of these is the social definition of skills. Women workers carry into the work place their subordinate status in society at large. The work of women is often considered inferior or unskilled simply because it is undertaken by women. In short, skill definitions may be no more than social classifications

Table 4.3 Women civil servants, 1982 and 1987

Grade	% of all civil servants	
	1982	1987
Administrative assistant	81	76
Administrative officer	61	61
Executive officer	27	34
Higher executive officer	12	18
Senior executive officer	6	18
Grade 7 (principal)	7	8
Grade 6 (senior principal)	8	9
Grade 5 (assistant secretary)	4	8
Grades 1–4 (permanent secretary to directing grades)	4	4

Source: *Financial Times*, 25 February 1988

based on gender. The same argument holds with respect to part-time jobs. Some jobs, such as cleaning or catering are socially constructed as part-time jobs because they are seen to be women's jobs; yet there is nothing inherent in the nature of such jobs which makes them full-time or part-time.

There are a number of mechanisms through which such social definitions are constructed. One of these is the emphasis placed on formal training. Unfavourable comparisons are drawn between the short formal periods of training in many women's jobs compared to say the traditional, long apprenticeships for many (male) jobs in manufacturing. Even if there was a factual basis to such an argument, the decline of the traditional system of apprenticeships in the UK would have undermined this in recent decades. However, even the factual basis of the argument is questionable for the emphasis on formal training undervalues on-the-job training and skills such as sewing and cooking learnt informally at home.

The largely male-dominated trades unions have also played a role in this through frequent failures to support women's claims for their jobs to be regraded. Until recently some unions also acted to thwart the entry of women into many better-paid and traditionally male-dominated industries such as shipbuilding. However, women have made some gains in the trades unions.[4] First, the proportion of women who were in trades unions has increased and by 1979 stood at 39 per cent. Secondly, women have become more active in union affairs as is evident, for example, in their role in a number of NHS disputes. In general, however, women still tend to be less active than men. This can partly be explained by the types of jobs they hold (especially part-time ones) and by their having to fulfil other roles as wives and mothers. Thirdly, there is also some evidence that women are gaining better representation amongst the full-time officials and the national executives of unions. Even so, in the TGWU, which had 16 per cent female membership in 1985, women formed only 3 per cent of the national executive. Similar underrepresentation can be found in most of the major unions. Fourthly, and more positively, there are signs that women have gained a greater recognition for their concerns within unions. Thus sewing machinists at Ford had a long but ultimately successful campaign to get the TGWU to back them in a struggle for pay parity with the majority of semi-skilled workers.

There may be indirect discrimination against women in firms' personnel practices. For example, a 1986 Equal Opportunities Commission report on British Rail found that a number of its employment practices discriminated against women. These included promotion based on length of unbroken service, word of mouth recruitment and height requirements. Such indirect discrimination may still exist even though direct discrimination has largely been made illegal.

The social expectation that women have 'dual careers' in which they combine paid jobs and domestic responsibilities also contributes to occupational segregation. Taking responsibility for child-rearing or caring for elderly relatives may mean that women are either unavailable for full-time work or can only take jobs with fixed hours which fit in with their domestic roles. This may exclude them from those management posts which require the working of flexible hours or spending periods of time away from home. Single women are not necessarily constrained in the same way but will suffer from the general social construction of what constitutes suitable work for women.

These social constructions have strong associations with the ideology of the family and the notion that men are the principal wage-earners while most women are their dependants. The ideology of femininity is also important. An emphasis on the glamorous aspects of femininity contributes to the attraction of women to such jobs as receptionists and hairdressers. This tendency is encouraged by many employers. For example, when discussing recruitment, one manager of a branch of a high street bank stated that:[5]

I think sex does come into it. Men would sooner be served by a pretty young thing, even at the risk of not getting quite the service that you would get from a keen young man. They are prepared to put up with that because they can stand there and ogle while they get paid the cash. Benefits in kind, isn't it?

Whatever 'benefits in kind' there may be for individual women employees, such stereotyping offers very few benefits for women as a whole.

Table 4.4 Levels of pay and hours for men and women, 1987

	Full-time employees on adult rates					
	Males			Females		
		Non-manual			Non-manual	
	Manual	manual	All	Manual	manual	All
Average gross weekly earnings (£) of which:	186	266	224	115	157	148
overtime payments	27	9	19	6	3	4
PBR etc. payments	14	10	12	10	2	4
shift etc. premium payments	6	2	4	3	2	2
Average gross hourly earnings (p)						
including overtime pay and overtime hours	417	680	527	292	418	388
excluding overtime pay and overtime hours	404	679	526	287	416	386
Average total weekly hours of which:						
overtime hours	5.5	1.5	3.7	1.6	0.6	0.8

Source: *Employment Gazette*, November 1987, p. 569

Men's and Women's Pay

Given occupational segregation, considerable differences are to be expected in men's and women's pay. Such differences do exist as can be seen from Table 4.4. In 1987 the average gross hourly earnings of women (excluding overtime) were only 74 per cent of average male earnings. While the gap has closed since, the ratio of 63 per cent recorded in 1970 (Table 4.5), most of the improvement occurred in the early 1970s. The relative position had already become static by 1979 and there has been no improvement during the Thatcher years. This only relates to average earnings and there is evidence that the general increase in income inequalities since 1979 has particularly disadvantaged women.

Women are concentrated in low pay industries. For example, footwear and clothing are notoriously poorly paid sectors, and women constitute three-quarters of all manual employees in these industries. Many women in these and other industries occupy posts which are below their real skill levels. This is frequently a problem for women returning to the labour market after having children. However, the problem goes far deeper than occupational segregation. There are significant inequalities between male and female earnings even within the same

Table 4.5 Women's earnings as a percentage of men's earnings in 1970–87

Average gross hourly earnings, excluding overtime, of full-time employees aged 18 and over			
1970	63.1	1981	74.8
1975	72.1	1982	73.9
1976	75.1	1983	74.2
1977	75.5	1984	73.5
1978	73.9	1985	74.1
1979	73.0	1986	74.3
1980	73.5	1987	73.6

Source: 'New Earnings Survey', report in *Employment Gazette*, November 1988, p. 570

occupation. According to the 1987 *New Earnings Survey*, female sales supervisors earn only two-thirds of the hourly rates of men, and footwear workers only some 70 per cent. Elsewhere there are more egalitarian pay-scales; for example, female nurses and police officers earn over 90 per cent of the hourly rates of their male colleagues.

Hourly rates do not measure the full extent of male–female inequalities, for men also work longer hours and have more overtime. According to *Social Trends*, amongst manual workers in 1986 only 23 per cent of women compared to 54 per cent of men had overtime earnings. Therefore when average *gross* weekly earnings are compared (Table 4.4), women's earnings fall to only 66 per cent of those obtained by men. The inequalities do not end there for women do not have equal access to the fringe benefits which are becoming increasingly important sources of real income. For example, 58 per cent of full-time and only 11 per cent of part-time women workers belong to occupational pension schemes. Taken as a single group, men are almost twice as likely as women to belong to such schemes. Even where women have pension rights, they are often on unequal terms. Most pension schemes allow men to pass on pension rights automatically to their wives, but only a minority of women can pass on their rights to their husbands. Unearned income for (single) men also tends to be consistently higher than it is for women by a factor of about 50 per cent according to the 1985 *Family Expenditure Survey*. Finally, the official retirement age also gives men five more working years than women in many occupations.

One of the underlying assumptions behind the historically low wages received by women is the notion that men needed to receive a 'family' wage while women's wages were little more than an additional luxury. Although this was never an accurate reflection of reality, the notion persisted well into the twentieth century. Single women were particularly disadvantaged economically by this sexist assumption. The unequal pay received by women has, in a sense, become even more significant in recent years. One quarter of all households now have female heads, whether single, divorced, widowed or separated. This has a direct bearing on their own welfare as adults and on the welfare of children brought-up in low-income, female headed households.

It has already been stressed that the ratio of male to female hourly earnings has been largely static in the 1980s. However, these figures conceal a far more worrying trend, the feminisation of poverty in the 1980s. A survey of living standards in London in the 1980s showed that the real earnings of men rose 9 per cent while those of women were static.[6] An important cause of this was the growth of female part-time jobs. As a result there has been an increasing concentration of poverty, especially in households headed by women. While only 20 per cent of all households were headed by women, they headed 62 per cent of households in the lowest quintile ranked by income. In the UK as a whole, the proportion of one-parent families amongst the poorest fifth of all households has increased by one half between 1979 and 1985. Consequently, structural economic changes and economic policies during the Thatcher years have increased the inequalities between men and women as well as between different types of households.

There has also been a deterioration of women's position with respect to benefits. It is true that gender inequalities were built into the welfare state from its inception. The Beveridge Report assumed that working women had a similar career pattern to men which, of course, ignored their career breaks for bringing up children. It also treated the family as a unit and made welfare provision for married women dependent on their husbands. This was seen, for example, in the way that separated wives received supplementary benefit rather than social insurance benefits; the underlying assumption was that women had been responsible for their own fates by allowing their marriages to fail.

Since 1979 the rights of women to benefits have been further weakened. Unemployment benefits are paid to those who are available for work. Since 1982 part of the test of availability has involved proof that adequate arrangements have been made for children and for dependants. Given the lack of state pre-school and out-of-school care facilities, this can be a major obstacle for many women. The Fowler Review had proposed to pay the new Family Credit through the pay-packet rather than directly to women, a move which would have further seriously undermined women's economic independence; however, sustained pressure led to this provision being dropped from the 1986 Social Security Act. Despite this victory, cuts in housing benefits, erosion of the value of child benefit and reductions in other welfare provision have disadvantaged women, especially those who are single parents.

Equal Pay Legislation

There have been some improvements in the legal provision of equal pay for women. One of the most significant landmarks was the 1975 Equal Pay Act which obliged employers to give equal pay and terms and conditions of employment to men and women employed on like work. This certainly helped many workers. However, because it only allowed for comparisons with men in the same occupations, many groups such as typists and secretaries were excluded. By 1983 only 26 applications were made under the Act to industrial tribunals in that year and only 6 of these were upheld.

The major weakness of the Act is that it does very little to break down occupational segregation and the concentration of women in low-paying jobs. The main effect has been to remove overt sex discrimination in recruitment as, for example, in job adverts. A small number of women have also been able to move into traditional male jobs such as lorry-driving or engineering apprenticeships. But the Act is essentially negative in that there is no obligation for employers to create equal opportunities. Thus a 1988 survey by the Labour Research Department showed that employers were still failing to take women workers seriously, despite the equal pay legislation. A survey of 21 large UK private companies found that all but one had an equal opportunities policy. However, with the exception of career breaks, only a minority had actually implemented measures to attract and retain women, especially working mothers. None had organised special nursery provision and only 7 per cent made specific payments towards child-care.

There is also no obligation on employers to break down occupational segregation – and in practice very few have done so. Instead many employers have taken actions to avoid having to comply with the Act. Examples include moving all men or all women out of previously mixed occupations, changing job contents or creating new grades so as to avoid direct comparisons of men's and women's wages. Therefore, while most women are receiving equal pay as defined by the Equal Pay Act, many women are not being paid in accordance with their skills.

Mrs Thatcher's government in the 1980s initiated no significant legislation to remedy the continuing weakness of women in the labour market. However in 1984 and 1986 it was compelled to change the UK's equal pay legislation to bring this in line with a 1975 European Commission directive that women workers should be paid the same as men for doing work of the same value. Following this, a number of judgments – many of which were contested by employers – have emerged from the courts. These could have profound implications for women's pay. The first major judgment concerned Ms Julie Hayward, a cook at Cammel Laird's Birkenhead shipyard. She won an appeal to the House of Lords for wages equal to those paid to male shipbuilders. In particular, the Law Lords ruled that fringe benefits paid to women workers could not be used to justify paying them less. A second judgment concerned Ms Rene Pickstone, a packer at Freeman's the mail order company; this prevented employers getting around the 1986 amendment by employing a token man in grades usually dominated by women.

Despite these legislative landmarks, only limited benefits have resulted to women in the 1980s. Those who have probably benefited most are a small minority of highly educated and professional women, for whom there has been some long-term opening up of jobs. Manual women workers have gained far less, especially compared to their gains in the 1970s. By the mid-1980s there were signs that the pay and employment conditions of women in manual jobs might even be deteriorating. While this was partly due to employers finding loopholes in the Equal Pay Act, it was also due to the growing incidence of part-time working, and to the rise of mass unemployment. Most companies did not have policies of positive discrimination. Indeed a survey by the British Institute of Management in 1989 found that only about one fifth of managers in the private sector considered that their companies had a coherent policy for or commitment to equal opportunities. There were some improvements in the late 1980s when a number of companies announced plans to introduce crêche facilities and to give favourable treatment to mid-career breaks. However, the stimulus to this was essentially economic – the increasing difficulties that companies in the South faced in recruiting sufficient labour.

Men, Women and Unemployment

Employment growth has been much more rapid for women than for men in recent decades. Between 1971 and 1983 the number of men in employment fell from thirteen to eleven-and-a-half million, while the number of women increased from 8.2 to 8.8 million. The reasons are partly to do with the relative concentration of men and women into sectors of growth or decline, but also to the partial substitution of women for men in several industries. In this respect the occupational segregation of women has actually benefited them.

The growth of female employment also obscures the growing incidence of unemployment amongst women. In absolute terms unemployed men still considerably outnumber unemployed women; the respective totals in 1987 were 2,008,500 and 898,000. However the rate of growth for women in the late 1970s and the early 1980s was double that for men. Given the number of single women in the workforce and the large number of households dependent solely on a wife's/mother's earnings, the significance of rising female unemployment should not be underestimated.

As a result of these trends, the experience of unemployment has become virtually universal amongst working women. According to one

Table 4.6   Unemployment by sex and
duration in July 1987

Duration of unemployment (no. of weeks)	Male	Female
	(Percentages)	
Up to 2	6.1	9.0
Over 2, up to 8	10.2	13.2
Over 8, up to 26	19.2	23.6
Over 26, up to 52	17.4	21.8
Over 52, up to 104	16.2	14.3
Over 104	30.9	18.1
Total	100.0	100.0

Source: *Social Trends*, 18, 1988, p. 78

survey, 83 per cent of economically active women had been
unemployed at some stage of their working lives.[7] The duration of
women's unemployment has also increased. In 1987 54 per cent of
those currently unemployed had been so for at least six months (Table
4.6). While the corresponding proportion for males was even higher,
this does underline the growing feminisation of unemployment. In no
small part this contributes to the increased feminisation of poverty
which was noted earlier.

Men, Women and Social Mobility

The generally unequal incidence of social mobility in UK society has
already been discussed in chapter 2. We now consider whether women
are in any way especially disadvantaged.[8] It is a question which has a
bearing on our understanding both of the constraints on women during
their own working lives and also between generations. Are they in
some sense divided forever from equal opportunities?

Inter-generational marital mobility is measured by comparing the jobs
of women's fathers to those of their husbands. In these terms one Scottish study found that 42 per cent of married women had upwardly
mobile marriages, while 37 per cent had downwardly mobile
marriages.[9] Of greater relevance is inter-generational occupational
mobility between fathers and their sons and daughters. Any such
analysis is made difficult by changing occupational definitions over time
and by the need to take into account career developments over life-
times. Nevertheless, the Scottish Mobility Study did find clear evidence
that men are more likely than women to be upwardly socially mobile.
The differences are greatest across the manual/non-manual divide.
Relatively few daughters of manual fathers entered non-manual occupations other than routine clerical-type posts.

Women perform equally badly in terms of intra-generational mobility.

They have far less overall occupational mobility than men and this is far more likely to be downwards. According to the Scottish Mobility Study three-quarters of men and women are downwardly mobile when they first enter the labour market, compared to their father's occupations. However, women are far less likely than men to be able to recover their positions over time. For example, amongst those with fathers in professional or semi-professional posts, 40 per cent of sons but only 12 per cent of daughters eventually achieved the same rank.

Apart from general discrimination in the labour market, the key to mobility is whether women have children. Childless women have far better opportunities to be upwardly mobile, although this still does not match the rate for men. For example, after having children 51 per cent of women return to work, but 37 per cent of these are downwardly mobile. They do not all recover their former positions, let alone achieve longer-term upward mobility. For many women the return to work also means a shift to part-time working. The structure of opportunities is such that part-time jobs tend to be poor quality which makes this shift detrimental to women's careers.

In concluding this section it is necessary to emphasise that class interacts with gender. But men are advantaged because they are men and women disadvantaged because they are women, in terms of both inter-generational and intra-generational mobility. One of the keys to this is unequal access to education.

His and Her Schooling: Men, Women and Education

The 1963 Robbins Report stressed that gender provided an additional dimension to class in under-achievement in schools. Despite progress in some areas this is still the case today. There has been some equalisation between boys and girls in their academic achievements at school but there are persistent differences in final academic achievements as well as sex stereotyping in the subjects studied. This contributes significantly to the types of jobs to which males and females have access and to the levels of incomes to which they aspire.

Between 1961–62 and 1973–74 the proportion of male school leavers with two or more 'A' level passes rose from 8 to 13 per cent while for girls the proportion increased from 5 to 11 per cent. Subsequently the gap has been narrowed further and by 1985–86 the proportions were 14.9 to 14.2 per cent (Table 4.7). In this respect there has been a real improvement in the position of women. However, there are still marked inequalities in the gender access to further and higher education (Table 4.8). Amongst school leavers there has been a decline in the proportion of boys intending to proceed to degree courses, while the proportion of girls so intending has risen more consistently. Even so, in 1985–86 the percentage of boys intending to go on to study for degrees was 8.4 per cent compared to 6.6 per cent for girls.

Table 4.7   School leavers' highest qualification, by sex, 1975–76 and 1985–86

| United Kingdom | (Percentages) | | | |
| | Boys | | Girls | |
	1975–76	1985–86	1975–76	1985–86
Percentage with:				
2 or more 'A' levels/3 or more 'H' grades	14.3	14.9	12.1	14.2
1 'A' level/1 or 2 'H' grades	3.5	3.6	4.0	4.3
5 or more 'O' levels/grades: A–C grades	7.2	10.0	9.4	11.9
1–4 'O' levels/grades: A–C grades	23.9	24.4	27.0	28.7
1 or more 'O' levels/grades: D or E grades, or CSE grades 2–5	29.9	34.0	28.4	30.9
No GCE/SCE or CSE grades	21.2	13.2	19.1	10.0
Total school leavers	100.0	100.0	100.0	100.0

Source: *Social Trends*, 18, 1988, Table 3.12

Table 4.8   Intended destinations of school leavers, 1970–71–1985–86

| England and Wales | (Percentages) | | | | | |
| | Boys | | | Girls | | |
	1970–71	1980–81	1985–86	1970–71	1980–81	1985–86
Leavers intending to enter full-time or higher education as a percentage of all school leavers – by type of course						
Degree	10	9	8	5	7	7
Teacher training	1	0	0	5	1	1
HND/HNC	1	1	1	0	0	0
OND/ONC/BTEC	1	0	2	0	0	2
GCE 'A' level	2	3	4	1	3	5
GCE 'O' level	2	2	2	1	2	3
Catering or nursing		1	1		4	3
Secretarial	5	–	–	11	5	3
Other full-time		7	7		10	10
Total leavers intending to enter full-time or higher education	20	22	25	24	32	33
Leavers available for employment	80	78	75	76	68	67
Total school leavers	100	100	100	100	100	100

Source: *Social Trends*, 18, 1988, Table 3.11

Table 4.9 Highest qualifications attained by men and women, 1984–85

	Professional	Skilled manual (Percentages)	Unskilled manual	Total
Persons aged 25–49 not in FT education *Socio-economic group of father*				
Degree or equivalent				
Men	52	7	6	12
Women	24	3	1	6
Other higher education				
Men	15	10	6	11
Women	23	7	3	10
GCE 'A' Level				
Men	11	12	9	12
Women	14	4	3	6
GCE 'O' Level or CSE grade 1				
Men	11	16	12	17
Women	20	18	11	20
Other				
Men	3	15	13	14
Women	11	17	14	16
No qualifications				
Men	7	40	54	34
Women	8	50	68	42
Total	100.0	100.0	100.0	100.0

Source: *General Household Survey*, 1985, 15 (HMSO, 1987)

While a larger proportion of girls intend to proceed to some form of full-time education, this can largely be explained by their presence on relatively low level courses. There is a marked intake of girls into secretarial and nursing courses and this, in itself, reveals much about the social and economic position of women. It is also true that boys are more likely to receive on-the-job training or to be on part-time or day-release courses. Differences in the level of education are confirmed by the types of courses that men and women are enrolled upon. According to *Social Trends*, of those in the 16–19 age group who were in full-time education in 1985, 31 per cent of men as opposed to 23 per cent of women were on university or polytechnic courses.

Gender deepens inequalities which already exist and stem from social class. For example, amongst the children of fathers in professional occupations the greater tendency for sons to secure degrees is partly counteracted by the higher proportion of daughters obtaining other higher educational qualifications (Table 4.9). This is not the case amongst the children of skilled manual workers where sons outshine daughters for all qualifications at 'A' level or above. With the children of unskilled workers the differences are even deeper-rooted and relate to all qualifications at 'O' level or above. Perhaps the differences are starkest at the lower end of the scale of academic qualifications. Considering those with no qualifications whatsoever, there is little difference between the sons and daughters of professional fathers but there is a yawning 14 percentage point difference amongst the children of unskilled fathers.

The actual position is even more worrying, for girls are overtaken by boys in terms of educational attainments during their school years. In the early stages girls outperform boys, learning to read more quickly and scoring more highly on intelligence tests. Up to the age of 12 they also outscore boys on arithmetic tests. Thereafter this lead declines while strong subject-streaming also occurs. Thus in 1980 97 per cent of those taking 'O' level cooking were girls, while the corresponding figures for French and Mathematics were 59 per cent and 40 per cent, and for woodwork just 1 per cent. Some subjects such as woodwork and cookery used to be socially categorised as boys' or girls' subjects. Although this formalised streaming is no longer practised, informal streaming by teachers and parents still occurs. This gender streaming is later extended into the subjects studied on higher or further education courses: engineering and technology remain largely male bastions while language and literature attract more female students. At 'A' level the differences are further exaggerated. According to the Equal Opportunities Commission, the ratio of boys to girls taking 'O' level physics was 2.5:1 in 1984–85 but for 'A' level physics it was 3.4:1.

Gender divisions are equally strong in the realm of training. While boys and girls are to be found in approximately equal numbers on full-time training courses, there are significantly more males than females on part-time or day release courses. The expansion of government-sponsored training courses in the 1980s has led to some equalisation of access to training (depending on how YTS is defined) – leastways in terms of numbers. However, there is still strong streaming: in 1980–81 women represented 97 per cent of students on shorthand and typing courses, 88 per cent on clerical courses, and 74 per cent on hairdressing courses. Even if the numbers of school-leavers receiving training have been more or less equalised, unequal access persists in in-service training. Amongst clerical workers 40 per cent of women but only 7 per cent of men do not receive any further training.

Educational Streaming

Streaming clearly influences the future educational and occupational opportunities which are available to males and females. Historically there had been a high degree of streaming in education and an opportunity was lost to rectify this in the immediate post-Second World War period. The 1944 Education Act established secondary education for all and was pervaded by notions of equality in most respects – save gender. Instead the importance of relating girls' schooling to their future roles as mothers was emphasised. This was also reinforced by social policy. Nurseries set up during the war were shut down and women were encouraged to see their primary responsibilities as home-makers.

Streaming is strongly grounded in childhood experiences in the home. The toys, books and games of boys and girls are very different and contribute to socialisation into highly differentiated roles. Sex stereotyping is particularly strong in the books produced for young children. These often show boys and girls doing very different types of jobs, while heroes and heroines have very different characteristics. At a later stage, school organisation further encourages stereotyping. This used to operate both through the types of subjects that were available in all-male and all-female schools, and in the types of subjects that were offered to boys and girls in mixed schools. The two types of schools had different types of practical streaming; for example all-girls schools offered a smaller range of science subjects than did mixed schools, but girls were more likely to select science options in the former than in the latter. Since the 1975 Sex Discrimination Act it has been unlawful to discriminate between males and females in either education or training and, consequently, the degree of formal streaming has declined substantially. Nevertheless the influences of childhood socialisation and of informal streaming remain strong. The use of gender in mixed schools to categorise pupils, to organise their daily school activities, their play activities etc. all reinforce the differences between the sexes.

The importance of streaming and of schools' expectations also extend into the realm of socialisation. Socialisation in schools is not only class specific but also gender specific. In working-class schools there is social pressure on males to conform to the notions of the masculine qualities of strength, dominance and bravery. Female roles tend to be portrayed as submissive, weak and home centred. In middle-class schools the roles are portrayed differently but there are still strong gender differences. Males are cast as the intellectual elite while for females there is more emphasis on being well dressed and well spoken. Gender stereotyping is not limited to state schools. In private schools masculinity, leadership and initiative are emphasised for boys while femininity and training in obedience are emphasised for girls. Consequently, the educational system – in all its various forms – has played and important role in socialising children into a view of the world that accepts and reproduces inequalities in terms of (*inter alia*) class and gender.

In the longer term such inequalities are reproduced in the labour market. The subjects chosen at school, the levels of examinations taken

Table 4.10   Men's and women's earnings and qualifications in the UK, 1985

| | Percentages earning | | | |
| | £120 or more | | £200 or more | |
Highest qualification attained	Men	Women	Men	Women
Degree or equivalent	93	86	70	33
Below-degree higher education	92	76	50	17
GCE 'A' level or equivalent	82	49	37	5
GCE 'O' level or equivalent/ CSE grade 1	79	38	32	5
CSE other grades etc.	74	28	20	5
No qualifications	66	24	16	2
Total	78	42	33	8

Source: *General Household Survey,* 1985, 15 (HMSO, 1987)

and the form of post-school education pursued all contribute to unequal gender access to jobs. The results of this have already been seen in occupational segregation. Differences in education also lead to persistent inequalities in pay. However, while educational differences contribute to job and pay inequalities, greater equality of opportunities in schools and universities will not guarantee greater economic equality. A comparison of pay and educational qualifications reveals that, at all levels, women earn significantly less than men (Table 4.10). A similar pattern can also be observed at the other end of the spectrum of educational qualifications. It is now realised that equality of opportunity is unrealisable without first achieving a greater degree of equality in society itself.

The contribution of Mrs Thatcher's governments to gender inequalities in education has been one of neglect, leastways in direct terms. However, the indirect effects of other educational policies have been considerable. Expenditure cuts, reductions in university places in the early and mid-1980s and increased centralisation of control on budgets and the curriculum do not address the issues of gender inequalities. Indeed, the harsh financial squeeze on resources can only make it more difficult to undertake any form of positive discrimination.

Women in the Household: the Conflicts of their Dual Roles

Over time the proportion of women who live as part of a married couple, with or without children, has fallen sharply. For example, the percentage of those aged 16 and over who lived alone had already reached 15 per cent by 1985. Between 1971 and 1985 the proportion of families headed by married couples fell from 92 per cent to 86 per cent, while the share headed by lone mothers increased from 7 per cent to 12 per cent. Nevertheless, the majority of women at some time live in a household where they are called upon to fulfil the roles of wife and mother. They may also be called upon to fulfil economic roles in the labour force. Given the limited time and other resources at their disposal, there may be, and usually are, conflicts between the demands of these different roles.

In the nineteenth century and in the first part of the twentieth century there was a growing separation between these roles. With this came other expectations concerning the behaviour and aspirations of women. Men were expected to be competitive, outward-looking, calculating and unemotional, while women were 'the angels' at home. They were supposedly warm and caring, giving unquestionable support to other members of the family. The English*man's* home may have been his castle but the bedrock for this was the emotional and material support provided by women.

Such stereotyped divisions of roles within the household have become less common. Instead there has been some shift to companionable marriages, based on greater equality between men and women. Nevertheless there are still strong differences in male and female roles within most households, especially in relation to the reproduction of labour power. However, only childbirth, by virtue of biological necessity, needs to be specific to women. The allocation of all other functions, such as child-care or looking after a husband or dependent relatives, is socially constructed.

In their roles as housewives many women enter into relationships of unequal exchange for they receive maintenance payments in return for their work inside the household. The nature of the exchange is not always clear because work for the family is usually portrayed as being done for love. Working for love supposedly brings happiness and contentment but it may constrain women's lives. It also places those women who do not have jobs outside the home in a position of complete or partial dependence on their husbands.

The effects of class and gender are not independent for the form of the unequal exchange of labour varies between classes. The middle-class housewife may receive help from servants or from a daily cleaning lady. The employment of domestic help has increased in the 1980s in high income households where both husbands and wives are in paid jobs. Yuppies are becoming 'Yuppeds' – young urban professional people employing domestic staff. The domestic staff may be employed informally (often in the black economy) or may be the employees of cleaning and maintenance companies. In either case their salaries and job conditions are worlds apart from those of the people whose homes they work in. Middle-class women are also more likely to have the use of more labour-saving devices such as dishwashers. Therefore, class does modify fundamentally patriarchial relationships. Yet both middle-class and working-class housewives exchange their labour indirectly for maintenance. The middle-class housewife may not actually do much manual housework herself but she does undertake household management.

Since 1945 women – especially married women – have been drawn increasingly into the labour force. As a result many have to work long hours in order to combine their two roles. Their total workload may be far greater than their husbands'. In addition many women provide unpaid assistance to their husbands in their businesses. This is often the case with small shops, farms and other small businesses. Their assistance may involve helping out with routine duties or with bookkeeping or other managerial responsibilities. The wives of businessmen may also be called upon to provide other forms of support for their husbands' careers, such as in entertaining clients to dinner. In farming, the farmer's wife is expected to undertake all her domestic duties and still be available to lend a hand with work on the farm; rarely is this formally recognised in terms of wages or joint ownership of the business.

Domestic Chores, Leisure and Consumption

The domestic division of labour is not constant between either classes or regions. For example, in the North more time is spent on preparing food while in the South there is more reliance on convenience foods. There are also differences between social classes. Amongst the working class, for example, some household chores tend to be raised to the status of obsessions. The same applies to the more marginal middle class whose anxieties sometimes approach a 'status panic'.[10] Housework has different meanings in different social strata, age groups and regions. As a result men share in housework to varying degrees, but, nevertheless, it remains overwhelmingly the responsibility of women.

Not only are there persistent differences in the amount of housework done but there are also increasingly subtle variations in precisely what is done by men and women (Table 4.11). Household repairs are still largely seen as a male preserve, as also are such tasks as cutting the lawn or washing the car. Men are taking on more household tasks but only in a very selective way. They are, for example, increasingly likely to be involved in shopping or in washing-up the evening dishes. However, they are less likely to prepare the evening meal or to do the household cleaning and rarely – if ever – do the washing and the ironing. These variations cannot simply be explained in terms of whether or not wives are also in paid jobs. Even when women are in paid jobs, they are likely to do most of the housework. Housework is rarely considered to be rewarding and the vast majority of women are very dissatisfied with having to do it. It is not love of housework but social conditioning which explains the unequal household division of labour.

Table 4.11 Household division of labour in Great Britain, 1984

	Allocation of tasks between couples Percentage[1] undertaken by		
	Men	Women	Shared equally
Household tasks			
Washing and ironing	1	88	9
Preparation of evening meal	5	77	16
Household cleaning	3	72	23
Household shopping	6	54	39
Evening dishes	18	37	41
Organisation of household money and bills	32	38	28
Repairs of household equipment	83	6	8
Child-rearing			
Looking after the children when they are sick	1	63	35
Teaching the children discipline	10	12	77

[1] 'Don't knows' and non-responses mean that some categories do not sum to 100 per cent.
Source: R. Jowell and S. Witherspoon (eds), *British Social Attitudes* (Aldershot: Gower Publishing Company, 1985)

Child-care is one of the most demanding of duties within the household and, as Table 4.11 shows, this is still largely construed as a female role. It is also a role which has changed in character over time. Women now have fewer children but they tend to stay in a protected phase of the life cycle (e.g. school) for longer. As a result of this extension of childhood, motherhood in the 1980s can be as long or even longer than in the past. After the period of breast-feeding – and, really, after childbirth – there is no inherent reason why these responsibilities should fall upon the mother. They do so primarily because of the strong myth of motherhood. Women are socialised from an early age to be mothers and this is part of the social conditioning which they receive via training at home or in the toys they have around them when young, such as dolls.

This does not necessarily mean that motherhood is an unrewarding experience. It can be rewarding and many women may choose it precisely because of this reason. Not least, motherhood can seem an attractive alternative to the drudgery of many paid jobs. While all of this is true, motherhood can also be exhausting and demanding.

There are a number of ways in which motherhood constrains the life-style and the life chances of the mother. First of all there is the additional housework to be done; for example, wives with one child do at least 40 hours of housework while those with two or three children do at least 70 hours.[11] The range of facilities open to mothers is also limited in that many restaurants, pubs, hotels and other centres of leisure simply do not welcome children. Even where children are welcome – as in shops and swimming pools – it may be very difficult for mothers to use these without help or without crêche facilities. In this respect there may be distinct differences between those mothers who can and cannot afford to buy in help – whether this is a professionally trained nanny or a neighbour who does child-minding. There are also differences between those whose children are at boarding school and those whose children are at day schools. However, the most severely constrained are single parents or wives who receive virtually no support from husbands.

One of the major constraints on the lives of all mothers in the UK has been the consistent failure to develop child-care facilities. Child benefit allowances are paid to mothers but these do not include specific payments for child-care, such as would free mothers for at least part of the day. Nursery provision is also poorly developed. The 1967 Plowden Report made a strong case for nursery provision and this coincided with growing demands for such provision as the result of the increasing numbers of married women in paid employment. By the late 1970s over 50 per cent of all four-year-olds were in state maintained nursery schools. However, only 15 per cent of three-year-olds were in state nurseries so that access to this type of provision was still largely dependent on social class. Instead, child minding has grown, often as part of the black economy, as one response by working-class mothers. Amongst middle-class mothers there has been more emphasis on private nursery schools and on voluntary self-help groups. Probably no more than about one half of those mothers who would like nursery provision for their three and four-year-olds are able to secure it. Access is of course conditioned by social class. However, the importance of nursery schools should not be exaggerated for even if a place can be secured, mothers will be constrained by their hours and school holidays.

Another important and potentially constraining activity which may fall upon families is the need to look after elderly relatives. More often than not most of the burden of physical care falls unequally on daughters. If the care work does not fall on the daughter, then it is daughters-in-law or female neighbours who take most of the responsibility. Again there is nothing intrinsically feminine in such work. Instead this division of labour seems to rest on the ideology of women being motherly and caring. This is a responsibility which is far more widespread than is commonly thought, for at some stage one in every two housewives can expect to look after elderly relatives. The state, via local authority social services departments, does offer some assistance both to the elderly living on their own and to those living with their

Table 4.12   Men's and women's use of time in a typical week, 1985

| Time spent on | Full-time employees | | Part-time employees | | |
	Males	Females	Males	Females	Housewives
			(Hours)		
Employment and travel to work	45.0	40.8	24.3	22.2	–
Essential activities[1]	33.1	45.1	48.8	61.3	76.6
Sleep	56.4	57.5	56.6	57.0	59.2
Free time	33.5	24.6	38.5	27.5	32.2
Free time per week day	2.6	2.1	4.5	3.1	4.2
Free time per week-end day	10.2	7.2	7.8	5.9	5.6

[1] Essential domestic work and personal care. This includes cooking, essential shopping, child-care, eating meals, washing, and getting up and going to bed.
Source: *Leisure Fortunes*, Summer 1986, The Henley Centre for Forecasting

families. Visits by nurses or by home helps can lighten the load but, ultimately, daughters still tend to become involved and hence constrain their own lives at the same time. Cuts in local authority services since the 1970s have only served further to intensify the expectations of and the responsibilities falling upon women.

As a result of this uneven division of household labour, it is not surprising that there are important differences in the amount of leisure time available to men and women (Table 4.12). Amongst full-time workers, males, on average, have half an hour more leisure time each working day. At weekends this rises to a three-hour difference. Even more striking is the difference between full-time male workers and housewives. Not only do housewives have almost five hours less leisure time on both Saturday and Sunday, but they also have less leisure time during the week!

It is not merely a question of the amount of time. Not only do husbands have more leisure time than do wives but its quality is different. Whereas wives have to snatch short periods of rest during the day, men tend to have solid periods of leisure. In contrast, even when women are at rest, the fact that they tend to assume the role of household manager means that they endlessly have to think of others.

The fact that many women are – or feel that they are – trapped in the home is well known. Household chores or caring for elderly relatives or children may make it difficult to be away from the home for any length of time. This again restricts the range of leisure activities which are available. In addition housewives form part of the 'transport poor' – that is individuals who lack access to adequate transport. This is partly dependent on social class, given the sheer lack of private car ownership in many working-class homes. However, even in many middle-class homes there may be transport-poor housewives as a result of husbands taking the family car to work during the day. This is not such a problem in two car families but these are still relatively rare. The differences are evident in car licence ownership patterns. In 1985 only 41 per cent of women compared to 72 per cent of men held car driving licences. While the gap between men and women had closed since the early 1970s – when the percentages were 21 per cent and 63 per cent – it remains substantial. It also represents one further constraint upon the range of leisure activities open to (some) women as opposed to men.

There has been little positive action by the Thatcher government to increase the amount of leisure time available to women or to reduce the burdens of care which habitually fall on them. Instead, cuts in existing services such as pre-school facilities and school meals for children, and in community and hospital provision for sick and elderly relatives, have tended to increase the responsibilities and the workloads of many women. It is very much a part of the Thatcher ideology to promote the need for families to take greater responsibility for such care activities. What is not specified is that in practice this means that women have to take on more responsibilities and duties. It is also not specified how low-income families which are dependent on the wife's earnings are to cope. This is not in any sense a problem for a minority. The Royal Commission on the Distribution of Income and Wealth calculated in 1978 that without the wife's earnings three times as many families would be below the poverty line. The growth of male unemployment in the 1980s has only served to exacerbate these problems. Except for a privileged wealthy minority, there is unlikely to have been any real improvement in women's access to leisure in Mrs Thatcher's United Kingdom.

'His' and 'Her' Consumption.

Differences between men and women are also prominent in consumption. These arise from the unequal pay received by men and women and from the unequal sharing of total household income. Even in the mid-1970s a number of surveys showed that only approximately one half of all women knew how much their husbands earned. Many husbands only give their wives a housekeeping allowance and one consequence of this is that mothers and children may live in poverty even within relatively high income households.

The payment of family allowances directly to mothers provides some buffer against such impoverishment but, of course, the real value of such benefits has fallen sharply during the Thatcher years. Child benefit allowances have been frozen in the late 1980s, leading to cuts in real terms. The Family Credit scheme provides some relief but for most households this has been cancelled out by cuts in housing, clothing and other benefits.

Working wives can use their earnings as a further buffer against such impoverishment but this only serves to underline class differences amongst women. The lower the family income, the greater the proportion of the wife's earnings which is spent on general housekeeping and the smaller the amount that is available to spend on herself and her leisure. This model does not apply to all households for there has been a growing tendency for husbands and wives to share their incomes and to make joint decisions on expenditure. Even so there are many women who are denied reasonable access to consumption even within prosperous households.

The consumption levels of women living alone with or without children are also likely to be more constrained than those of men living in similar circumstances. This is because of the low pay received by women, a structural feature of British society which persists despite equal pay legislation. In this respect their lower levels of consumption are the end product of a long chain which originates in the streamed education and training which they receive. The resulting deprivation – both absolute and relative – is more widespread than is commonly imagined, for one quarter of all households in the UK are headed by women. There are also lasting inter-generational implications to be noted for this has a direct bearing on the welfare of the next generation.

Unequal consumption is evident in several spheres. One of the most basic is in terms of food. In working-class households, for example, there is a tradition for boys to be put before girls and for families to be put before mothers when food is in short supply. Similarly, space within the home is not allocated equally and, where there are conflicts, boys will usually be given priority over girls. This has implications in terms of doing homework and, hence, in terms of educational achievements. In this, as in so many respects, the fundamental inequalities stem from class differences in the availability of resources but they are then deepened along gender lines.

The most important gender differences in consumption probably relate to housing. As can be seen from Table 4.13 the actual distribution of men and women between housing tenures is highly uneven. Households headed by men are far more likely to be owner-occupied than those headed by women. In contrast 42 per cent of all households headed by women live in council owned properties. Women are also far more likely than men to be living in unfurnished privately rented dwellings. These differences in housing tenure relate to fundamental differences in the wealth, housing mobility and independence of men and women.

Table 4.13 Men's and women's housing tenure, 1985

| | By sex and marital status of head of household | | | |
| | Males | | Females | |
	Single	All males	Single	All females
Owner-occupied, owned outright	16	22	23	30
Owner-occupied with joint mortgage	35	45	18	12
Rented with job/business	2	3	2	1
Rented from local authority/ new town housing association	27	26	36	45
Rented privately unfurnished	6	3	11	9
Rented privately furnished	15	2	11	3
Total	100	100	100	100

Source: *Social Trends*, 18, 1988

While women's wages continue to be much lower than men's, it will be difficult for them to gain independent access to owner-occupied houses. They will instead continue to be relatively dependent on the public sector. As such, they are one of the groups which have to bear the brunt of Mrs Thatcher's governments' cut-backs in council house building. They also suffer from the residualisation of council housing whereby sales and a lack of new building have led to a sharp deterioration in the quality of the remaining council housing. The decontrolling of rents in the private sector will also increase the difficulties for many women. In future they will have to pay full market rents for new tenancies. Not all women, or even all low-paid women, will suffer from these changes in housing conditions. At present separated women with children are most dependent on council accommodation; approximately one half of all women whose marriages break down end up in council housing.

There are other class differences among women in the access to housing, not least in that separated middle-class women are more likely to be able to benefit from continued occupation of, or the proceeds from, the sale of the family's owner-occupied home. This is a relatively recent improvement for, traditionally, the ownership of the home in which a married couple lived was in the the name of the husband. In the last twenty years it has become common for building societies to register properties in the names of both spouses. Since the 1967 Matrimonial Homes Act, divorce courts have also tended to let wives claim possession of at least part of the marital home, irrespective of whether their names appeared on the property deeds. In this way there has been a gradual improvement in the position of women, but it is largely confined to the middle class and the higher income end of the working class. Even within this group there may be continuing difficulties of access to good quality housing. Mortgages have to be paid, while the proceeds from the sale of part of a house may be insufficient to cover the costs of buying a new home for the wife. In this way the housing market position of women is fundamentally undermined by their weak labour market position.

Women's weak position in housing markets is not in any sense just a product of the Thatcher years. But it is equally true that there has been little positive action to improve the situation during the 1980s. The principal emphasis of Thatcherism has been on extending 'the property-owning democracy'. Owner occupation has been extended but the ability to purchase is based on the assumption of pooled family income. This may benefit married women but it does little to assist single women. It is also to the detriment of those women (and men) who are reliant on a dwindling stock of council housing.

Housing construction in the UK is conditioned by ideological notions of the family. Local authority allocation rules and mortgages tend to favour family occupation of dwellings. This, in turn, leads to an over-whelming emphasis in house building on family dwellings which, consequently, conditions the future possibilities for household occupancy, whatever the tenure. There is a hierarchy of social groups in terms of access to housing and it is probably headed by two-income middle-class households. At the bottom end are to be found single persons, especially those who are working class and/or women.

Mrs Thatcher's governments have had a far from benign influence upon many of the developments in consumption which have been outlined. Public expenditure cuts have fallen most heavily in the sphere of social consumption, that is, upon education, housing and some forms of social services. Women have been more affected than men by most of these cuts, and this is especially true of single parents and working-class women.

Men, Women and Political Power

Women's battle for formal access to political power was completed in 1928 when they gained the vote, on an equal footing to men. However, in many senses the real battle has still to be won for despite – and perhaps because of – Mrs Thatcher becoming Prime Minister, most of the positions of political power in the UK are held by men.

Parliament provides the most obvious stage on which to view the struggle for political power. After rapid initial gains, the proportion of women MPs has changed little over the last fifty years. For a long time, the high point in terms of the number of women elected to parliament was 1964 (Table 4.14). In that year there were 28 female MPs and subsequently the number fell to 23 at the 1983 election. At only 3–4 per cent of the total, this is a long way from the notional 50 per cent of seats which should accrue to women.

The Labour and Alliance parties are apparently more progressive in their selection of candidates and at the 1987 election had, respectively,

Table 4.14 Women candidates in General Elections, 1918–87

Election year	% of candidates	% of all MPs elected	No of women MPs
1918	1.0	0.1	1
1922	2.3	0.3	2
1923	2.4	1.3	8
1924	2.9	0.7	4
1929	4.0	2.3	14
1931	4.8	2.4	15
1935	5.0	1.5	9
1945	5.2	3.8	24
1950	6.8	3.4	21
1951	5.6	2.7	17
1955	6.5	3.8	24
1959	5.3	4.0	25
1964	5.1	4.6	29
1966	4.7	4.1	26
1970	5.4	4.1	26
1974 February	6.7	3.6	23
1974 October	7.1	4.3	27
1979	8.4	3.0	19
1983	10.9	3.5	23
1987	14.2	6.3	41

91 and 99 candidates; that is, about one in every six or seven candidates. The Conservative Party was less receptive to female candidates and only fielded 42 in that election. However, all these figures are rather deceptive, for women were disproportionately selected for seats for which the parties had no realistic hopes of victory. Nevertheless, there were some advances in the results of the 1987 election with the Conservatives having 17 women MPs, Labour 21 and the Liberals, SDP and the Scottish Nationalists one each. Despite this near doubling in the number of women MPs, one half of the UK's population still has only 6 per cent of the representatives in Parliament.

Within Parliament there has also been little advance in women's progression into the Cabinet. All Cabinets since 1945 have had at least one woman in them but again the high point came in the 1960s when, at various times, Harold Wilson appointed Barbara Castle, Shirley Williams and Judith Hart. In the 1980s the election of a Conservative government has had mixed consequences for women. On the one hand it brought a woman to the office of Prime Minister but she, in turn, has not notably championed the cause of other women. Except for a brief period when Baroness Young was Lord Privy Seal, there have been no other women in the Cabinet. The way in which she has conducted her government has also had ambiguous effects for women. It has been argued that her obvious toughness and competence may have reduced men's prejudices against women in power. However, the tendency to project her as 'the best man' in the Cabinet tends to single her out as a very atypical woman.

Outside Westminster there are signs that women have made more progress. They form about one quarter of all local government councillors in the UK and about one sixth of Britain's Euro MPs. However, the powers of local government have been severely constrained by Mrs Thatcher's governments and those of the European Parliament remain restricted.

Women also continue to be seriously under-represented in most of the other areas of the state. There are, for example, very few women on the boards of nationalised companies, few women in the upper echelons of the civil service, few women judges and no female chief constables. Their under-representation in the legal services also contributes to the lack of confidence that many women have in legal justice. There have been a series of court cases, especially with respect to rape, where judges have revealed strongly sexist attitudes in their summing-up or their sentencing.

Outside Parliament women have made some notable inroads in the political scene. The feminist movement has gained strength since the 1960s and since the first national meeting of the Women's Liberation Movement was held in 1970. The movement has sought more than just legal equality, for it has also been concerned to try and reduce the inferiority complex of women. This general movement has spawned a number of smaller organisations which have focused on more specific issues. One such group was Women in The Media which protested at the way women are portrayed by the media as well as their previous exclusion from jobs such as newsreading. Another such organisation was the Women's Aid Federation which has campaigned for refuges for battered wives. However, it is in the 1980s that women have gained greatest prominence in the political sphere. Two very different milestones were the largely middle-class Greenham Common movement and the essentially working-class support committees set up by miners' wives during the 1984–85 coal strike. Although the direct 'victories' of these movements may have been limited, they were important as assertions of a greater self-confidence amongst women in terms of their capacity for effective political action.

It is appropriate to end this chapter by returning to consider how these broader women's movements have influenced the major political parties themselves. There is a long tradition of special provision for women within the Labour Party. In the post-war period there has been a National Women's Advisory Committee and there have been statutorily-reserved places for women on the National Executive. However, until the late 1960s the women's organisation was largely peripheral to the real centres of power within the party. Subsequently the Labour Party has been influenced by feminist demands and has strengthened its commitments to positive discrimination. For example, since 1986 there has been a formal party commitment to creating a post of Minister of Women's Rights, and it has also been obligatory to include at least one woman on every short list of parliamentary candidates.

In contrast the Conservative Party is far less well disposed towards women's rights and is far more patriarchial. The party is, of course, overtly against sex discrimination and has supported the major legislative advances in this field. However, Mrs Thatcher has been resolutely opposed to all forms of positive discrimination. Indeed, the Prime Minister stated on Thames Television on January 1st 1981 that '. . . there is nothing more that you can do by changing the law to do away with discrimination. After all, I don't think there's been a great deal of discrimination against women for years'. Instead Mrs Thatcher's government has emphasised 'individualism' and individual initiative to overcome disadvantages. As such it does not recognise structural inequalities in UK society and is against policies to assist specific groups, whether defined by sex, class or race. In addition, as has already been noted, the weakening of the wages councils and cut-backs in the welfare state have severely disadvantaged many women.

This is not to say that the Conservative Party has been untouched by feminist demands for greater rights. For example in 1983 Emma Nicholson became Vice-Chairman of the party with special responsibility for women. However, as with some of the other concerns of Mrs Thatcher, such as environmental issues in 1988, it is difficult to see this as little more than window-dressing. Under the Thatcher government there have been few initiatives to further improve the position of women. Instead many of the government's policies have seriously harmed the opportunities open to women and their living conditions.

It is significant that in the 1970s the UK was at the forefront of legislation to give women and men equal rights, notably with the passing of the 1970 Equal Pay Act and the 1975 Sex Discrimination Act. In contrast, in the 1980s the UK has appeared before the European Court on sex discrimination charges more times than any other EC country.

Notes

1. S. Walby, 'Gender, class and stratification: towards a new approach', in R. Crompton and M. Mann (eds), *Gender and Stratification* (Cambridge: Polity Press, 1986).
2. R.E. Dobash and R. Dobash, *Violence Against Wives* (London: Free Press, 1979).
3. This view is exemplified by J.H. Goldthorpe, 'Women and class analysis: in defence of the conventional view', *Sociology*, 17 (1983), pp. 465–88.
4. A. Carter, *The Politics of Women's Rights* (London: Longmans, 1988).
5. D. Collinson, *Barriers to Fair Selection* (Manchester: Equal Opportunities Commission, 1988).

6. I. Bruegel, 'Women: the feminisation of poverty', *Interlink* (1987), p. 9.
7. R. Martin and J. Wallace, *Working Women In The Recession: Employment, Redundancy And Unemployment* (Oxford: Oxford University Press, 1984).
8. There is a considerable literature on the relationship between gender and class mobility. See S. Dex, *Women's Occupational Mobility: A Lifetime's Perspective* (London: Macmillan, 1987); P. Abbot and R. Sapsford, *Women And Social Class* (London: Tavistock, 1987); A. Heath, *Social Mobility* (London: Fontana, 1981).
9. Abbot and Sapsford, op. cit.
10. R.E. Pahl, *Divisions of Labour* (Oxford: Basil Blackwell, 1984).
11. A. Oakley, *The Sociology Of Housework* (London: Martin Robertson, 1974).

Further Reading

A good general introduction is provided by V. Beechey and E. Whitelegg (eds), *Women in Britain Today* (Milton Keynes: Open University Press, 1986).

The concepts of patriarchy and of the relationships between gender and stratification are discussed in R. Crompton and M. Mann (eds), *Gender and Stratification* (Cambridge: Polity Press, 1986); P. Abbot and R. Sapsford, *Women and Social Class* (London: Tavistock, 1987). J.H. Goldthorpe, 'Women and class analysis', *Sociology*, 17, 1983, pp. 465–88; S. Walby, *Patriarchy at Work* (Cambridge: Polity Press, 1986).

Women's role in the workforce is reviewed in V. Beechey, *Unequal Work* (London: Verson, 1987); V. Beechey and T. Perkins, *A Matter of Hours* (Cambridge: Polity Press, 1987); *Feminist Review* (ed), *Waged Work: A Reader* (London: Virago, 1986); S. Dex, *The Sexual Division of Work* (Brighton: Wheatsheaf, 1985); J. Jenson et al., *Feminization of the Labour Force* (Cambridge: Polity Press, 1988).

For a discussion of gender and class mobility see S. Dex, *Women's Occupational Mobility* (London: Macmillan, 1987).

Gender inequalities in education are discussed in M. Arnot, 'State education policy and girl's educational experiences', in V. Beechey and E. Whitelegg op. cit. 1986; T. Blackstone, 'Education' in N. Bosanquet and P. Townsend (eds), *Labour and Equality* (London: Heinemann, 1980), R. Deem (ed), *Schooling for Women's Work* (London: Routledge & Keegan Paul, 1980).

The household division of labour is considered in A. Oakley, *The Sociology of Housework* (London: Martin Robertson, 1974); see also R.E. Pahl, *Divisions of Labour* (Oxford: Basil Blackwell, 1984).

For a discussion of women and politics see A. Carter, *The Politics of Women's Rights* (London: Longmans, 1988).

5
Divided by race

The Division Begins: Immigration And The UK

Immigration is not a new phenomenon in the UK for it is a process with deep historical roots in slavery. There has also been a constant stream of immigration from Ireland throughout both the nineteenth and the twentieth centuries. By 1981, for example, there were an estimated one million first and second generation Irish people in the UK. In the post-1945 period the UK has become a multi-racial society and there are now several relatively large ethnic and national groups in UK society. This chapter will concentrate only on the 'black' population of the UK, that is those who are mostly of Afro-Caribbean or Asian origin. These are by far the largest racial minority groups and their study provides insights into the experiences of all non-white racial minorities with respect to education, jobs, housing and political power in the UK.

The incorporation of black people into UK society has passed through three main phases.[1] The first is the 'pre-competitive' period 1948–62. At this stage there were urgent shortages of labour in the UK and these were met by dual sourcing from the rest of Europe and from the colonies. 'Traditional' immigration from Ireland was augmented by an estimated 460,000 workers recruited in war-torn continental Europe. There was also active recruitment in the West Indies by companies such as London Transport, as well as a generally open-door policy towards immigration from the colonies. As can be seen from Figure 5.1, this phase of immigration peaked in the early 1960s before the introduction of legislation to control immigration.

The 1962 Commonwealth Immigration Act marked the beginning of a second phase of immigration, the 'competitive' period 1963–76. In this period immigration from the Indian sub-continent was dominant. The general level of immigration fell with occasional fluctuations such as the arrival of some 27,000 Ugandan Asians in 1972. As a result of legislative changes, immigration was increasingly dominated by the

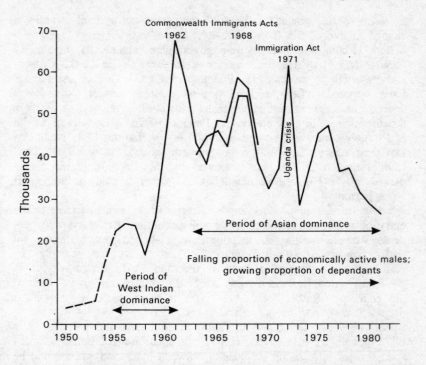

Figure 5.1 Immigration to the UK, 1950–82. (After C. Brock (ed.), *The Caribbean in Europe*, London: Frank Cass, 1986)

arrival of dependants, that is women, children and elderly relatives; by 1979 they constituted 90 per cent of all the new arrivals from the New Commonwealth. In the third phase, after 1977, the level of immigration has fallen further.

Meanwhile, it had become increasingly clear that black workers in the UK were not making the transition in the labour force from being unskilled to being skilled workers. Instead there was evidence that the labour market was becoming increasingly segmented along both class and racial lines, and that black workers were becoming part of an underclass.

Popular attitudes towards immigrants have also changed over time. In the 1950s there was a tendency to see West Indians as 'happy-go-lucky' and as being grateful to have any job. Needless to say, the view from within the West Indian community was very different. By the 1960s popular racism was taking root, especially in work places. It was fanned by the racialist comments of several MPs. Remarks such as that accredited to Conservative MP Martin Lindsay who referred to 'the future of our own race and breed' inflamed popular prejudices. Popular newspapers also tended to present immigration as a flood awaiting a chance to overwhelm British society.

Both Labour and Conservative governments shamefully gave in to popular racism by passing a series of immigration acts. The Conservatives began by passing the 1962 Immigration Act which the Labour Party opposed. After the 1963 general election Labour initially was against further immigration controls. However, when it lost the safe Smethwick seat in a by-election to Peter Griffiths, a Conservative who had largely campaigned on immigration issues, Labour Party strategists lost their nerve. The Wilson government passed the restrictive 1968 Immigration Act. This was followed by the 1971 Immigration Act passed by the Heath government which further limited the issuing of work permits.

These Immigrations Acts imposed increasingly strict barriers to the entry of immigrant workers while still permitting the entry of dependants. The legislation was inappropriately labelled because it was not really concerned with immigration. There were, for example, no restrictions on immigration from Ireland, and short-term guest workers were still welcome, indeed were essential to the labour-power needs of the economy. Rather these Acts were a racist response to popular prejudice and short-term political gains.

The UK only developed immigration problems and policies when black people were involved. It was not a question of immigration as such, but of how social boundaries between black and white could be maintained to the advantage of white people. One means of achieving this was through the creation of two kinds of citizenship and two kinds of British passport holder. This was the principal objective of the 1971 Act, which restricted UK nationality to patrials and to those who were registered citizens. Alternative citizenship – without automatic rights of residence – was granted to the (largely black) residual. This legislation, although not couched in overtly racialist terms, is not colour blind for the concept of patrials most severely impinged upon blacks.

By the mid-1970s race and immigration were again in the forefront of political concern. Both Labour and Conservatives stressed the need for strict controls on immigration, but there were differences in the attitudes of the parties. These differences are epitomised by the following quotations from the parliamentary debate on immigration on 5 July 1976:

Roy Jenkins (Labour):
  The British people occupy a largely urban, densely populated, industrialised island of limited size . . . Our imperial history, combined with the maldistribution of wealth and prosperity in the world has traditionally produced strong pressures to migrate to this country. These are basic facts. They necessitate both a strict limit on the amount and rate of inward immigration for settlement.

Winston Churchill (Conservative):
> We cannot fail to recognise the deep bitterness that exists among ordinary people who one day were living in Lancashire and wake up the next day in New Delhi, Calcutta or Kingston, Jamaica . . . I believe that generous arrangements should be available to anyone who wishes to return to the country that he regards as his homeland.

More severe restrictions on immigration were to follow after the Conservatives were returned to power. From the late 1970s Margaret Thatcher increasingly associated herself with the issue of immigration. In January 1978 she appeared on a World In Action programme on immigration and stated that 'people are really rather afraid that this country might be rather swamped by people with a different culture'. She then went on to promise a clear prospect of an end to immigration. Labour, to its credit, resisted the popular calls for further controls at this time, despite a rising tide of racialist hysteria in the country.

Once the Conservatives had been returned to power, further immigration legislation followed. The 1981 Nationality Act broke new ground by depriving UK-born children of immigrants of the automatic right of citizenship. The discretionary qualifications were such that, of course, they tended to favour white rather than black children. Then, in 1987, the Home Secretary, Douglas Hurd, introduced another Immigration Act which was designed to make 'sensible and limited changes' to earlier legislation. What this really meant was that the right was taken away from every male citizen of marriageable age to bring his (non-citizen) wife and children to the UK. The 1971 Act, which had provided for this right, was undoubtedly sexist in that it did not extend the same rights to women. However, Mrs Thatcher's government's response was to equalise rights by taking these away from men! As usual the legislation had racist undertones, for those with patrial connections (mostly white) were excluded from the restrictions. The real target of the legislation was young men of Asian origin who had been born in or brought up in the UK. They had had the right to marry and to bring to the UK anyone that they chose. The 1987 Act was an attempt to close what was seen as a serious loophole, albeit this meant a retrospective removal of fundamental rights. At the same time, overtly sexist legislation was replaced by implicitly racist laws.

Over time the nature of the Asian and Afro-Caribbean communities in the UK has changed. Partly as a result of legislation, and partly because of the onset of economic recession in the 1970s and 1980s, the number of new arrivals has fallen (see Figure 5.1). It is becoming less and less accurate to describe it as an immigrant community. By 1983–85 the black population of the UK was estimated to be approximately 3.4 per cent of the total population and 40–50 per cent had been born within the UK. Of these, about one third were of West Indian origin and about one half originated from the Indian sub-continent. This certainly provides a contrast with 1951 when only 0.4 per cent of the UK population was estimated to be black. However, the black population of Britain is, in numerical terms, no more than a small minority. Yet it is a minority which is on the wrong side of most of the social divides in the UK.

The important issues for this chapter are to identify the precise nature of racial inequalities in the UK and the ways in which these have changed over time. Such inequalities are not new features of UK society but they have become increasingly visible over time. The inequalities span education, politics, housing and many areas of consumption but, above all, they are grounded in economic realities. Herein also lie many of the problems of racial inequalities and of racial tensions, for black people in the UK made the transition from immigrant community to settled population at the same time as the post-war economic boom came to an end.

Black and White People In The Labour Market

Race and Class

There are at least three different views of the relationship between class and race in UK society. A 'class'-based view is that those at the bottom of British society have many overlapping disadvantages. Black people form one part of this class mainly by virtue of the jobs which they hold. Although they have some additional disadvantages resulting from racism, they share many class disadvantages with the white working class. In opposition to this a 'race'-based view stresses that it is white racism which keeps ethnic minorities at the bottom of the social hierarchy. A third view, and one that we would accept, is that there is some truth in both views.

The economic and social requirements of UK society create disadvantaged positions in the class structure of the country while racism ensures that black people continue to occupy a disproportionate number of these.[2] This was the view of the 1975 White Paper (Cmnd 6234) on racial discrimination:

Beyond the problem of cultural alienness, there are the problems of low status, of material and environmental deprivation which coloured immigrants and, increasingly, their children experience. To the extent that they share all or some of these problems with other groups in society, a general attack on deprivation will be relevant to their problems. But there may be a special dimension to their problems to the extent that the factor of racial discrimination multiplies and accentuates the disadvantages which are shared in part with others.

It is only a short leap from this position to viewing the black population as an underclass.[3] The black population forms an underclass below the white working class. It is characterised by being comprehensively disadvantaged in terms of jobs, housing and education. In terms of employment there is some overlap between the white and the black working class but blacks are far more concentrated in the dirtiest and lowest paid jobs. To this extent there are dual but not exclusive labour markets. The colonial legacy also contributes to the formation of an underclass. In the process of colonial exploitation black people were treated as socially and often legally inferior. These notions persist to fuel racism in the post-colonial era.

Although black people have been classified as an underclass, this does not mean that all black people belong either to this class or to the working class as a whole. After all the epithet 'black' is being used in this instance to describe people from several continents with very different colonial histories, languages and cultures. For example, some Asians have been able to channel their savings into small business formation and may associate themselves with the middle class. Indeed, when looking at the Asian communities there is a need to discard many of the traditional views concerning the economic position of black people. There are both rich and poor Asian families. Growing numbers of both Asian men and women have jobs in the professions or in city financial houses. Many middle class families are also investing in private education for their children so that their position in the class hierarchy will be consolidated in the next generation.

In contrast, West Indians tend to fare far less well both in the educational system and in the job market, and they are becoming increasingly conscious of these failures. While some have gained or will gain entry into and acceptance by the white working class, many others will not. Given the constancy of racialism in British society, and a growing alienation from the system of legal justice and enforcement, West Indians are increasingly likely to pursue separate black identities and alternative forms of political and community action.

Black and White Employment in the UK

Black immigrants initially came to the UK largely as a replacement labour force. They occupied the least skilled, the dirtiest and the lowest paid jobs. With hindsight it is clear that the flexible and cheap source of labour which they provided was an invaluable ingredient in the moderate but sustained expansion of the UK economy in the 1950s and the 1960s. A similar role was played in other Northern European countries by guest-workers from Southern Europe and North Africa. However, with the passage of time, it has become clear that black immigrants in the UK have made little progress in the labour market. In part this is because of the economic recessions of the 1970s and the 1980s which led to reduced openings in the job market. However, there are also other reasons, including widespread discrimination, poor access to education and cultural alienation. The result is that, despite

Table 5.1 Economic status by sex and ethnic group, 1984–86

Percentages of those aged 16–59/64 in Great Britain
(Percentages)

	Males			Females		
	White	West Indian or Guyanese	Indian/ Pakistani/ Bangladeshi	White	West Indian or Guyanese	Indian/ Pakistani/ Bangladeshi
Economically active in employment						
Employees – full-time	64	53	47	31	41	22
– part-time	2			24	14	7
Self-employed	11		15	4		4
On government scheme	1			1		0
All in employment	79	63	64	60	58	34
Unemployed	10	21	17	7	13	9
All economically active	88	84	81	67	71	43
Economically inactive						
Looking after home	4		10	22	14	41
Full-time student	2	7		4	9	7
Retired	6		7	1		
Other inactive				8	4	4
All economically inactive	12	16	19	34	29	57
Total	100	100	100	100	100	100

Source: *Social Trends*, 18 (1988), (CSO: HMSO) Table 4.6

Table 5.2 Occupations by ethnic group and sex in 1984–86 (Great Britain)

(Percentages*)

	Males			Females		
	White	West Indian or Guyanese	Indian/ Pakistani/ Bangladeshi	White	West Indian or Guyanese	Indian/ Pakistani/ Bangladeshi
Non-manual						
Managerial and professional	34	10	38	25	27	26
Clerical and related	5		6	30	27	23
Other	6		5	10		9
Total Non-manual	46	21	48	65	58	58
Manual						
Craft and related	26	34	19	4	16	16
General labourers	2					
Other	26	40	30	31	38	24
Total Manual	54	78	51	35	42	42
Total	100	100	100	100	100	100

*Small percentages suppressed so totals do not add to 100%
Source: *Social Trends,* 18 (1988), Table 4.13

individual successes, black workers have become trapped into a niche at the bottom end of the hierarchy of jobs, income and status.

The economic status of whites, Asians and West Indians is shown in Table 5.1. Amongst males there are higher activity rates for whites than there are for Asians or West Indians. However, for women the pattern is different and it is West Indians who have the highest activity rates. For cultural reasons, Asian women have had a very low activity rate. Even in the mid-1980s it was only 43 per cent which is no more than two-thirds that of the other two groups. There are also variations within the Asian group with Pakistani/Bangladeshi women having activity rates of only 17 per cent. Although these differences are partly to be explained by age structures, the main reason lies in the proportions who are 'looking after the home'.

There are further major differences between whites, Asians and West Indians in terms of their jobs (Table 5.2). West Indian males are less than half as likely as white or Asian males to be in non-manual jobs. West Indians are even more poorly represented in managerial and professional occupations than Asians and whites who are three to four times more likely to gain access to these jobs. Within manual jobs whites are more likely than West Indians to end up in craft-level work. In contrast, there are fewer variations amongst female workers. White women are more likely to obtain non-manual jobs but there is only a 7 percentage point difference. Perhaps, surprisingly, there are similar proportions of all three groups in managerial and professional jobs. However, looking at manual jobs, West Indian women – like West Indian men – seem to be strongly concentrated into below craft-level jobs.

The aggregate data seem to suggest that, in general, Asians are performing almost as well as whites in the labour market while West Indians are considerably disadvantaged. However, the real picture is different for non-whites consistently underachieve *within* most of these broad categories. They are, for example, given supervisory posts far less frequently than are whites. The largest difference is amongst skilled manual workers: 26 per cent of whites are supervisors compared to only 17 per cent of Asians and West Indians. Furthermore most non-white supervisors are likely to be in charge of the work of non-white employees, which confirms the highly segregated nature of the labour market. This is particularly evident in shift work, with much of the unpopular night time work being done by non-whites. In the textile industry in Yorkshire and Lancashire some nightshifts are manned almost entirely by Asian workers. Of course, not all black workers are doing similar types of jobs; one basic difference is the relative concentration of Asians in manufacturing and of West Indians in transport and the services, especially the NHS.

There are also differences between whites and blacks at the other end of the occupational scale. Only 5 per cent of West Indians are employers, managers or professional workers compared to 13 per cent of Asians and 19 per cent of whites. There are also many subtle divisions within seemingly identical occupations. For example, although Asians make up 27 per cent of the hospital doctors in the UK, they are concentrated into the least popular branches of medicine such as geriatrics. If such fine degrees of job distinctions within this and other occupations are taken into account, then there is clearly strong occupational segregation along ethnic lines in the UK.

The one area in which Asians (but not West Indians) seem to have made some progress is in self-employment. According to Table 5.1 a higher proportion of Asians than of whites are self-employed. A 1982 PSI survey[4] found even larger differences: amongst Asians 18 per cent of men and 14 per cent of women were self-employed compared to 14 per cent and 7 per cent for whites. Two-thirds of the self-employed Asians are in distribution, catering, repair and hotel work. Asians have certainly gained access to self-employment, and also to being small-scale employers; for example, they are increasingly to be found running corner shops or restaurants. Sometimes they survive only through the long hours worked by the owners and their families, a form of self-exploitation. Many of these businesses initially tended to be reliant on the ethnic community for their custom but their trade is becoming more widespread. The economic progress of the Asians is not to be denied. It also represents one of the rare successes of Mrs Thatcher's enterprise culture. However its obvious visibility tends to obscure the fact that four out of every five Asian workers are employees. Indeed many – especially the women – work in very low paid jobs either in 'sweat-shops' or as homeworkers. Moreover, West Indians have had a singular lack of success in becoming entrepreneurs. The Conservative Party's attempt to attract the electoral support of the black community is, in reality, directed at one small segment of it at the upper end of the occupational hierarchy for the Asians.

Lack of Skills or Discrimination?

It would be easy to dismiss the occupational segregation of black people as being due to their lack of employable skills. They came to the UK as replacement labour migrants and, therefore, is it not to be expected that they occupy the lowest rungs in the occupational hierarchy? Even if such an argument were true of the initial immigrants, it does not apply to the second generation who now form approximately one half of the black population.

However, the above argument was never accurate, even in the early period of immigration. Black people did come to the UK as replacement workers and they therefore tended to be drawn into those areas and those industries which had employment vacancies at the time. They were therefore to be found in low-paid and low-skilled jobs in the health service, transport and a few manufacturing industries in London and the larger cities. However, the posts which they took were often less skilled than their previous jobs. Many West Indians and Asians had to accept inferior positions to the white-collar and skilled jobs which they had held before. Not surprisingly the result was bitter disappointment.

Immigration was therefore accompanied by deskilling. The problems faced by the immigrants – and their children – were not overcome even if they had or were to acquire educational qualifications. Black people generally have lower educational qualifications than white people. However, even if this is taken into account, they still do less well in the labour market than might be expected. Qualifications do help. Amongst those with 'A' levels or higher qualifications, 84 per cent of whites compared to 75 per cent of Asians have non-manual jobs. The West Indians do even worse. In contrast, amongst those with no qualifications, the proportions of whites who have non-manual jobs is four times higher than the proportion of West Indians and twice as high as the proportion of Asians. Therefore, inequalities persist across all levels of educational qualifications. Even taking into account language difficulties amongst newly-arrived immigrants, non-whites still do far less well in the labour market than is to be expected according to any objective criteria.

Persistent inequalities in employment, over and above those to be expected on the bases of education and previous job-training, can mainly be accounted for by discrimination. This exists at the individual and the institutional level, and in direct and indirect forms. Since the Equal Opportunities Act most forms of racial discrimination are illegal and, consequently, this has disappeared in many of its open forms. However discrimination still persists in the UK in many indirect practices. It is underwritten by a colonial legacy and reinforced by the bitterness of race conflict over the four decades since large-scale post-war immigration was initiated.

Many immigrants faced discrimination as soon as they had arrived in the UK. One West Indian in the 1950s described his experiences thus:[5]

I arrived on a Sunday night. On the Monday morning I was taken to the Labour Exchange to go through all the formalities. I remember very clearly the cold stare given to me by the man behind the counter when I told him that I was interested in a job as a tracer in a drawing office. The reason I chose that job was because I had done about three years of evening classes doing a City and Guilds course in architectural draughtsmanship and although I had no formal drawing office practice I was confident that I could at least pull lines because of the experience I had in drawing basic plans for my father, who had been a building contractor. The job vacancy pages of the daily and evening papers were full of thousands of vacancies for this kind of job. But the Labour Exchange clerk paid no attention to my request and went straight to the filing cabinet labelled either manual workers or labourers.

It was not only institutional discrimination which immigrants had to face. Discrimination was common amongst employers and amongst their white fellow-employees. There are numerous examples of white workers refusing to work with black people. In one notorious incident in 1955, white workers at the West Bromwich Corporation Transport Department went on strike against the employment of Indian trainee bus conductors. Official trades unions policy was to oppose racism but, in general, unions were inactive in this field while many local shop stewards were blatantly racist.

Black people continue to face discrimination in the job market at the present time. For example, a number of test situations in which whites and blacks with equal qualifications or experience have applied for the same jobs have shown that the latter are less than half as likely to get the jobs. Furthermore, discrimination has not diminished over time. A comparison of two surveys undertaken in 1974 and 1982 found that *increasing* proportions of West Indians and female Asians had personal experience of discrimination when applying for a job.[6] About a quarter of the sample claimed to have experienced discrimination in the 1982 survey, a disturbingly high figure. Discrimination is greater at the lower end of the occupational hierarchy, hence black unskilled manual workers experience most racial discrimination over jobs. This group has disadvantage heaped upon disadvantage.

The low rates of reported discrimination probably understates its true extent. In the face of their own and their parents' experiences of the job market, many black people set their aspirations relatively low. If they were to raise their aspirations to match those of, say, whites with equal qualifications, the reported incidence of racial discrimination would probably be much greater.

Race and Earnings

Occupational segregation goes hand in hand with unequal earnings. In the early 1970s black, male non-manual workers had only 77 per cent of the earnings of white, male non-manual workers. The differences were less amongst manual workers, and the corresponding ratio for those in skilled jobs was only 89 per cent. For semi- and un-skilled workers there were no significant differences, but this reflects the greater amount of shift work done by black workers rather than genuine equality of pay. For women the picture was more complex, not least because blacks were more likely to be in full-time jobs than were whites but, taking this into account, the usual racial differences emerge.

The reasons for inequalities in earnings are clear. Black workers are more concentrated into low-pay industries and occupations, both manual and non-manual. In addition older workers usually earn more than younger ones and this is to the disadvantage of the black community which is relatively young. However, of greater consequence is the

Table 5.3   Gross earnings by race and age, 1982

| | Full-time employees in Britain Median earnings (£s) per week | | | |
| | All | | Aged 25–54 | |
	White	Black	White	Black
Males				
All males	129	110	137	115
Professional etc.	185	152	187	171
Other non-manual	136	130	144	138
Skilled manual	122	112	127	115
Semi-skilled	111	101	115	104
Unskilled manual	100	98	117	111
Females				
All females	78	79	92	82
Professional etc.	107	122	105	130
Other non-manual	82	86	99	97
Skilled manual	67	74	71	74
Semi- and unskilled manual	67	72	72	76

Source: C. Brown, *Black and White in Britain* (London: Heinemann, 1984), Tables 111 and 113

failure of blacks to gain promotion within particular occupational groups; racial discrimination plays a key role in this.

There has been little narrowing of income differentials during the 1970s and the 1980s. According to the 1982 PSI survey, white men earn about £20 more than West Indian men and £18 more than Asian men. For women the differentials are smaller, being £4 less for Asians and £3 more for West Indians than for whites. While the differences are partly due to occupational segregation they persist across *all* the main occupational groupings (Table 5.3). In the 25–54 age group, the gap between blacks and whites appears far more significant. This is because most workers are paid fairly minimal wages when training or when on the first rungs of a career ladder, while many older workers may be partially retired, or are more likely to be working part-time. The earnings gap is also larger than it appears at first sight because more black workers than white workers are involved in higher-paid shift work.

Aggregate figures show that black women and white women earn approximately equal wages. If age is controlled for, then the difference is reversed in favour of white women (Table 5.3). This confirms that black women are still failing to achieve higher paid jobs in proportionate numbers. However, there are no major differences in earnings between black and white women in each separate occupational group. One reason for this similarity in earnings is that the large gender

Table 5.4 Unemployment rates by gender and race, 1984–86

	(Percentages)	
	Males	*Females*
White	10	7
West Indian	21	13
Asian	17	9
All	10	7

Source: Central Statistical Office, 1988

differential in pay between men and women leaves little scope for further disparities along racial lines. In other words most women are already earning minimal wages within any particular occupational group, so that further differences between black and white women are minimal. This combination of gender and racial inequalities is an important example of multiple deprivation, a theme which we return to later.

Race and Unemployment: Young Black People's Inheritance?

The economic disadvantages of black people are further compounded by higher unemployment rates compared to white people. Male unemployment rates are about twice as high for black workers as for white workers (Table 5.4). There is a similar differential between whites and West Indians amongst female workers, but a far smaller one for Asians. All these unemployment rates have been affected by changes introduced by the Conservative government in the 1980s in the recording of unemployment; the true rates are probably higher for all ethnic groups.

Unemployment is even greater amongst young black people. According to the 1984 Labour Force Survey the unemployment rates for males aged 16–24 were as follows: whites 20 per cent, Asians 25 per cent, and West Indians 40 per cent. The equivalent rates for women were 15 per cent, 35 per cent and 25 per cent. In addition, young people of Pakistani or Bangladeshi origin face a higher probability of unemployment than these data suggest. The immigrants of the 1950s and 1960s had faced considerable discrimination in the labour market but they did at least find jobs. Unfortunately this is far less likely to be true of their children. There has been even less of a welcome – in economic terms – for black children than there had been for their parents.

Not only is the rate of unemployment higher for black people but the differential with white people has increased over time. While total unemployment increased twofold during the 1970s, black unemployment increased fourfold. One reason for this is the concentration of black people in the types of jobs which have been most severely affected by the recession; that is, traditional and marginal industries concentrated in the hard-hit inner cities. In addition the young age profile of the black community has meant that disproportionate numbers have first entered the labour market at a time of recession. It has also meant that disproportionate numbers have been in their first jobs only for short periods of time; consequently they were particularly vulnerable to the 'last-in-first-out' rule that often applies at a time of redundancies. Over and above this, there is also the constant discrimination against black people, which may make it difficult for them to obtain jobs in the first place, and to retain them subsequently. Until recently the trades unions have opposed such racism passively rather than actively.

Black Workers and the Trades Unions: Reluctant Support

If trades unions do not represent the needs of black workers, it is not because they are not members of the unions. On the contrary, in the 1980s black workers are far more likely than white workers to be unionised. While only one half of white workers belong to unions, more than 70 per cent of Asian and West Indian workers in the formal economy are members. Black workers are, generally, more likely to be in firms which have high rates of union membership.

While black workers tend to support the trade unions, they do not necessarily obtain the support from the unions which they expect or to which they are entitled. Black workers are poorly represented at virtually every level of trade union organisation, except for the actual membership. There are relatively few black full-time officials, black delegates to conferences or black shop-floor representatives. The critical period was probably the 1950s and the 1960s when the unions were at the height of their power and the UK economy was expanding, hence creating new opportunities. This was when the unions could have fought and probably achieved substantial improvements for the black working class. That challenge was not taken up. Ironically the unions have become more aware of the needs of their black members in the 1980s but at a time when their powers have been severely curbed by Mrs Thatcher's governments.

It has taken many years of struggle by black workers to get the unions to take up their causes. There have been a number of hard-fought benchmark disputes through which black workers have gradually won better rights. The first two of these were in the Midlands, at the Wolf plant in Southall and at Mansfield Hosiery Mills in Loughborough. In both cases Asian workers were frustrated at being allocated the least desirable jobs and the most unsociable shifts. Frustrated also by a lack of support from the local unions, they took unofficial action to remedy their complaints. After long struggles and with the reluctant support of the unions, they eventually won their struggle. In this, as in many other struggles by black workers, Asians rather than West Indians took the lead. This was not because West Indians had no grievances – far from it. However, they tended to be employed in a more dispersed way through a variety of workplaces unlike the Asians who had a far stronger tradition of community-based job recruitment. In other words the grievances of the West Indians were less visible, less dramatic and less easy to organise.

The next major dispute was again in the Midlands, this time at the Imperial Typewriter Company in Leicester. The Asian workers at the factory felt that they were being set far harder production targets than the white workers. Furthermore, they did not feel that the largely-white shop stewards committee was responsive to their grievances. In the end they staged a walk-out. At first the strike was opposed by the local TGWU committee and it only backed the strike under pressure from the union's national committee.

In the 1980s the focus of attention switched to London with the Grunwick strike. The largely Asian female workforce walked out in protest at the lack of union recognition at the factory, but the underlying causes were intense frustration with low wages and appalling working conditions. This was to be a major landmark because the small Asian workforce was able to win massive support from a number of sections of the white working class. Whether white workers turned out on the picket lines to defend trade unionism or to defend the rights of the Asian workers is less important than the fact that they were there.

By the 1980s there was a fuller awareness of the needs of black workers in the trade union movement. This was developing anyway in the 1960s and the 1970s but it has intensified in recent years. In part Mrs Thatcher's government is responsible for this, not least in the way that its attacks on organised labour have served to unify black and white workers in a common cause in a number of disputes. Against this, however, the tensions stemming from the growth of unemployment in the 1980s had the potential to divide the working-class, especially along racial lines. The fact that it has not done so, leastways in the work place, is in part due – almost perversely – to the way in which the Conservative government, through its policies, has undermined the influence of the National Front and other right-wing groups. This applies as much to its stance on immigration as it does to specific employment policies.

Race and Occupational Mobility: Unequal Progress

While black workers occupy some of the lowest rungs in the occupational hierarchy, it is possible that over time they have improved their status and their access to better jobs. One indicator of occupational mobility is to be found in a comparison of the proportion of each ethnic group which was in the highest socio-economic category in 1974 and

1982.[7] The proportion of whites was constant but there was a two-fold increase for Asians and a four-fold increase for West Indians. Therefore, there would seem to be a marked degree of upward social mobility amongst the black population. As ever, care must be exercised in interpreting such data.

Rather than a general upward social mobility of black workers, there has been increased polarisation between and within ethnic groups. At the lower end of the social scale there has been an increasing *relative* concentration of black workers in semi- and un-skilled jobs. The proportion of Asians in this category has fallen by an eighth, but the proportion of whites has fallen even faster, by approximately one quarter. However, the proportion of West Indians in this lowest occupational category has actually increased. Black workers in general, but West Indians in particular, are becoming increasingly locked into an underclass. There may be some upward mobility at the other end of the occupational hierarchy but even this is limited. For example, the net movement of black workers from manual to non-manual jobs between 1974 and 1982 was only 3 per cent.

The previous analysis was based on aggregate numbers in particular occupational groups at two different dates. Such an approach does not tell us how individuals have fared. Longitudinal data are required for this purpose and these have been used in a major study of the London labour market between 1971 and 1981.[8] This shows conclusively – leastways within London – that in the 1970s black workers have suffered more from unemployment, and have become relatively more concentrated in the lower rungs of the occupational hierarchy. Black workers have become increasingly marginalised, and have been left 'high and dry' as jobs have disappeared in many traditional industries.

The experiences of black workers in London in the 1970s have been far from homogeneous, however. Male Asian workers have been moving into skilled manual work even though the size of this sector has declined. West Indians have also made some gains, notably in obtaining low status clerical jobs in the rapidly expanding service industries. However, West Indians were also the only group to increase in number in the declining manual sector, and they also recorded the most severe rates of unemployment.

Employment provides a critical test of the degree to which black people have been integrated into UK society. The evidence suggests little if any success for black people as a whole. Of course there are individual success stories, and parts of the Asian community have prospered, gaining entry to the professions or becoming small-scale business owners. Nevertheless, the impression remains that, as a whole, second generation black children are still getting the same types of low pay and low skill jobs as their parents. The limited shift into the higher social categories does little more than reflect structural changes which are occurring in the UK economy. Nevertheless, West Indians have remained firmly rooted at the bottom end of the occupational hierarchy and have shared least in upward social mobility. One of the keys to this is educational performance.

Education And Race

Education is important both because of its influence on job opportunities and its role in socialisation. The education of the first wave of immigrants had largely been determined before they arrived in the UK – although, of course, some were to enrol on further education courses. However, with the second generation immigrants, it is important to review their performance within the UK educational system.

There is no simple and direct link between education and employment for any ethnic group, let alone black people. For example, one study of young black people in Leeds and Manchester found that even the children of immigrants who have grown up in Britain, speak English fluently and have good educational qualifications have difficulties in obtaining jobs which match their qualifications.[9] This was highlighted by the fact that over two-thirds of black graduate students were turned down by employers without being interviewed compared to only about one fifth of white students. In a sense educational qualifications seem to create additional problems for black people. The ratio of white to black unemployment is actually far higher for those with qualifications than it is for those without any qualifications.

Despite this cautionary note about the limits to an educational route to better jobs, it is still an important indicator of the progress of black people in UK society.

Educational Achievement and Underachievement

The 1981 Rampton Report on the education of black children found clear evidence of differences in performance between various ethnic groups. The worst results were achieved by West Indian children. Asian children usually did at least as well as, and sometimes better than, white children. The differences can be summarised in terms of a number of indicators:

a) Only 5 per cent of West Indians compared to 20 per cent of Asians and 23 per cent of all UK school leavers had high grades in CSE and 'O' level mathematics.
b) Only 3 per cent of West Indians compared to 18 per cent of Asians and 21 per cent of all UK groups had 5 or more 'O' levels.
c) Only 2 per cent of West Indians compared to 13 per cent of Asians and 13 per cent of all UK groups had one or more 'A' levels.
d) Only 1 per cent of West Indians compared to 3 per cent of Asians and 5 per cent of all UK groups went on to university.

e) West Indian children were four times as likely as other schoolchildren to be in ESN schools.

While Asian children as a whole did outperform West Indians, their achievements were far more polarised than these data suggest. High achievements at one end of the scale were matched by some very poor results at the other. If all CSE or 'O' level results are considered, then Asians do *less* well than West Indians and both groups perform far worse than white children. The differences are particularly acute for girls: one half of young black Asian girls compared to only one fifth of West Indian girls had no qualifications at all. The Rampton Report gave rise to the mistaken assumption that all Asian children are doing well. This is not the case and some Asian children – especially from working-class backgrounds – share the educational disadvantages of the West Indians.

Table 5.5 Highest qualification level by sex and ethnic group in 1984–86

| | % of population aged 25–29 | | | |
	White	West Indian/ Guyanese	Indian	Pakistani/ Bangladeshi
Highest qualification held				
Males				
Higher	17	6	24	12
Other	47	36	34	21
None	36	58	42	67
Total	100	100	100	100
Females				
Higher	14	16	15	6
Other	36	30	29	14
None	50	54	56	80
Total	100	100	100	100

Source: *Social Trends*, 18 (1988) Table 3.22

The need to further disaggregate the data for Asians is confirmed by Table 5.5 which treats the Indian and Pakistani/Bangladeshi groups separately. The male Indian adult population is as well qualified as the white adult population. In contrast, while 12 per cent of the male adult Pakistani/Bangladeshi group have higher educational qualifications, 67 per cent lack any qualification; this is considerably higher even than for West Indians. The position of Pakistani/Bangladeshi women is worse still, for 80 per cent have no formal qualifications. In contrast, Indian and West Indian women have similar qualifications to white adult women.

Explaining Educational Underachievement

The reasons for the poor educational performance of black children include the home environment, social class, lack of fluency in English, the type of school attended and racism. None of these alone provides a sufficient explanation and not all the reasons apply equally to all ethnic groups. However, taken as a whole they explain a large part of the observed disadvantages.

The educational performance of all children is affected by the emotional and material circumstances of their home environment. It has been argued that the children of black parents are doubly disadvantaged in that they tend to come from low income homes in which parental concern for education is often absent. While the first part of this argument is certainly true, most of the evidence shows that the pressure for educational performance and excellence is as strong amongst black parents as it is amongst white parents.

One of the supposed sources of disadvantage amongst West Indian families is the higher incidence of single families which may lead to a lack of emotional support. Yet, if social class is controlled for, there are no significant differences in the educational performance of children in single and two-parent families. Furthermore, as the structure of the family does not seem to harm the educational performance of West Indian children in the West Indies, it is unlikely to be the primary reason for their poor performance in the UK.

Black children do suffer disadvantages, however, as a result of their home backgrounds. Some are disadvantaged by a linguistic handicap if their parents are not used to speaking standard English at home. The difficulties this causes, given that schools only teach in standard English, are considerable. Large family sizes, poor living conditions and a lack of quiet working space may also contribute to poor educational performance. But these multiple disadvantages are shared with many white children from poor backgrounds.

Social class certainly does contribute to poor educational performance. As black families, and especially West Indian ones, are disproportionately represented amongst the working class, particularly among unskilled manual workers, it is to be expected that they will underachieve. On this basis alone poor educational achievements are likely. The importance of class is confirmed by the fact that there is no real difference in the performance levels of middle-class West Indian and white children.

The type of school attended is also influenced by social class. This is mediated through both the neighbourhood effect (middle-class areas tend to have better schools) and the public/private divide. Purchasing a private education is not a realistic option for most black parents, although it is becoming so for growing numbers of middle-class Asians. This lack of access to private education contributes to underachievement in examinations. White parents, whose children are of marginal ability (in terms of examination results), can buy the additional assistance provided by low staff–pupil ratios in private schools. Such a strategy is financially impossible for many black parents. Instead, their children depend on the education available in local state schools. Given the residential distribution of the black community, this often means a decaying and under-resourced inner-city school. Furthermore, black children are disproportionately likely to attend schools where the average ability level and aspirations are low. This also leads to underachievement by individuals.

Within the school black children suffer disadvantages resulting from linguistic difficulties. This was more of a problem in the early days of immigration when it was compounded by tardy provision of teaching English as a second language. It has become less of a problem as second and third generation black children pass through the school system, but large numbers still suffer some form of linguistic disadvantage. One of the most common of these is a lack of English practice outside the school especially in Asian homes. In the early 1980s one fifth of Asian men and one half of Asian women spoke little or no English; this must adversely affect their children's performance at school. West Indian children may also suffer educationally because many of their parents speak Creole or patois at home. Such problems are, of course, much more common in working-class than in middle-class homes.

Until recently school teaching was heavily influenced by the history and culture of white Britain. This did not necessarily affect educational achievements as such. However, apart from the fact that it may have encouraged or reinforced racist ideas amongst white children, this may have contributed to low self-esteem amongst black children. There has been some shift to a more multi-cultural education precisely in order to apply some positive discrimination to this problem. There is certainly a need to oppose racist stereotyping wherever it is found. However, the heavy emphasis given to multi-cultural education can also be criticised for it distracts attention from the fundamental way in which class and race interact to produce educational disadvantage.

Racism also contributes to under-achievement by black children. This operates in a number of ways. There are some overtly racist teachers, while racism in the job market may discourage black children from pursuing educational qualifications. More important than overt racism are the low expectations that many teachers have of black children, especially West Indians. Low expectations contribute to low self-fulfilment.

Black children do underachieve in the educational system but this does not apply to all individuals or, in equal measure, to all ethnic groups. It also does not apply equally to both black males and females. Nevertheless, the broad class, home and school conditions outlined above do explain a large part of the educational disadvantage of black children. These disadvantages tend to have a multiple character. Not least, inequalities in the job market and in schools feed upon each other and add significantly to the cumulative disadvantages of black youngsters.

Race and Education Policy: From the Plowden Report to Thatcherism

The response of the state to racial disadvantage has been relatively muted, leastways at central level; the response of local authorities has been more mixed but often more positive. The dominant ethos of educational policy is probably best represented by the views of the 1967 Plowden Committee. This argued that black and white children in inner-city areas were equally disadvantaged. The policy response was measures such as Educational Priority Areas and Educational Disadvantage Units. The Rate Support Grant was also weighted in favour of urban areas, while Section 11 of the 1966 Local Government Act had been specifically directed at the educational needs that arise from the presence of immigrant children in an area.

In so far as there is an underlying philosophy to this approach, it was to avoid identifying race as a source of disadvantage per se. Instead class, low income or location were seen as the major underlying causes. Hence the emphasis was on the needs of immigrant rather than of black children. As such, there was a tendency to see the educational difficulties of black children as being temporary, linked to the difficulties of transition to or assimilation in white UK society. This underestimated the persistent difficulties faced by second and third generation immigrants. It also meant that the issues of how to represent black culture in the school curriculum were played down.

Another failing of this approach was that it treated all black children alike, even though there are both high and low achievers and disadvantaged and non-disadvantaged. In its most pernicious form this also involved associating black children with the causes of educational disadvantage in some areas. It was a view which was also present in the Plowden Report, for it used the proportion of immigrants in an area as one indicator of educational disadvantage. The same theme emerged in a more political and blatantly racist form in West London in the early 1970s. Parents at two schools complained of the presence of large numbers of immigrant children. The Tory Education Minister suggested that 30 per cent should be the upper limit for such children in any one school and that dispersal or spreading might be necessary to achieve this. In practice, few local authorities ever practised this policy. It was abandoned in 1975.

By the late 1970s the context for policy formulation was changing. In particular the minority communities and black parents began to demand multi-cultural education. Initially such parents had wanted their children to be completely assimilated into British society through the educational system. This was perceived as a route to better jobs and to upward social mobility. However, the experiences of the 1960s and the 1970s had been disappointing. Partly in reaction to this, and partly as a reflection of the growing self-assurance of the black communities, there was now a demand for a less Euro-centred education which recognised the values and the cultures of non-whites.

The Labour government in the later 1970s started to move in the direction of multi-racial education. Its 1977 Green Paper on education stressed that there was a need to review an educational curriculum which was still firmly rooted in an imperial past. Mrs Thatcher's government at first showed little sign of responding to these pressures, but it was galvanised into action by the 1981 civil disturbances. The Scarman Report pointed to school failures and unemployment as being linked to the 1981 riots. This led the Department of Education, in the same year, to issue guidance that schools should promote greater tolerance of other races and cultures.

Local authorities reacted to this advice in various ways. Some simply ignored it while others, such as the Inner London Education Authority, set out to develop new curricula and other teaching resources. It was probably inevitable that there would be some sort of backlash to the introduction of multi-cultural education. This surfaced with a vengeance in Bradford. Ray Honeyford, headmaster of a largely Asian school, published an article in the *Salisbury Review* in which he voiced concern that an emphasis on multi-cultural education could lead to a neglect of the needs of indigenous white children. The article received national publicity which sharpened the political debate on multi-cultural education. This was taken a step further when some white parents in Bradford's inner city refused to send their children to local schools. Multi-cultural education was the underlying issue although it was also presented as a confrontation over parental choice. The parents eventually won their case in the courts on a technicality. As a result, the issue has faded somewhat from the media spotlight but the serious dilemmas posed by multi-cultural education remain. Not least there is the need to balance the rights and needs of white and black children.

What, if anything, has Mrs Thatcher's government contributed to the debate on the education of black children? The answer is that it has made very little direct contribution to the evolution of policy. Not least this is because Mrs Thatcher's view of individual responsibility and individual initiative ignores structural disadvantages in society, whether derived from class or race. However, in the longer term it is possible that Thatcherite educational policies will be detrimental to the needs of the black community. The emphasis on parental choice (both within the public sector and between the public and private sectors) and on schools being allowed to opt out is unlikely to benefit the vast majority of black children. This is precisely because much of educational disadvantage is structural, being linked to home, class and neighbourhood. The children of a few middle-class black parents may benefit from private education, but it is difficult to see how 'parental choice' will benefit most working-class children, let alone black working-class children, in any practical way.

Race And Housing: Black And White In Separate Worlds?

Race and class are closely intertwined in the field of housing. Immigrants tend to be concentrated in the worst quality housing but this can not be accounted for simply by class. For black people within each class tend to occupy the worst housing. There are also persistent differences in the housing tenure of white and black families and of Asians and West Indians which go beyond those which could be expected simply on the basis of class.

Racial exclusion or channelling effects in housing is produced by a variety of mechanisms. There is, of course, outright discrimination in all the tenure sectors but legislation in the 1970s has removed at least the more overt manifestations of this. Abolishing institutional discrimination does not of course guarantee the removal of more individual and informal forms of racism. However, the removal of institutional discrimination has assured better access to local authority housing for black people. The problem is that improved access in the 1970s has been followed in the 1980s by Mrs Thatcher's governments' policies to reduce the size of and the role of public sector housing.

In the private sector racial exclusion has been achieved via the market mechanisms of prices and ability to pay. As the black population has lower incomes relative to whites, higher prices for properties in some areas disproportionately exclude them. Therefore class discrimination becomes linked to racial discrimination to produce a form of housing segregation which is beyond the scope of existing legislation. We see here the difference between the rhetoric of legislation and the realities of how an unequal society operates.

This is not to imply that the position of black people in housing markets has been static. Quite apart from the effects of anti-discrimination legislation, the competitive ability of black groups has changed over recent decades. Longer established immigrants and second and third generation black people have become more linguistically adept, more aware of their housing rights and, in some cases, more powerful in terms of purchasing power. It is therefore to be expected – and indeed this is the case – that black people would

Table 5.6　The housing tenures of ethnic groups in 1982 (Great Britain)

	White	*(Percentages)* West Indian	Asian
Owner-occupied	59	41	72
Council rented	30	46	19
Privately rented	9	6	6
Housing association	2	8	2
Total*	100	100	100

* 'Others' excluded so the columns do not add up to 100%
Source: C. Brown, *Black and White in Britain* (London: Heinemann, 1984) Table 29

have improved their housing conditions. However, the overall housing conditions of white people have also improved in the same period. Consequently, in relative terms, black people still tend to do less well in the housing market; this applies particularly to West Indians.

Divided Ways: Race and Access to Housing Tenure

By the early 1980s there were relatively simple patterns of housing tenure. West Indians, in comparison to whites, were far more concentrated in council housing and housing association dwellings: the corollary to this was the smaller proportion of West Indians in owner occupation (Table 5.6). In contrast, Asian households were more likely than white households to be in owner occupation – by 72 per cent compared to 59 per cent. They were far less likely to be in the public sector.

Taken in isolation, housing tenure data say little about either the presence or absence of discrimination or about housing conditions. However, some insights into housing conditions are provided by the 1982 PSI survey (see Table 5.7). Both Asians and West Indians have less satisfactory conditions than the white population with respect to every one of the principal indicators. West Indians are especially likely to be living in flats rather than in detached or semi-detached houses. Asians are more likely to be in older dwellings which lack basic amenities and are overcrowded.

It could be argued that these differences in housing conditions are no more than is to be expected given the different tenures of the three groups. However, this is not the case as can be seen from considering the main tenures separately (Table 5.7). Amongst owner-occupiers, Asians and West Indians are less likely than whites to be living in detached dwellings (instead being in terraced dwellings), and more

Table 5.7 Housing conditions of ethnic households in 1982

	% in flats	% in detached or semi detached houses	% in dwellings built pre-1945	% lacking exclusive use of both hot water and inside wc	% with > 1 person per room
(Percentages)					
All tenure groups					
White	15	54	50	5	3
West Indian	32	23	60	5	16
Asian	16	26	74	7	35
Owner-occupiers					
White	5	67	56	3	2
West Indian	1	37	84	3	13
Asian	4	29	81	5	33
Council tenants					
White	27	39	27	3	5
West Indian	54	9	34	3	20
Asian	54	11	35	7	43
Private tenants					
White	32	33	87	27	2
West Indians and Asian	24	21	83	32	22

Source: C. Brown, *Black and White in Britain* (London: Heinemann, 1984) Table 35

likely to be in older properties lacking amenities. They are also more likely to be living at higher occupational densities – and this applies particularly to the Asians. The same pattern of inequality is present in the local authority sector. Only in the privately rented sector is there some blurring of differences. This reflects the way in which this tenure has become the 'last resort' for many of the poorest members of all ethnic groups.

The class differences between Asians and West Indians are simply not substantial enough to explain such sharp variations in access to tenure. In order to better appreciate inequalities in access to housing each type of housing tenure is considered separately.

Private renting: the last resort

Until the early 1970s private renting was the principal source of housing for the black population, especially immigrants. They lacked sufficient priority to be housed by the public sector and lacked the money to buy a home. In contrast there was a relatively large stock of privately rented dwellings available, especially in the inner cities, which were also the principal labour markets for immigrants. The quality of such dwellings was often poor, while their leases were short and insecure. Even so immigrants often encountered discrimination in this sector.

One response to such discrimination was for black immigrants to seek black landlords, a process which contributed to class divisions within the black community. While this provided an immediate response to the housing needs of immigrants, it could not offer a long term solution to their housing needs and aspirations. Even if they chose to remain or were constrained to remain in the private sector, they were likely to encounter discrimination when they eventually moved. This was especially likely if they tried to move outside their communities or if their command of English was poor.

Over time the importance of private renting has declined for the black community as the overall size of the sector has shrunk. However, it is encouraging that the reported level of discrimination has also fallen sharply in this sector. In the 1960s a series of controlled experiments was undertaken whereby whites and blacks of similar incomes and ages telephoned for advertised rented flats or rooms. Discrimination against West Indians occurred in 62 per cent of the test cases. By the mid 1970s similar experiments found a discrimination level of 27 per cent against West Indians and Asians. As the most informally allocated type of housing, this is the tenure where direct discrimination can be expected to be greatest. There is therefore some comfort to be drawn from these data. Similar data are not available for the 1980s but the 1982 PSI survey did ask whether Asians and West Indians had ever been refused accommodation by a private landlord on the grounds of race or colour. About one half of the West Indians and one third of the Asians had such personal experiences. Any case of discrimination is of course serious but the decline of private renting means that it has become less of an explanation for the overall position of black people in the housing market.

Council Housing: Administrative Discrimination

In the 1950s and much of the 1960s black people were severely disadvantaged in their access to local authority housing. It was not so much that housing departments operated openly racist or discriminatory systems of housing allocation. Instead, there was indirect discrimination in that many housing departments had residential qualifications which tended to exclude newly-arrived immigrants. In allocating priority to applicants, they gave disproportionate weight to length of time on the waiting list rather than to housing need; this also discriminated indirectly against the black community. Furthermore, out of desperation at being unable to find satisfactory rented housing, many immigrants had purchased very poor quality houses. Yet the fact that they were house-owners – never mind the quality – also excluded them from many housing waiting lists.

With time, the residential qualifications became less of a barrier for immigrants, especially the longer-settled West Indians. Consequently by the time of a PEP survey in the mid-1970s the proportion of West Indians in council housing was approaching that for the white population – if social class was controlled for. At a later date Asians were also able to secure better access to council housing. In Blackburn, for example, only one Asian household a year was allocated a council tenancy between 1968 and 1972. By 1978 there were 56 allocations in a single year.[10] However, even by the mid-1980s the proportion of Asians living in council houses was far smaller than for white or West Indian people. In part this was due to slowness in the catching-up process, but it also reflected a cultural preference for home ownership and, increasingly, their greater purchasing power compared to West Indians.

Better treatment on council waiting lists still left scope for discrimination in the allocation process. This is evident in a comparison of the types of council dwellings occupied by the major ethnic groups (Table 5.7). Black people are twice as likely to be allocated flats than houses, and are four times less likely to be allocated semi-detached or detached dwellings. They are also more likely to be allocated pre-1945 dwellings. There are also many other forms of unequal access. For example, black people tend to have to accumulate more points on the waiting list before being made their first offer of a council house. They are also less likely than white people to be given their first-choice area of residence.

Inequality of access to better quality council dwellings is partly due to discrimination by housing department officials, especially by the housing visitors who prepare reports on prospective tenants. However, the major barrier to greater equality of access lies in the way that housing department rules are framed. These tend to discriminate against certain groups and black people tend to belong to these groups. Housing officers are under pressure to minimise the numbers of vacant properties and also to maximise their rent yields. They therefore tend to offer better quality dwellings to 'respectable' applicants and offer rougher quality dwellings to their lowest-rated tenants. Such a strategy is also seen as a way of minimising conflicts between tenants and of easing the general problems of housing management. The result is that racial and class discrimination are an inherent part of housing allocation.

The inequalities which have been described existed before 1979 and had evolved slowly throughout the post-1945 period. However, the policies of Mrs Thatcher's governments have exacerbated the difficulties of access for the black community. Council house sales are leading to a process of residualisation as better quality dwellings are sold to the better-off tenants. This leaves a residue of poorer quality dwellings for those in greatest need and with the least resources at their disposal. Poor black people – especially West Indians – are therefore increasingly in competition with poor white people for a dwindling stock of poor quality council housing.

Owner-occupation: Housing Market Discrimination

In the 1950s and the 1960s the only real alternative to private renting was home purchase if the immigrants could secure sufficient capital or a mortgage. This was often the preferred option of the Asian community. Through hard work and savings, even relatively poor Asians managed to buy homes. Hence, by the 1980s, almost four in every five Asian households owned their own homes.

This simple statistic should not be taken to mean that Asian families had somehow unlocked the access gate to large detached homes in leafy suburban lanes. Instead for many immigrants their first purchase was a low-price, short-leasehold, low-quality property. Given their incomes, it was often all that they could afford. In this respect housing-market position reflected job-market position. There has subsequently been a marked improvement in the position of black owner-occupiers as they have gradually moved up-market. However, even in the 1980s they still occupy distinctly poorer quality owner-occupied dwellings than do white owner-occupiers (see Table 5.7). These homes also tend to be disproportionately concentrated in the inner areas of the large cities.

Both race and class contribute to the residential concentration of black people in the inner cities. Nevertheless, black families face more obstacles than do white families of the same social class. For example, in Birmingham a larger proportion of whites have been able to secure building society loans. Whites are also less likely to face building society refusals of their mortgage applications: the respective rates are 39 per cent, 51 per cent and 53 per cent for whites, West Indians and Indian families.[11] The precise way in which this operates is unclear. But in part it is because building societies generally do not favour lending on inner-city properties. This applies to both whites and blacks in these areas but black people are more likely to apply for mortgages on inner-city properties – either from community preference or because these are the only properties which they can afford.

Yet, it is more than a question of the area of purchase. Black applicants are more likely to have insecure incomes or jobs and this is a common factor in building society refusals of mortgages. Alternatively, it may be that past discrimination against black people has led to fewer applications by those who may have a realistic opportunity of obtaining a loan from some other source. Another possibility is that there may be discrimination practised by estate agents, surveyors, valuers or other professionals. We lack comprehensive information on the behaviour of all of these professions, but even in the 1970s – that is after the Race Relations Act – 12 per cent of black people in Birmingham were discriminated against when they tried to buy homes. Estate agents are particularly influential. Many try to steer black purchasers towards certain areas and properties – those which already have black residents. White sellers have also been known to refuse to sell on racial grounds to black purchasers. As a result, while black families, especially Asian ones, have secured access to owner-occupation, this has gone hand in hand with their continued segregation in particular segments of the housing market and particular areas.

Housing and Racial Segregation: Black and White Worlds

Britain's black population is heavily concentrated geographically. One half live in just two metropolitan areas, London and the West Midlands. There are black people living in small towns and in rural areas but they are disproportionately concentrated in the metropolitan areas. Not only that but they are also concentrated in the inner areas of these large cities. As a result, one half of the black population lives in enumeration districts (small census areas of about 1,000 people) where they constitute at least 12 per cent of the population. This is not simply segregation along the lines of white v. black or even of Asian v. West Indian. Instead there is a finer-grained segregation between West Indians according to their island of origin and between Asians according to religion, country and region of origin.

Concentration need not be undesirable per se. It could be the outcome of ethnic preferences for living together as a community with access to appropriate shops, social and religious organisations. There certainly are elements of this in the residential concentration of black people in the UK, especially amongst Asians. In addition, clustering tends to occur in the early stages of immigration for all groups, no matter what their ethnic or racial origins. Newly arrived immigrants usually rely on previous immigrants as their contacts in job and housing markets; they therefore tend to concentrate in particular areas. Over time such residential segregation declines markedly for most immigrant groups; in the UK, for instance, this is the experience of the Italians and the Irish. It is not the experience of black immigrants. There has certainly been some suburbanisation of black people but the overall level of concentration has changed little during three decades of immigration and settlement.

Some residential segregation of black people is to be expected on the basis of social class. Black families tend to be working class – or, indeed, form part of an underclass. As working-class families tend to be concentrated in particular residential areas, then segregation of black families is to be expected on these grounds alone. However, this can only provide a partial explanation of black segregation. For example, research on the distribution of West Indians in London has shown that only about one half of their segregation can be accounted for by socio-economic characteristics.[12] Even this understates the argument, for the socio-economic characteristics of black people – such as their occupational segregation – are in part the outcome of racial discrimination. The same applies to black people's position in the housing market, which is the principal cause of their residential segregation. Black people are concentrated in particular housing tenures which would partly explain their residential distribution. However, their presence in certain tenures is conditioned by racial discrimination.

There are also other reasons for the residential segregation of black people. In part it is a reaction to the hostility of the white community, for residential concentration provides some protection – but not immunity – against racial abuse and attacks. The reverse of this is that there is sometimes a flight of white people from particular neighbourhoods once the proportion of black residents reaches certain perceived critical levels. This may be due to outright racism or to a fear that house prices are likely to fall in the area. Of course, outmigration turns this into a self-fulfilling prophecy and contributes to the residential segregation of black families

It would be wrong to suggest that there have been no changes at all in the residential segregation of black people in the UK. While there has been an increase in segregation of Asians, there has been a decrease for West Indians in several large cities. This is mostly due to their changing relative positions within the housing market. In the 1970s West Indians gained better access to local authority housing – even if not equal access to the better quality dwellings. In the process of being rehoused by local authorities, they have been dispersed, to some degree. This has contributed to a decline in their segregation, albeit only within working-class areas. In contrast, Asians have opted more for owner-occupation. This has not lead to any significant decline in their residential segregation because the types of properties purchased – both through choice and constraint – tend to be in the inner city.

Residential segregation remains one of the most potent symbols of the failure to intergrate black people into UK society. It is also an indicator of the continued inequalities between ethnic groups in the UK. The question of the relationship of the black population with the larger society and with the state is the focus of the final section of this chapter.

Black People, Politics And Civil Disturbances

The relationship of black people to the state, politics and the larger majority white community are all major topics which cannot adequately be addressed here. Yet these are of fundamental importance in understanding the limited integration of the black population and racial inequalities in the UK. Some insights into these larger issues are obtained from a consideration of a small number of specific themes: the relationship of black people with British politics, race relations legislation, racial attacks, relationships with the forces of law and order, and civil disturbances.

The Politics of Race

During the 1950s there was broad party political consensus between Labour and the Conservatives with respect to most issues relating to black people. Immigration control was the principal issue and while the introduction of the 1962 Immigration Act strained the party consensus it was not ruptured. If there was a decisive break it came in 1968 with Enoch Powell's infamous 'rivers of blood' speech. This gave the appearance of political respectability to an undercurrent of racism within the Conservative Party which had gradually been surfacing for some time. Once race had been made an election issue, neither Labour nor Conservative governments were able to resist the demands for stronger immigration controls.

The Labour Party did, however, take a more liberal stance than the Conservatives on most racial issues. As a result – and in the context of Powell's speeches – Labour was able to mobilise considerable support from the black community in the 1970 election. However, race had also become an issue amongst white voters; opinion polls showed that it was ranked as their fourth most important concern. In retrospect, therefore, it seems that Powell made an important contribution to the 1970 election victory of the Conservatives and his political rival, Edward Heath.

The way in which the major parties approached racial issues was also influenced by developments on the far right of British politics, especially the growth of the National Front (NF). The National Front was formed in 1966 but it had roots in earlier right-wing movements such as the British National Party and the National Socialist Movement. In the 1970 election the NF fought 10 seats and gained 3.6 per cent of the vote in these. Some right-wing Conservatives were willing to cooperate with the blatantly racist NF and, following the crisis over the Ugandan Asians, the local Monday Club did support the NF candidate in the 1972 Uxbridge by-election. This was too much for the party leadership, especially the relatively liberal Edward Heath, and the Uxbridge Monday Club members were expelled from the party.

Immigration continued to be a contentious issue. In the February 1974 general election the NF candidate secured 7.4 per cent of the vote in Leicester East. It then recorded a new high in the October 1974 election with 9.4 per cent of the vote in Hackney South. Racial issues were again prominent in 1976, especially following press hysteria over the temporary housing in the UK of Asian families from Malawi. This and other issues were capitalised upon by the NF which in that year secured 16.6 per cent of the vote in local elections in Leicester. However, this was to be its electoral high point. By the 1979 general election its share of the vote in the 303 seats it contested had fallen to 1.4 per cent. Even in Leicester it only secured 2.4 per cent of the vote. By the early 1980s the National Front was in political disarray and it fragmented.

How is the decline of the NF to be explained? In part it was due to its own political incompetence and to reduced publicity for racial and immigration issues. However, the explanation is also to be found in the changes which occurred in the Conservative Party. Edward Heath had been relatively liberal on racial issues. He had, for example, sacked Powell from his Cabinet and had forbidden Tory candidates to exploit race issues in the elections. The Tory Party was also beginning to try and attract support from black voters, especially the Asian owners of small businesses. Margaret Thatcher was to change this approach after her election as party leader.

The critical turning point was a speech which Mrs Thatcher made in January 1978 on the World in Action programme, referring to the dangers of being swamped by immigrants (see the introduction to this chapter). There is no doubt that this interview harmed racial harmony in Britain. Bernard Levin commented in *The Times* that 'If you talk and behave as though black men were some kind of virus that must be kept out of the body politic then it is the shabbiest hypocrisy to preach racial harmony at the same time'. Following this speech there was both a sharp increase in public concern about immigration issues and a rise in support for the Conservative Party; the two facts were of course connected.

In the 1979 general election the Conservatives stated a commitment to tighten-up immigration controls and to introduce a new British Nationality Act. Substantial swings to the Conservatives in the seats where the NF had previously done well suggest that Mrs Thatcher probably had been successful in attracting ex-NF voters. Her election victory therefore went hand in hand with the defeat of the NF. The 1981 British Nationality Act, which provided further indirect discrimination against black immigrants, probably sealed the demise of the NF. This is not to be lamented, but the price of sinking the NF was high; Mrs Thatcher's government had given further political respectability to thinly-disguised racist politics.

The discussion thus far has treated black people as an object of political debate, but black people also have a potentially more active role in UK politics. They represent approximately one in every twenty voters in the UK and, in a small handful of seats, may account for as much as one third of the electorate. The nature of two-party politics – where the parties have to try and occupy the middle ground – generally means that they tend to ignore the interests of minorities. Even so, there has been a growing awareness in both parties of the relative importance of the black vote.

Traditionally Labour has been favoured by the ethnic vote. In the 1960s it regularly attracted about 90 per cent of black support. Subsequently it has been argued that the growth of a black middle-class, and especially of small-scale Asian businesses, has created potential votes for the Conservatives. In practice however, surveys in the late 1970s found that 95 per cent of West Indians and 92 per cent of Asians were still intending to vote Labour. Under Mrs Thatcher there have been further attempts by the Tories to woo the black vote. The second and third Thatcher governments have played down the prominence given to immigration and racial issues by the 1979 administration. However, this shift has been constrained by their continuing awareness of the importance to the party of the anti-black vote.

Although both the principal parties have become more aware of the potential of the black vote, they have been slow to adopt black parliamentary candidates. Again this is probably due to an awareness of a depth of anti-black feelings amongst the British electorate, and an assumption that black candidates would be vote-losers. This has discouraged black candidates from seeking nomination. The historical record makes very dismal reading: there was one candidate in the February 1974 general election, none in October 1974 and five in 1979. None were elected. It was only in 1987 that a critical breakthrough was achieved in terms of parliamentary representation. Four black people were finally elected as MPs – they were all Labour Party candidates. Conservative MPs have remained all-white during Mrs Thatcher's three election victories.

Formal Equality?: Race Relations Legislation

While immigration has been a contentious party political issue, there has been broad consensus about the need to provide legal protection for black people living in the UK. In particular, between the mid-1960s and the mid-1970s a series of Acts was passed which made racial discrimination illegal. With the exception of a few individual MPs, there was broad agreement about the need for such legislation.

The first important measure was the Race Relations Act passed by Harold Wilson's government. This established the Race Relations Board which was charged with working for conciliation in cases of racial conflict. The Act did not introduce criminal penalties for racial discrimination but the Board could request the Attorney-General to take out injunctions to stop individual acts of discrimination. Soon after this a number of PEP reports were published which provided convincing evidence that racial discrimination was widespread. This led to the passing of new and far stronger legislation, the 1968 Race Relations Act. This extended legislation to discrimination in the fields of housing, jobs and financial services. The Board was to try conciliation in the first place but ultimately could pursue legal actions against discriminating parties. The third important legislative milestone was the 1976 Race Relations Act. This established the Commission for Racial Equality with powers to conduct strategic investigations into racial discrimination and to issue non-discrimination notices. It was under this legislative umbrella that the notorious racist, Robert Relf, was imprisoned for distributing racialist literature.

The legislation contributed to reducing some of the problems faced by black communities. It was particularly useful in removing instances of large-scale or institutional discrimination and some of the more blatant acts of individual discrimination. However, as with all legislation of this nature, it could not actually change attitudes or eliminate more informal and subtle acts of discrimination. The fact that all three Acts were passed by Labour governments is to the credit of that party. So are the progressive policies and positive discrimination introduced by many Labour-controlled local authorities. Nevertheless, until the late 1970s there was broad party consensus on the need for such legislation. Mrs Thatcher's government has certainly not turned its back on such legislation but neither has it introduced any major new initiatives to assist the black community. Urban aid has been directed at the inner cities but this is considered to be a problem of general deprivation, as well as a specific reaction to the civil disturbances of 1981. Indeed, given the Thatcherite emphasis on individualism, structural inequalities deep-rooted in UK society are overlooked.

Racial Attacks and Relationships with the Police

Throughout the last four decades black people in Britain have been subject to racial attacks. Immediately after the Second World War there was a series of attacks on black people. These took the form of collective violence. Amongst the most serious incidents were attacks on hostels which housed Indian workers in Birmingham in 1949, attacks on immigrant homes in Camden Town in 1954, three week-ends of violence against immigrant communities in Nottingham and severe riots against black people in Notting Hill in 1958, and racial attacks in Dudley in 1962. This marked the end of large-scale collective white violence against black people.

It did not, unfortunately, mark the end of racial violence. By the 1960s 'Paki-bashing' was increasingly reported in the press and the 1970s saw a sharp escalation of racially-inspired attacks. This initially culminated in the murder of a young Asian in London's East End in July 1980. Thereafter the wave of racialist violence seems to have intensified further and the 1980s have seen a number of racialist murders, as well as petrol bomb attacks on Asian churches and businesses. In one of the worst incidents, Mrs Barene Khan and her three children were murdered in an arsonist attack in July 1981. The true extent of racially-inspired violence is not known but a 1981 Home Office Report estimated that there had been at least 7,000 such attacks in the UK in 1980–81. Almost as worrying as the escalation in violence has been the growing disillusion within the black community with the ability of the police to stop such attacks. This, in turn, is linked to a general deterioration in relationships between the police and the black communities, especially young black people.

Young blacks have been represented in the press during the 1980s as the major source of mugging and other violent crime in large cities. This image is partly due to the age structure of the black population, for violent street crimes are mostly committed by young people. However, even taking into account the age factor, it is still true that black youths are more likely than white youths to commit violent crimes. The problem is that this has evoked a massive response from the police which many commentators consider to be disproportionate and provocative. The police response is linked to strong racism within the police force.[13] By the early 1980s a relationship between crime and black people, especially young people, had developed in many police minds, and an association between 'police and illegality' had grown in the minds of many young blacks.

Particularly contentious was police use of Section 4 of the Vagrancy Act, the so-called 'sus-laws'. This empowered the police to stop and search individuals in public places if they were considered to have intent to commit arrestable offences. The problem is that the law has consistently been used more against young blacks than against any other group. For example, in London West Indians aged 15–24 were two or three times more likely than young white people to have been stopped by the police. This heavy-handed and sometimes racialist approach to policing has contributed to the alienation of young black people from the police, and bred a sense of profound distrust between them. In its most extreme form this type of policing has involved massive police swamping of particular areas, such as Lambeth and Lewisham, with intensive stop-and-search procedures. This is the polar opposite of community policing and it has been labelled 'fire-brigade policing'.

It is certainly not true that all or even a majority of the police are directly racialist. However, a substantial minority of police officers hold hostile or suspicious views of black people in general; the situation is not helped by the fact that less than one per cent of police officers in the mid-1980s were black. Racially-offensive language is also frequently used by many police officers and this must influence the way in which they carry out their policing duties.[14] The tip of the iceberg was revealed at the 1984 Police Federation Conference when Peter

Johnson, speaking from the platform, referred to 'our coloured brethren or nignogs?' Although the remark was quickly repudiated the damage had been done. Such racism is important for it is one element in the inequality of access to legal justice. It is also important as one of the critical elements in the major civil disturbances in UK cities in the 1980s.

Inner-City Civil Disturbances

A series of civil disturbances rocked the UK's inner cities in the 1980s. The first was in St Paul's in Bristol in April 1980, but this was followed by more widespread disturbances in the summer of 1981. There were major outbreaks of violence in Brixton and in Toxteth (Liverpool) as well as lesser disturbances in over thirty other cities. Two-thirds of those arrested during the major disturbances were black, which led some commentators to brand them as race riots.

However, the disturbances were anti-police rather than racial in nature. They were based on resistance to heavy-handed police methods. Because black youth had had the most bitter experience of such methods it was young blacks who took the lead. This is illustrated by the infamous police operation 'Swamp 81' which was taking place at the time of the Brixton disturbances. More than a hundred officers were involved in stop-and-search procedures to try and apprehend criminals on the streets of Lambeth. In early April they stopped 943 people: over two-thirds were aged under 21 and one half were black. The Scarman Report on the major disturbances was unequivocal on this point for it saw the root cause as being a spontaneous outburst of anger by young black people against the police. The report also criticised other aspects of policing in Lambeth especially the collapse of the police liaison committee, hard policing methods and racially-prejudiced police behaviour.

This is not to say that unemployment, poor housing conditions and general urban deprivation did not also contribute to the disturbances. They were important, as the Scarman Report confirmed, and indeed were essential preconditions. But the outbreak of disturbances was highly selective. It did not include predominantly white areas of high unemployment such as South Wales or Tyneside, while West Indians were far more likely than Asians to have been involved. In other words, West Indian-police relationships were the critical factors influencing which areas experienced disturbances.

In 1985 violence erupted again. The first outbreak was in Handsworth, Birmingham, and a night of violent clashes ended with £10 million of damage and the death of two Asian brothers when their shop was set alight. By late September Brixton had become the central focus. This time the disturbances were sparked when police, trying to arrest a black suspect, accidentally shot and seriously injured his mother, Mrs

Groce. However, the most serious violence was reserved for Broad-water Farm estate (in Tottenham). During a police raid on the estate a black woman, Mrs Jarrett, collapsed and died. There followed a long and extremely bitter confrontation. Guns were fired at the police and a police officer was hacked to death. The police were on the verge of deploying plastic bullets and CS gas.

What had brought the UK's inner cities to the verge of full-scale riots, murder and the apparent collapse of police-black youth trust and respect? In part the roots lay in deprivation and, for example, unemployment rates in Handsworth were 36 per cent at the time of the disturbances. Young blacks were the subject of police harassment although this was not always the result of racism and discrimination. Sometimes it was the result of legitimate attempts to crack down on street crime or the drugs trade. Whatever the precise causes, the result was a deepening sense of resentment amongst young blacks about their living conditions, restricted opportunities and racist discrimination. Lacking direct access to any of the formal channels of political power, they often felt that street action was the only form of political expression for them.

Neither inner-city deprivation nor racialist attacks and harassment were products of the 1980s. As was shown in the introduction to this chapter, cities such as Nottingham and Liverpool experienced racialist attacks in the 1950s. However, we would contend that, wittingly or unwittingly, Mrs Thatcher's governments have exacerbated the difficulties of the black communities. In the run-up to the 1979 general election she cynically manipulated popular white racial prejudices, with respect to immigration. In office her policies have consistently disadvantaged the underclass in UK society and black people are disproportionately represented in this group.

Furthermore, the government's insistence on the role of market forces and individual enterprise has made it blind to structural disadvantages. After Handsworth, Douglas Hurd insisted that the disturbances were 'not a social phenomenon but crimes' and Norman Tebbit condemned events on Broadwater Farm as being due to 'wickedness'. We would not wish to excuse the events which took place or deny that there were examples of wickedness and crime. But virtually all objective evidence, including the report of the esteemed Scarman inquiry, identified the role of racial tensions and of social and economic disadvantages in these disturbances. The seeds of racial distrust and disadvantage may have been sown a long time before Mrs Thatcher's government came to power. But its policies helped fertilise the bitter harvests which were reaped on the streets of London, Liverpool and Birmingham.

Notes

1. See M. Cross, 'Migration and exclusion: Caribbean echoes and British realities', in C. Brock (ed.), *The Caribbean In Europe* (London: Frank Cass, 1986).
2. N. Abercrombie and A. Warde, *Contemporary British Society* (Cambridge: Polity Press, 1988), p. 265.
3. J. Rex and S. Tomlinson, *Colonial Immigrants In A British City: A Class Analysis* (London: Routledge & Kegan Paul, 1979).
4. C. Brown, *Black And White in Britain* (London: Heinemann, 1984).
5. T. Carter, *Shattering Illusions: West Indians in British Politics* (London: Lawrence & Wishart, 1986) pp. 32–3.
6. Brown, op. cit.
7. S. Field, 'The changing nature of racial disadvantage', *New Community*, 14, no. 1/2 (1986), pp. 118–22.
8. C. Hamnett and B. Randolph, 'Ethnic minorities in the London labour market: a longitudinal analysis, 1971–81', *New Community*, 14, no. 3 (1988), pp. 333–46.
9. I. Martin, 'Racial Equality', in N. Bosanquet and P. Townsend (eds.), *Labour And Equality* (London: Heinemann, 1980).
10. V. Robinson, 'Asians and council housing', *Urban Studies*, 17 (1980), pp. 323–31.
11. V. Karn, 'Race and housing in Britain: the role of the major institutions', in N. Glazer and K. Young (eds.), *Ethnic Pluralism And Public Policy* (London: Heinemann, 1983).
12. T.R. Lee, *Race And Residence* (Oxford: Clarendon Press, 1977).
13. M. Cross, op. cit., p. 103.
14. J. Benyon, 'The spiral of decline: race and policing', in Z. Layton-Henry and P.B. Rich (eds.), *Race, Government And Politics in Britain* (London: Macmillan, 1986).

Further Reading

There are good reviews of immigration to the UK in C. Brock (ed), *The Caribbean in Europe* (London: Frank Cass, 1986); C. Brown, 'Ethnic pluralism in Britain', in N. Glazier and K. Young (eds), *Ethnic Pluralism and Public Policy* (London: Heinemann, 1983).

The 1982 PSI survey of ethnic groups is reported in C. Brown, *Black and White in Britain* (London: Heinemann, 1984).

The class position of immigrants is specifically analysed in J. Rex and S. Tomlinson, *Colonial Immigrants in a British City: A Class Analysis* (London: Routledge & Kegan Paul, 1979); R. Ramdin *The Making of the Black Working Class Britain* (Aldershot: Gower, 1987).

Educational disadvantages are reviewed in Brown op. cit; and B. Parekh, 'Educational opportunity in multi-ethnic Britain, in N. Glazier and K. Young op. cit.

An excellent starting point for the discussion of race and housing is J. Henderson and V. Karn, *Race, Class and State Housing* (Aldershot: Gower, 1987). Also see N. Glazier and K. Young op. cit.

Relationships with the police and the 1980s civil disturbances are the subject of Z. Layton-Henry and P.B. Rich (eds), *Race, Government and Politics in Britain* (London: Macmillan, 1986); C. Peach, 'A geographical perspective on the 1981 urban riots in England', *Ethnic and Racial Studies*, 9, (1986), no. 3, pp. 396–401.

Disillusion with the political process is outlined in T. Carter, *Shattering Illusions* (London: Lawrence & Wishart, 1986); I. Crewe, 'Representation and the ethnic minorities in Britain', in N. Glazier and K. Young op.cit., 1983.

6
Divided by location

Introduction: where you live matters

Pronounced inequalities between and within regions are certainly not unique to the 1980s. They are endemic to capitalist development and nowhere is this more true than in the UK. From the earliest days of capitalism, pre-existing patterns of spatial inequality were radically reshaped, generating new contrasts in economic and social conditions between areas: for example, between the cities and the countryside and between regions. From the moment in 1928 when a Conservative government acknowledged that regional inequalities constituted a political problem, spatially uneven development, usually defined as a 'regional problem', has never been far from the political agenda. Despite a long period of state engagement with regional problems via regional policies, they have been a persistent feature of the UK scene. The form of the problem, and the processes generating it, have certainly altered somewhat, but the regional problem has persisted despite this. It has done so despite – some would say because of – state policies. From the mid-1970s though, regional problems have increasingly taken second place to urban problems.

In the 1980s, however, despite increasing governmental focus on urban problems – or, again, perhaps because of it – the regional problem and, more specifically, the growing divide between the two nations of North and South has re-emerged politically centre-stage. It has been a persistent focus of media attention as the following selection of national newspaper headlines, all taken from the *Financial Times*, testify:

South east increases lead in wealth (23 March 1984).
Prosperity gap widens between North and South (22 May 1985).
Job census figures will fuel concern over 'two nations' divide (5 January 1987).
North–South disparity confirmed' (2 February 1987).
Regional wealth disparity 'growing' (18 February 1988).

Indeed, the growing North–South divide has become an issue of international interest, with the Canadian *Globe and Mail* proclaiming:

England's great divide: the South prospers while the industries of the North crumble (7 February 1987).

Such newspaper headlines register a growing recognition of and interest in the deepening divide between a booming South and a declining North. Broadly speaking, the 'South' is defined as the Standard Regions of the South-East, South-West, East Anglia (and on occasion the East Midlands) whilst the 'North' is defined as the remainder of the UK (Fig. 6.1). Like most newspaper headlines, those highlighting the growing North–South divide contain elements of truth, in this case substantial ones. At the same time they necessarily oversimplify more subtle patterns of spatial inequality in the UK in the 1980s.

The growing North–South divide is commonly represented, not least by Mrs Thatcher's government, as a simple product of the operation of the hidden hand of market forces. We wish to argue, strongly, that this is not the case. On the contrary, the North–South divide has deliberately been redefined and enhanced as part of the political strategy of Thatcherism. It was and is intimately connected to its electoral prospects.

Unemployment, employment and incomes in the 'North' and in the 'South'

In many ways the most commented upon aspect of the growing divide between North and South in the 1980s is the difference in unemployment levels and rates. By 1986 registered unemployment had reached over 20 per cent in Northern Ireland. Some 55 per cent of unemployed men had been out of work for over a year. Whilst unemployment in the northern part of Great Britain did not attain these levels, there was still a 7–10 per cent difference in rates between it and most of the South (Fig. 6.2). Again, long-term unemployment was most pronounced in the North. Conversely, the vacancy rate in the South averaged twice that in the North. As a result, people continued to migrate and increasingly to commute from North to South in a desperate search for work, despite enormous differences in house prices and housing markets. In 1985, for example, there was a net inter-regional, permanent in-migration of 50,000 into the South and a corresponding net loss from the North (Fig. 6.3). Moreover, temporary short-term migration into the South for work, a new form of long-distance commuting, has grown sharply. These differences in unemployment, vacancies and net migration are a reflection of the deepening employment divide between North and South in the 1980s (Fig. 6.4).

At its simplest, this growing employment divide can be summarised as follows. Between mid-1979 and mid-1987 employees in employment

Figure 6.1 Standard Regional Boundaries

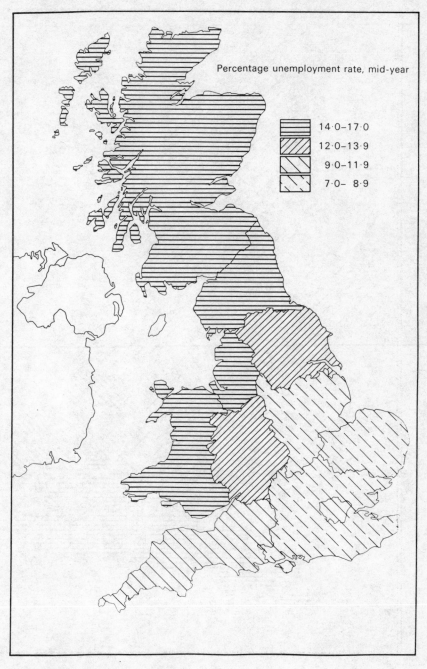

Figure 6.2 Unemployment, 1986

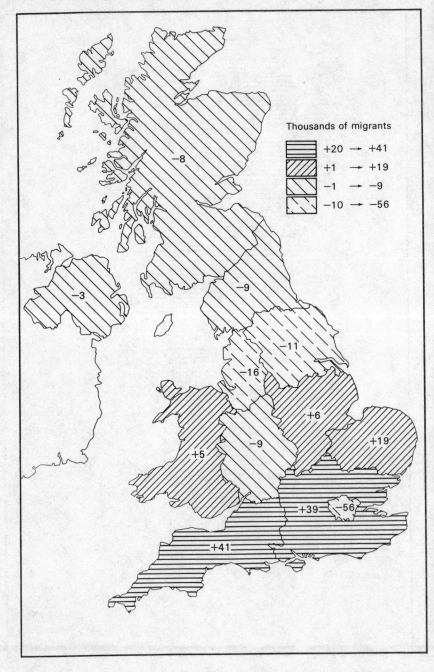

Figure 6.3 Net inter-regional migration, 1985 (000's)

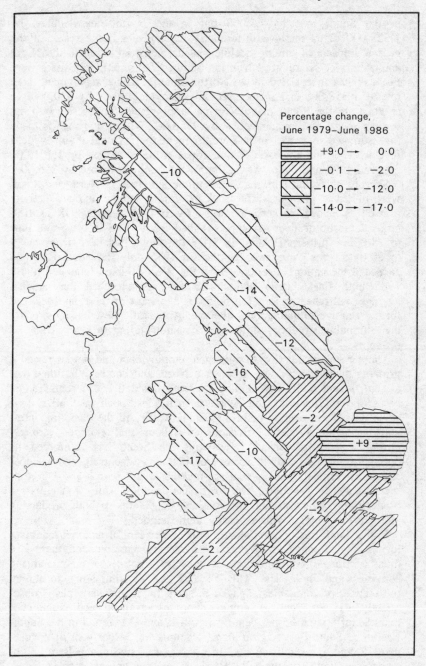

Percentage change,
June 1979–June 1986

+9·0 ⟶ 0·0
−0·1 ⟶ −2·0
−10·0 ⟶ −12·0
−14·0 ⟶ −17·0

Figure 6.4 Employment change, 1979–86

in the South rose by 66,000 but in the North they declined by 1,328,000. This massive difference was, above all, the result of the greater impacts of mining decline and de-industrialisation in the North and of service sector growth in the South. Coal mining job losses were exclusively concentrated in the North. Manufacturing employment there fell by 1,358,000 and service sector employment grew by 330,000. In contrast, in the South manufacturing employment fell by 678,000 but service sector employment grew by 935,000. When allowance is made for estimated increases in self-employment the regional divide widens further. The total employed labour force in the North fell by 1,101,000 between 1979 and 1986, whilst that in the South-East rose by 356,000.

Sharply diverging patterns of economic activities in North and South were linked to growing differences in regional output and productivity as well as labour market conditions. By 1985 (taking the UK as 100) gross domestic product per capita ranged from 114.8 in the South-East to 74.8 in Northern Ireland; in 1975 the range had been from 112.9 to 80.0, for the same two regions. In 1975 only the South-East had exceeded the national average whilst the West Midlands equalled it. By 1985 both East Anglia and the South-East exceeded the national average. All other regions fell below it and most of these had declined further relative to the national average. Above all, these changes reflect the continuing structural shift from a manufacturing to a service-based economy.

These numbers relating to aggregate employment and output reveal a growing quantitative division between North and South. What they hint at, but do not really reveal, is a growing qualitative differentiation in types of job, functions and economic activities. Such qualitative divisions have their origins before 1979, however, in the changing intra- and international spatial divisions of labour that emerged strongly during the 1960s. Broadly speaking, the South has reinforced its dominance in key growth sectors of both manufacturing and services and in the crucial control, decision-making and Research and Development (R and D) functions. The North has been left with a concentration of declining industries and the routine occupations in both production and service sectors. This is easily demonstrated.

In the South-East Region alone, with 27 per cent of national manufacturing employment and 39 per cent of service employment, there is a disproportionate concentration of jobs in 'high-tech' manufacturing activities and industries. This reflects the discriminating locational preferences of companies engaged in such 'high-tech' activities. Consequently 41 per cent of employment in advanced and 'high-tech' manufacturing and 55 per cent of that in R and D is found in the South-East. The South-East Region alone accounts for 54 per cent of government R and D establishments. In so far as a sunshine belt of 'high-technology' industry, typically based on new non-unionised small firms, is to be found in the UK it is concentrated within the South in areas such as Silicon Fen (as Cambridge has become known) and around the M4 corridor and the M25 London orbital motorway.

Secondly, there is a disproportionate concentration of business (or producer) services employment in the South. The South-East Region has over one half of total national employment in this sector, closely linked to the role of the City of London. Of course, London held a position of historical pre-eminence in financial and money markets before 1979. However, this has been reinforced in the 1980s as a result of a variety of interrelated changes: the growing importance of inter-national finance; new markets such as those for Eurodollars; the influx of foreign banks; and de-regulation of the Stock Exchange.

Thirdly, in so far as an 'enterprise culture' is being created in the UK, it is disproportionately concentrated in the South. The South-East Region accounted for almost 39 per cent of all new business registra-tions between 1980 and 1984 (Fig. 6.5). Moreover, between 1984 and 1985 the rate of small firm creation was higher in the South as the North–South divide widened further. There are several reasons for this. The existence of numerous well-paid jobs and high incomes in the South-East creates market opportunities for personal services, the main area of small firm growth. The concentration of R and D activities also creates market opportunities for small sub-contracting companies to emerge. In addition, the disproportionate presence of financial services in the South-East creates a bias in favour of lending venture capital in what is perceived as a known, low-risk region.

In contrast to the South, the North tends to have a distinctly higher proportion of unskilled and semi-skilled labour in routine manufacturing and service jobs. These workers are more likely to be unionised and militant, at least to the extent that trades unions actually do engage in strike activity and other forms of industrial action in the 1980s (Fig. 6.6). In addition, there are relatively few new firms created there as the 'enterprise culture' finds considerable difficulty in establishing itself, a consequence of the previous cultural and political history of much of the region.

Changes in employment patterns are one important reason for the growing divide in incomes and wealth between North and South (Fig. 6.7). For example, by 1985 and 1986 average weekly household incomes in the South-East and South-West were £269.06 and £232.63, respectively. Only these two Regions exceeded the national average of £225.36. At the other extreme were the North (£187.27) and Northern Ireland (£192.78). The fact that average household incomes in the Northern Region of England had slipped below those of Northern Ireland takes on an added significance in the context of newspaper headlines such as 'Northern Ireland poverty "second worst in Europe"'. It says much about regional divisions in the UK in the 1980s that the point of comparison has become Calabria, the most poverty-stricken region of the south of Italy.

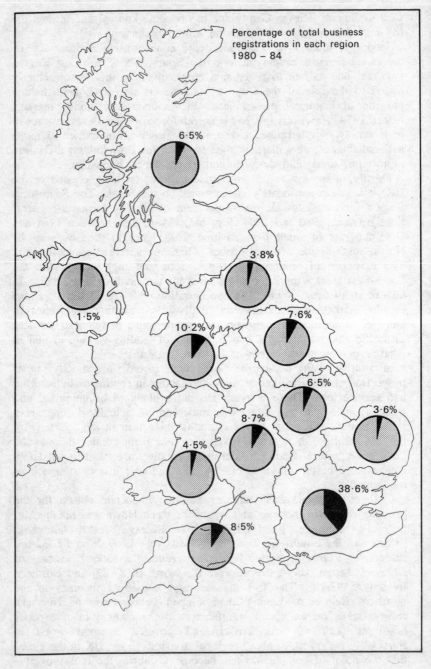

Percentage of total business
registrations in each region
1980 – 84

Figure 6.5   New firm formation, 1980–84

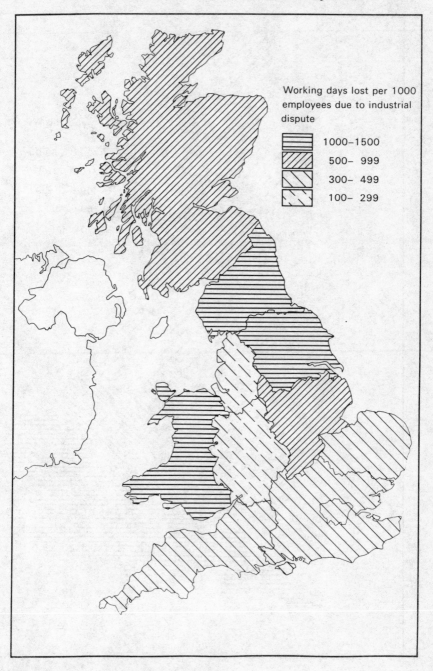

Working days lost per 1000
employees due to industrial
dispute

	1000–1500
	500– 999
	300– 499
	100– 299

Figure 6.6 Industrial militancy, 1980–84

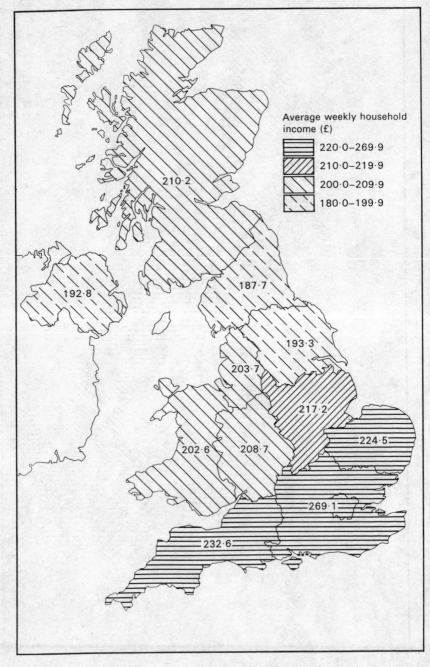

Figure 6.7 Average weekly household income, 1985–86 (£)

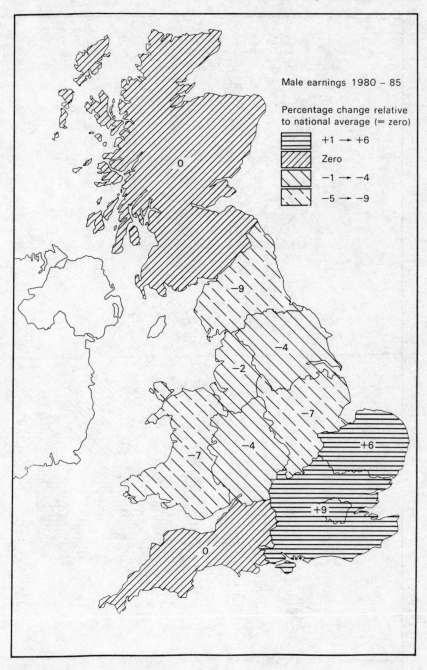

Male earnings 1980 – 85

Percentage change relative
to national average (= zero)

+1 ⟶ +6

Zero

−1 ⟶ −4

−5 ⟶ −9

Figure 6.8 Relative changes in male earnings, 1980–85

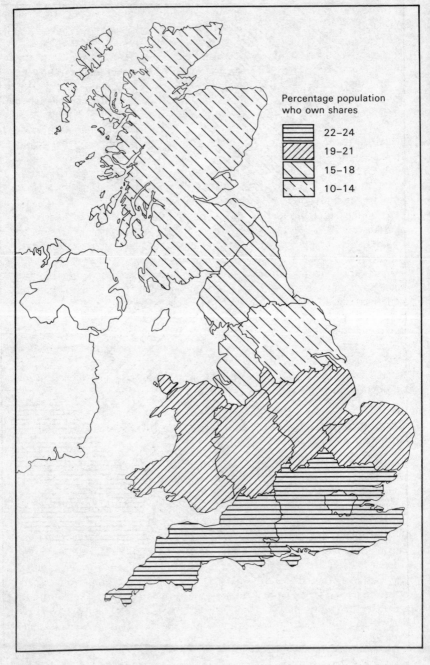

Percentage population
who own shares

	22–24
	19–21
	15–18
	10–14

Figure 6.9 Popular capitalism, 1986

In general terms, these wide and growing regional income differentials reflect the effects of several factors. In part, they arise because of differing industrial and occupational mixes. Wage supplements to workers within the South-East exacerbate these differences. Companies in the South-East pay up to 50 per cent more in allowances to try to recruit or retain staff in the face of chronic shortages of skilled labour. This is also an important contributory factor to the more rapid growth of wages in the South-East in particular (Fig. 6.8).

There is much greater incidence of unearned incomes in the South, which further exacerbates the income divide between it and the North. In the South-West, this is related to the age structure of the population, with over 25 per cent of personal incomes deriving from dividends, rents and pensions accruing to people of retirement age. Share ownership is generally more prevalent in the South (Fig. 6.9): over 22 per cent of the adult population in the South-East and the South-West are share-owners. In contrast, over much of the North less than 15 per cent of adults are share-owners. This again is indicative of strong regional differences in receptivity to 'popular capitalism'.

In contrast, in the North there is a much greater dependence upon state transfer payments, notably unemployment benefits, supplementary benefits (Fig. 6.10) and retirement pensions. In 1985 9.5 per cent of total household income in the South-East was from social security payments but in Northern Ireland it was 21 per cent. More generally, 25 per cent of the population of Northern Ireland claimed supplementary benefit or family income supplement. This contributes to Northern Ireland's unenviable position of being second only to Calabria in terms of poverty in the European Community.

Consumption, life-styles and living conditions in the North and South

In the latter years of the 1970s, immediately prior to the election of Mrs Thatcher's government, there were marked regional inequalities in household expenditure patterns. Not surprisingly, they reflected differences in incomes. Household expenditure in 1978–79 was highest in the then 'traditionally prosperous' South-East and West Midlands, the only two regions to exceed the UK average. It was lowest in the North, South-West, and Yorkshire and Humberside. By 1985–86 this pattern had altered significantly. Only in the South-East (considerably) and East Anglia and the South-West (marginally) did household expenditure exceed the national average. The greatest relative and absolute increases in income and expenditure occurred in the South-East. There had been a considerable alteration in the regional pattern of household expenditure, polarising around a North versus South divide.

There were also considerable regional variations in patterns of expenditure on goods and services. If anything, the 1980s have further

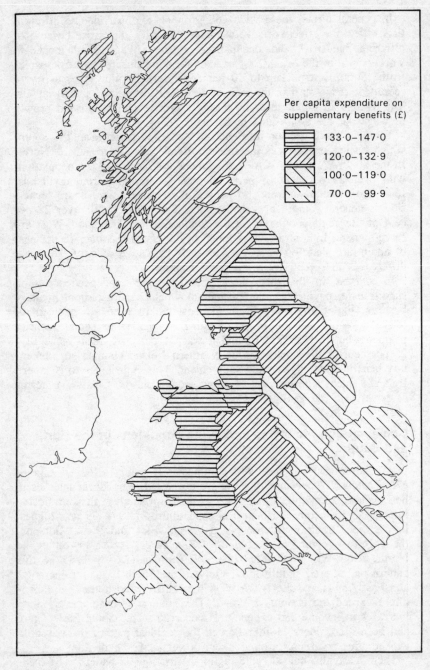

Per capita expenditure on
supplementary benefits (£)

133·0–147·0
120·0–132·9
100·0–119·0
70·0– 99·9

Figure 6.10   Dependency on supplementary benefit, 1984–85

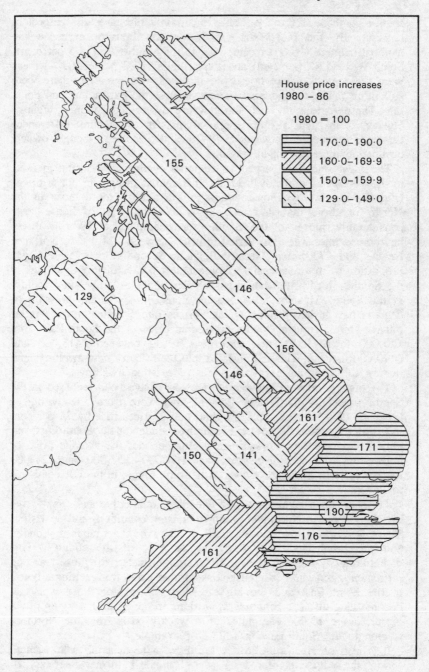

Figure 6.11 Dwelling price increases, 1980–86

reinforced these differences. This is certainly the case with respect to housing. By the mid-1980s expenditure on housing exceeded the national average (16.6 per cent) only in the South-East (18.5 per cent), South-West (17.2 per cent) and East Anglia (17.0 per cent). As these were the regions where household incomes were greatest, there were still more marked regional variations in absolute expenditure on housing. These regions are also those where owner-occupation is highest. However, in general, the regional pattern of tenure differences remained unaltered between 1978–79 and 1985–86, though owner-occupation increased in all regions.

The most significant aspect of regional changes in housing markets in the 1980s has probably been the differential growth in house prices (Fig. 6.11). Average house prices in the South exceed those in the North for three main reasons. First, a given type of house costs considerably more in the South: for example, in 1986 a three-bedroomed inter-war semi varied in price between £24,000 in Northern Ireland and £73,000 in Greater London. Secondly, there is a bigger proportion of more expensive, larger and/or higher quality dwellings in the South. Thirdly, the housing stock continues to grow more rapidly in the South. This increases average house prices as the pressure of demand has pushed residential land prices into a higher upward inflationary spiral. Housing land increased in price in the South-East from £40,000 to £169,000 per acre in 1979 to between £415,000 and £490,000 in 1986. This is translated into the price of new dwellings and in turn these influence re-sale prices of existing dwellings.

The highest rates of house price increases have been recorded in the South, especially in Greater London, and were from already higher levels in 1979. For example, in 1986 house prices rose by 25 per cent in Greater London, 20 per cent in the remainder of the South-East, but only 7.6 per cent in Yorkshire and Humberside; the average price of a dwelling in these three areas was £64,000, £57,000 and £27,000 respectively. In this respect the North–South divide in the UK continues to widen.

There are then significant, and widening, qualitative and quantitative divisions between North and South in housing conditions and provision. There is now not one housing market but two. The first is in London and the South-East. The other is the rest of the country. This dichotomous housing market is of great significance for those reaching retirement age, who can realise considerable gains from selling a house in the South-East and moving elsewhere. And, for those who can become long-distance commuters, working in the South but living in the North. Some 10,000 commuted on a weekly basis from the Northern Region to the South-East in 1988, for example.

It is also of great significance for those without a job who wish to follow the advice proffered by Mrs Thatcher's former Secretary of State for Employment, Norman Tebbit, to 'get on their bikes' to search for work.[1] Differences in housing markets between the North and South make it prohibitively expensive for a family to come South to look for work. They also present a formidable barrier to attempts to solve regional unemployment problems via inter-regional migration.

Compared to housing, the absolute and relative variation between North and South in other categories of household expenditure is generally less pronounced. This is particularly so in the case of 'basic' items such as foodstuffs, fuel, light and power and clothing and footwear. In a sense, expenditure on such items is both unavoidable and relatively income inelastic. This means that beyond a certain income level that enables needs for these items to be met, expenditure on them tends to rise more slowly than income. In so far as it does vary, such expenditure tends to be absolutely greatest but relatively smallest in the more affluent South and vice versa. This implies important qualitative variations in consumption of these 'basic' commodities because of income differences. In part, these differences reflect varying regional cultural traditions, and lend some credence to the persistence, in modified form, of a socially constructed North–South divide in tastes.

Inter-regional differences in expenditures on consumer durables and various services are rather more pronounced. Spending on these is higher in the more affluent South both relatively and absolutely. Even so, falling real prices and slowly rising average real incomes over much of the North have resulted in a narrowing of the North–South divide in household ownership rates of some more basic consumer durables in the 1980s. By the mid-1980s household ownership rates varied between regions over a narrow range for refrigerators (97 per cent to 91 per cent), washing machines (85 per cent to 75 per cent) and telephones (86 per cent to 71 per cent). Ownership rates tended to be both lower and more variable for more sophisticated and expensive consumer durables such as deep freezers (71 per cent to 43 per cent), videos (32 per cent to 22 per cent), and dishwashers (9 per cent to 3 per cent), with in all cases the highest rates of ownership in the South. Moreover, the North–South gap tended to widen in the 1980s in ownership of these consumer goods.

There are also marked variations which tended to grow in the 1980s, in expenditure on transport. It is greatest in the South. One reason for this is greater spending on commuting, especially in the South-East. In 1979, household car ownership was highest in the South-West (65.4 per cent) and lowest in the North (50.9 per cent). By 1986 it had increased to a maximum of 72 per cent in the South-West and South-East, outside of Greater London, but only up to 52 per cent in the North (Fig. 6.12). Moreover, households having two (or more) cars are far more prevalent in the South. In part this is because of the concentration there of those in well-paid jobs which include a car as part of their remuneration.

It is important to remember, however, especially in the context of de-regulation of buses in the 1980s, that household car ownership rates

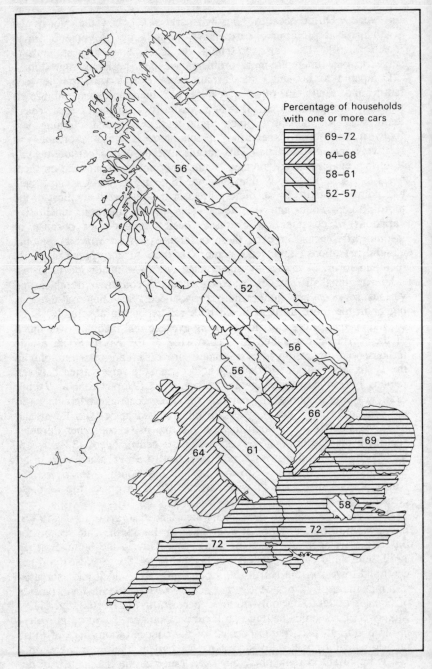

Figure 6.12 Household car ownership, 1986

also reflect the (non)-availability of public transport. In both East Anglia and the South-West there are rural areas that have wholly lacked public transport for well over a decade. For many households in such areas, having a car is a matter of necessity. Household car ownership, especially in one-car households, should also not be confused with personal mobility.

There are significant regional variations in another sort of mobility: people's propensity to go on holiday. These existed in 1979 and in some ways the North–South divide has increased in the 1980s. In several regions in the North rather more households took no annual holiday in 1986 than in 1979. Residents of the South-East took a disproportionate share of all holidays outside the UK in both years. The disproportionate number of people from the South-East taking not just one but two or more holidays a year is decisively related to the concentration of higher incomes there. Holiday making from the affluent South-West and East Anglia is no more than one would expect on the basis of their share of national population, but this must be seen in the context of many people migrating there to retire.

So far, we have concentrated on regional variations in private consumption, which directly reflect those in incomes. Increasingly in the 1980s, there has been a growing emphasis upon purchasing education and health services in the market. This redrawing of the private-public sector boundary has been particularly focused in the South. Almost one half of all private school places in the UK are located in the South-East. This reflects regional variation in the ability to pay for education but, more significantly perhaps, the persistence of the public school system, which plays a crucial role in reproducing the class structure of UK society. The expansion to 10,000 acute beds in privately-owned hospitals has also been heavily concentrated in the South-East. This has sharpened the North–South divide in the amount and quality of provision of these services.

A review of the National Health Service revealed the continued existence of marked inter-regional variations in resource allocation (as well as intra-regional ones). The Resources Allocation Working Party (RAWP) was established to remedy this situation. Even so, at the start of the 1980s there were still marked regional variations in resourcing. The four Thames Regional Health Authorities and Oxford all had between 6 and 15 per cent above the level of resources calculated as necessary to secure equal access to health care for people of equal need. The remaining nine Regional Health Authorities (RHAs) were between 4 per cent and 10 per cent below this level. There were also considerable regional and sub-regional variations in levels of provision of, and access to, medical facilities. For example, hospital waiting lists, *tended* to be lower in the North than the South, although the pattern was a complicated one. Moreover, despite national norms, doctors' and dentists' list sizes were generally greater in the North than the South.

Although this does not necessarily imply corresponding differences in quality of health care, it does suggest variability in ease of access to facilities.

Between 1979 and 1983, the Thatcher government attempted to alter the regional pattern of resource allocation in line with the RAWP proposals via differential growth in revenue allocations. After 1983, for the first time, growth in 'underfunded' regions was to occur at the expense of real cuts in 'over-provided' ones. This has certainly resulted in a closer convergence of regional spending around the target norms of RAWP but at the same time, given that needs increased more rapidly than NHS funding, there has been a deterioration in public provision of health care. For example, hospital waiting lists increased in nine of the fourteen English RHA's and in Northern Ireland, Scotland and Wales, although the pattern is more complicated than a simple North–South split. Nevertheless, differential provision of medical facilities is at least related to variations in death rates and health conditions, even if it does not cause them. Research at St Thomas's Hospital Community Medicine Department (reported in *The Sunday Times*, 27 March 1983) revealed that those areas in England with the highest probability of unnecessary deaths – people dying because of the non-availability of medical treatment that could prevent death – are the old industrial areas of the North. Probability of death is lowest predominantly in the South. The former tend to be areas with relatively poor levels of medical provision. The latter are relatively well-provided for. In this sense, whether you live in North or South may literally still be a life-and-death matter in the UK in the 1980s.

Although less dramatic, regional variations in educational provision and participation have a profound effect on life chances. There were important differences in these in 1979. In part, these reflected the concentration of private sector education in the South, and this has strengthened in the 1980s. There were also considerable regional variations in average levels of attainment in state schools, despite nominally equal levels of provision, which if anything have widened in the 1980s. Children in the South are more likely to do even better in school exams. For example, between 1981–82 and 1985–86 the percentage of male school leavers with three or more 'A' levels rose in the South-East, South-West and East Anglia to 10–11 per cent but it fell in two regions in the North of England and only exceeded 10 per cent in one of them (Fig. 6.13). This understates the growing gap between North and South as more children in the latter stay on beyond minimum school-leaving age and take these exams, and more go on to courses in further and higher education.

An important objective of the post-war welfare state was to eliminate differences in access to, and levels of provision of, education and health services. Important regional differences remained in 1979, despite – and in part because of – the way in which state provision of these

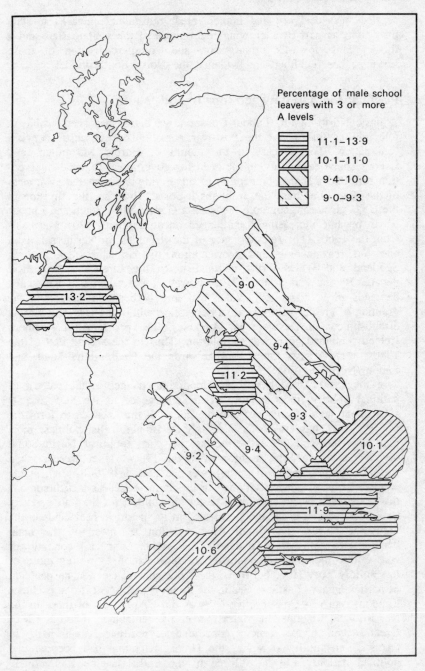

Figure 6.13 Educational attainment, 1985–86

services was designed and implemented. Substantial cutbacks in state provision, as part of a growing redefinition of the welfare state and a further shift towards privatisation and commercialisation of these services, has redefined and widened the North–South divide.

Politics: the gap between 'north' and 'south'

A basic North–South, Labour-Conservative divide has been visible in UK politics throughout the post-war period. The consensus between 'one-nation' Tories, cast in the mould of Harold Macmillan, and Labour social democrats on the need for government regional intervention reflected a shared perception of this divide and a shared awareness of the need to address the problems it posed. Even so, this division in the UK's electoral geography between a Conservative South and Labour North became increasingly challenged on an explicitly territorial basis from the 1960s. The re-emergence of the 'troubles' in Northern Ireland and the reawakening and reorientation of nationalist sentiment in Scotland and Wales thrust nationalism to the forefront of political debate. By the end of the 1970s, however, it seemed that nationalist demands in Scotland and Wales had largely been contained via the granting of greater administrative devolution within the UK state via the establishment of Development Agencies. The problems of Northern Ireland remained no nearer to solution. Thus in the second half of the 1970s, there was a move back towards the Conservative/South and Labour/North division.

In the 1980s there have been important changes in the pattern of national politics, most notably in the emergence of the SDP and its subsequent saga of alliances and merger with the Liberals to form the SDLP. There has also been a resurgence of nationalist politics, most markedly in Scotland. Nevertheless the party political North–South divide has been sharply reinforced in the 1980s. There were marked shifts in the geography of voting over the period 1979–87 that, at the simplest level of generalisation, can be characterised as a dichotomous divide between North and South. Electoral support for the Labour Party both declined and became concentrated in its historical heartlands in the industrial North. The South, the location of most of the main beneficiaries of Mrs Thatcher's neo-right political economy of competitive individualism, showed its appreciation by voting more or less solidly Tory (Fig. 6.14). In the 1987 general election 88 per cent of parliamentary constituencies in the South (96 per cent if one excludes London) returned Conservative MPs as did 67 per cent of those in the two Midland Regions. In contrast, over the remainder of the North of Great Britain, 67 per cent of constituencies returned Labour MPs. In terms of electoral geography, the United Kingdom had become two political nations. The third force of the SDLP has been effectively frozen out, via a series of two-way contests with the Tories in the

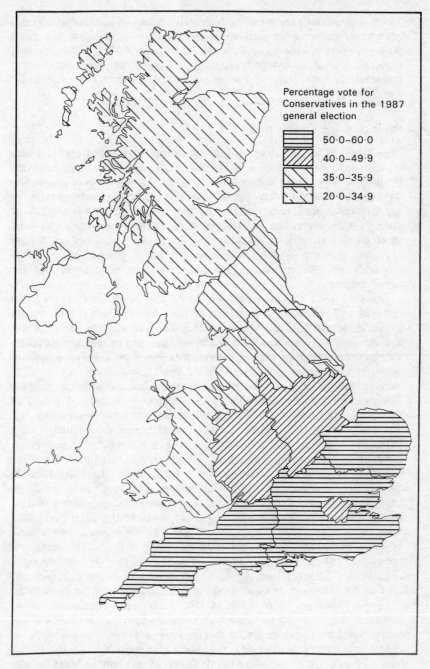

Percentage vote for
Conservatives in the 1987
general election

50·0–60·0

40·0–49·9

35·0–35·9

20·0–34·9

Figure 6.14 Conservative Party support, 1987

South and Labour in the North. Nationalist votes in Scotland and Wales became subdued as the nationalist parties there declined to the point where they were little more than parties of protest, though they showed signs of revival in by-elections in 1988 and 1989. Northern Ireland followed its own tragic political trajectory but remained effectively marginalised.

Divisions within regions

Important though the deepened North–South divide is over so many areas of life in the 1980s, it is important not to reduce spatial divisions in the UK to this one dimension. For there have also been increasing intra-regional inequalities in the 1980s. Some commentators have suggested that settlement size has become one of the principal lines of division while increasing polarisation between urban and rural areas and inner cities and affluent suburbs, has deepened. The broad picture of a deepening North–South divide hides pockets of great affluence in the country's more depressed regions and areas of relative poverty in the richer regions.

The pattern of spatial inequality in the UK in the 1980s is a more complex and subtly-differentiated one than just a North–South divide. Contrasts at sub-regional scales can be found in all regions, in North and South alike. This has been acknowledged and in part generated by a burgeoning range of central government 'small area' policies such as those for Enterprise Zones and Urban Development Corporations. They have helped produce a competition between Local Authorities for the locational advantages associated with designation in one (or more) of these categories brings in the competition for new jobs. More generally, this competition in the place market has expanded dramatically.

To illustrate the point about growing intra-regional inequalities, consider the following examples. Within the South-East, there are considerable variations in the economic fortunes of different places. In the 1930s, another era of mass unemployment, Luton held its unemployment rate at 2 per cent yet, by 1986, associated with a decline in the motor vehicles industry, unemployment in the Luton area had risen to 12.9 per cent. This was considerably above the average level of the affluent South. Luton contrasts sharply with the booming job honey-pots of the South, such as Milton Keynes, Peterborough, Huntingdon, Thetford, Basingstoke and Bracknell (many of which, of course, are New Towns developed via considerable public expenditure). Their problems are more those of labour shortages than surpluses.

Within the South, London stands out as not just a major national but international financial centre. Between 1981 and 1987, employment in banking, insurance and finance in London rose from 568,000 (or 16 per cent of total employment) to 697,000 (or 20 per cent). Much of the increase was associated with the growing penetration of foreign banks and finance houses. This in turn helped fuel a dramatic escalation in residential property prices: the price of a typical Chelsea or Kensington family house rose from £65,000 in 1975 to £450,000 in 1985, with overseas buyers making the running. Around 40 per cent of sales of residential property in Kensington, Mayfair and around Hyde Park are to non-UK citizens. The prices are far above the levels of the rest of the South and make the prospect of 'four-bedroomed luxury from £133,000' in Basingstoke positively alluring to those accustomed to London prices.

Yet although in many respects London's economy is booming, indeed over-heating, there are growing divisions within London itself. Standards of living between rich and poor are continuing to diverge, and to do so faster in London than in the UK as a whole. London may have a low unemployment rate, but it has large numbers of unemployed concentrated within its area. Even on the basis of official statistics, which certainly under-estimate the severity of the problem, in parts of London there are registered unemployment rates of 35–40 per cent. Moreover, unemployment has been increasing disproportionately in those areas where it was already most severe.

Associated with this, there has been a disproportionate increase in London in other forms of deprivation, linked to unemployment and poverty. This is undoubtedly linked with (though not in any simple sense the cause of) the concentration of crime in London: two-thirds of armed robberies in England and Wales, a third of homicides and more than half of all robberies take place there. A wide and growing gulf in social and economic conditions exists between inner boroughs such as Hackney, Tower Hamlets, Islington, Lambeth and Newham, and outer ones such as Harrow, Sutton, Bexley, Bromley and Havering.[2] This is a theme to which we return in the next chapter.

There are similar contrasts between relatively affluent urban boom areas and areas of decay and decline within the North too, although there are proportionately far fewer of the former and more of the latter than in the South. Within North-East England, for example, towns such as Durham City, Hexham and Morpeth stand out as islands of *relative* affluence, low unemployment and high house prices. They are residential locations for the new middle classes, in a sea of poverty, high unemployment and depressed house prices, typified by the ex-colliery villages and steel towns of the region. Within the region's major conurbations, there are sharp contrasts between – say – the environmental dereliction and high unemployment of parts of inner Newcastle or peripheral council housing estates such as now-demolished Killingworth Towers, and the more salubrious suburban middle-class enclaves of Darras Hall or Ponteland.

The political construction of spatial inequalities in the UK in the 1980s

Spatial inequalities have long been a characteristic feature of life in the UK. In this sense, the 1980s do not differ markedly from the years that preceded them. In another sense, however, they do differ radically. Before 1979, over a period of 50 years, governments had acknowledged that such inequalities were economically inefficient and socially divisive and had pursued policies to reduce them. After 1979, Mrs Thatcher's government deliberately pursued policies that would increase them, particularly the North–South divide, whilst diverting attention from this via a plethora of cosmetic 'small area' policies. The North–South divide, and more generally spatial inequality, has been redefined as a result of a series of policy and political choices that are an integral part of the Thatcherite project.

One element in this is the cut-backs in nationalised industry spending. These have been decisive in deindustrialising large swathes of the North as coal, shipbuilding and steel have been drastically restructured as a prelude to privatising the remaining rump of these industries. At the same time regional policy expenditures in the North have been drastically curtailed. The plethora of new 'small area' initiatives in no way compensates for this. Indeed, the urban aid programme was cut back by about 25 per cent in real terms between its peak in 1983–84 (after it was increased in response to the 1981 inner city riots) and 1986–87. As this has been both cut and focused into smaller areas, government funding for Urban Development Corporations has risen. This is one aspect of the strongly centralising tendency in government policies as 'small area' policies became the responsibility of appointed government organisations rather than elected local councils. As automatic regional development grants were cut in the North, government spending on industry was increasingly channelled into selective schemes and into the South. Between 1981 and 1984, just under 25 per cent of selective industrial assistance – via support schemes such as those for micro-electronics, fibre optics and robots – was given to companies in the South-East alone. Much of the expansion of such sectors was a consequence of the concentration of government spending on defence-related production. The great concentration of government defence spending in the South has increased in the 1980s. In 1977–78, 61 per cent of Ministry of Defence procurement expenditure was within the South and by 1985–86 this had risen to 64 per cent. Thus the widening of the 'gap' between North and South in the 1980s is in part a consequence of the remilitarisation of the British economy. Once again, the burgeoning North–South divide is an integral element in the political-economy of Thatcherism.

State support for the new 'enterprise culture' has, directly and indirectly, also been channelled the the South, especially the South-

East. This is exemplified by the disproportionate concentration of beneficiaries of the Business Expansion Scheme in the South-East. In 1983–84, 53 per cent of investments supported by the Business Expansion Scheme were located there. In 1984–85, this rose to 63 per cent. This overwhelming concentration reflects the fact that, because of past patterns of social and economic development, the most favourable preconditions for the successful implementation of policies to promote 'the enterprise culture' are generally to be found in the South-East.

This favourable environment for the flowering of the enterprise culture in the South and in particular places within it, is further underpinned by other state policies and expenditures. In particular, both directly and indirectly, it is strongly reinforced by the concentration of state expenditure on defence and R and D into the South. But overlaying all these specific government policies that have both widened inter- and intra-regional inequalities, are the effects of the government's overall economic policy. This again has been sharply divisive both between and within North and South. The main thrust of economic policy, to re-position the UK in the international economy, centred around an expansion of internationally competitive financial services and a decline in manufacturing activities, has been a major reason underlying the growing North–South divide. Expansion of financial services has been overwhelmingly concentrated in the South, above all in London. Industrial decline has been disproportionately concentrated in the North, often focused on specific communities as a direct consequence of the run-down of nationalised industries.

This strategy has simultaneously involved severe reductions in public expenditure to support industry in the North and a selective expansion of public expenditure to underpin growth in the South. As well as the redirection of state aid to industry to the South, there has been a considerable increase in other sorts of public expenditure to subsidise economic growth there. Provision and expansion of major international airports at Gatwick and Heathrow, in conjunction with associated motorway developments such as the M11 and M25, are good examples. These have been crucial, both in relation to the South-East's international role in financial services and business administration and in the location of new 'high-tech' manufacturing. In addition, state investment in infrastructure itself results in considerable employment growth. London's airports, for example, generate a large number of jobs, both directly and indirectly (for example, both in hotels and in the numerous firms servicing the airport). The decision taken in 1985 to develop a third major international airport at Stansted will further reinforce the dominance of the Gatwick-Heathrow-Stansted triangle within the South. Along with the impacts of the Channel Tunnel, this will further widen the North–South divide. However, the vigorous campaign against the proposed routes for the Channel Tunnel rail link in solidly Tory Kent may be indicative of growing environmentalist opposition to further concentration of growth in the South-East.

Conclusions: the UK's map of divisions

By the mid-1980s, there were deep locational divisions within the UK, and they were more sharply etched than they had been when Mrs Thatcher became Prime Minister. The North–South divide had widened with a vengeance. Within cities, physical distances between affluent suburbs and gentrified inner-city areas on the one hand, and deprived local authority peripheral housing estates and decayed inner cities on the other, may have stayed the same. But the social distances between them grew markedly. Within rural areas there is a growing differentiation between the residential areas of the affluent middle classes and those of the remnants of the rural working class. Such locational divisions are closely intertwined with those of class, ethnicity and gender and this point is developed in the next chapter.

Notes

1. D. Brindle in 'Crumpled leaves in Roseland', *Financial Times*, 23 February 1986, caustically points out that house prices varying from £51,000 for a 'starter home' to £133,000 plus for 'four-bedroomed luxury' in Basingstoke hold out 'not much promise . . . for a nurse from Skelmersdale or a cook from Middlesbrough'.
2. B.L. Elliott graphically describes life in the inner city as '. . . rich only in fear: fear of the next unpayable fuel bill; fear of another humiliating and probably frustrating encounter with the officials in the DHSS offices; fear, especially of the isolated elderly, of robbery or physical violence; fear among the young and the black that once again they will be stopped and questioned by the police if they gather on the streets'. 'Cities in the eighties: the growth of inequality', in P. Abrams, and R. Brown (eds), *UK Society: Work, Urbanism and Inequality* (London: Weidenfield & Nicholson, 1984) p. 40. If that judgement was true in the early 1980s, it is doubtful whether the situation has changed for the better in the succeeding years.

Further Reading

For a much fuller analysis of regional, urban and rural inequality in the UK, see R. Hudson and A. Williams, *The United Kingdom* (London: Harper and Row, 1986). R. Martin 'The Political economy of Britain's North–South Divide', *Transactions, Institute of British Geographers, New Series*, 13 no, 4, 1988, pp. 389–419 specifically discusses regional inequalities in the 1980s. J. Lewis and A. Townsend (eds), *North versus South* (London: Paul Chapman, 1989) and J. Mohan (ed.) *The Political Geography of Contemporary Britain* (London: Macmillan, 1989) provide recent analyses of spatial inequalities in the 1980s. R. Hudson, 'Nationalized industry policies and regional policies: the role of the State in capitalist societies on the deindustrialization and reindustrialization of regions', *Society and Space*, 4, 1986, pp. 7–28 discusses the decimation of the nationalised industries and its effects on the North. N. Thrift, P. Daniels and A. Leyshon, 'Sexy/Greedy: The New International Financial System, the City of London and the South East of England', Working Paper, University of Liverpool, Department of Geography, 1987, analyse the reasons for the expansion of financial services in London and J. Lovering and M. Boddy, 'The geography of military industry in Britain', *Area*, 20 no. 1, 1988, pp. 41–51 demonstrate the significance of the defence sector to the South. Spatial variations in aspects of health care are considered by P. Townsend and N. Davidson, *Inequalities in Health* (Harmondsworth: Penguin, 1982) and by J. Mohan, 'Restructuring, privatization and the geography of health care provision in England, 1983–7', *Transactions, Institute of British Geographers, New Series*, 13 no. 4, 1988, pp. 449–65. R.J. Johnston, C.J. Pattie and J.G. Allsop, *A Nation Dividing?* (London: Longman, 1988) provide a detailed account of the changing geography of party political support in the 1980s. *Regional Trends* provides a wealth of relevant data, as does the *Financial Times*.

7
Divided and divided

Inequality And Inequality

We have argued that there are a number of distinctive dimensions to inequality in the UK. The most important of these are class, race, gender and location although they are by no means the only such dimensions. Age, for example, can be deeply divisive. The fact that they are interrelated has also been suggested. Not least class has been shown to have a profound mediating effect on the experiences of gender, race and location.

In this chapter we wish to show that the interrelationships between these various dimensions take a systematic form. This has a considerable influence on the life chances of individuals and social groups. For example, the probability of being unemployed is considerably greater for black than for white people, for men than for women, and for those living in the inner cities or the North of the UK. Therefore, it is of no surprise that one of the groups with the highest probability of being unemployed is young, black men living in the North or in the inner cities. There is no simple additionality in this concentration of disadvantage. The separate dimensions can and do frequently overlap and the effects are cumulative. Not least this is because class is so strongly associated with each of these cleavages in UK society.

The ways in which the various dimensions inter-mesh is far from simple. Women living in the North face disadvantages both from being women and from living in a particular part of the UK. While women in both North and South face discrimination at work, the range of jobs available in the North is likely to be less and the probability of being unemployed is likely to be greater. This does not necessarily make it any 'easier' to be a woman in the South than in the North. The two groups will face different types of disadvantages but, in total, their disadvantages will usually be greater than those faced by men in each region. It could similarly be argued that there are systematic but

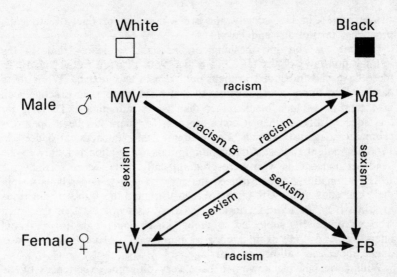

Figure 7.1 Racism and sexism

different disadvantages faced by black people living in the North and in the South. However, as an illustration of the way in which different sources of inequality are inter-meshed we concentrate here on the example of race and gender.

Race and Gender

The ways in which race and gender are interlinked are shown in Figure 7.1. Both sexism and racism are in general operation but, in addition, black men and white women are engaged in a form of exchange of discrimination. But the exchanges of racism and sexism are not necessarily equal. Not least the ability to exercise discrimination or to take advantage of inequalities is also dependent on class. Hence, it is probably rarer for black men to be in positions of power – as employers, bank managers etc. – in which they can actively discriminate against white women, than vice versa.

The group which is likely to encounter the greatest disadvantage is black women; they have to face both racism and sexism. Given the poor job prospects that confront them and their families, black women – especially West Indians and Bangladeshis – are also likely to experience the inequalities faced by all working-class families. Consequently their life chances may be more constrained than those of almost any other social group. There are layers of inequalities in society and these tend to rest disproportionately heavily on the shoulders of particular groups such as black women. Such layers of inequalities are firmly rooted in UK society and are a complex product of attitudes, practices, institutions and laws.

Nowhere is the intermeshing of inequalities clearer than in the immigration laws of the UK. From the 1960s through to the late 1980s these have had imbedded in them both racism and sexism. While there has been no overt discrimination against black people, in practice such laws tend to exclude black rather than white individuals. There is far less squeamishness when it comes to sex, for there has been open discrimination against women. For example, the vouchers introduced in 1968 for potential East African immigrants were allocated only to the heads of households who were predominantly male. More recently the 1981 Nationality Act constrained the right of female dependants to join their husbands in the UK far more than it limited the rights of husbands to join wives. In addition, in the 1970s it was women rather than men who were usually subjected to embarrassing and degrading personal interviews and body examinations by immigration officials if there was doubt about the validity of marriage.

Within the UK black women have very different experiences of the labour market from those of white women. The labour market is heavily segmented and black women are systematically channelled to some of its lowest paid segments. Again there are differences between different sub-groups of black women. However, it is commonplace, for example, for West Indian women to be found in the most physically-demanding and lowest-paid jobs such as nursing ancillaries, cleaners or factory workers. In applying for new jobs or for promotion within their present firms, they face two considerable access barriers: discrimination against women and against black people.

The difficulties faced by black women also extend to unemployment. Traditionally black men faced higher unemployment rates than did black women. However, in the 1980s unemployment has had a disproportionate greater effect upon black women than upon virtually any other social group.[1] This is mainly because they have been concentrated in those segments of the labour market which have been most affected by recession and restructuring. Government policy has played an important role in this. Monetary policies and public expenditure cuts have led to job losses in both the public and the private sectors. Moreover, privatisation and specific cut-backs in the welfare state have led to employment losses in occupations such as cleaning and hospital ancillaries where black women have been particularly numerous. To make matters worse, black women have made very few inroads into those sectors – such as finance – which have been expanding in the 1980s. Consequently, the unemployment effects of the 1980s recession, which have been adverse for women in general, have been particularly disastrous for black women.

Economic difficulties spill over into other areas of life. This is certainly the case for black women. Low incomes and unemployment tend to lead to inferior housing. This is compounded by racial discrimination in both the public and the private sectors. To this has to be added a number of other disadvantages: the reduced real value of child benefit in the late 1980s, and the lack of adequate child care facilities for working mothers. The latter is particularly important for young West Indian mothers as a disproportionate number are single parents. Consequently this group has experienced very real enhanced difficulties as the result of public expenditure cut-backs.

Although we have emphasised the inter-meshing of inequalities, there is a need to guard against making unwarranted inferences. The fact that a particular social group suffers from disadvantage or inequalities does not necessarily imply that all members of that group are equally affected or equally able/unable to overcome such social obstacles. It is no more true that all black women are poorly housed and lowly paid than it is that all white men are well housed and well paid. Not all members of a social group are equally deprived or privileged.

However, it is true that particular social groups are systematically disadvantaged so that all their members face difficulties of access to improved life chances. By virtue of being black and a woman an individual will be doubly disadvantaged. If working class (which is likely if black), she will be further disadvantaged. Of course some black working-class women are able to overcome these disadvantages and gain access to better jobs or housing. In other words life chances are the outcome of individual initiative and chance operating within a set of socially-produced structural constraints. But the constraints are particularly strong when individuals face a series of mutually-reinforcing inequalities.

Multiple Deprivation And Areas Of Multiple Deprivation

Multiple deprivation arises when an individual or social group suffers disadvantages in terms of a number of social dimensions. However, the term implies more than a simple additionality; instead it suggests that these inequalities are linked and mutually reinforcing. The result is cumulative disadvantage which is greater than the sum total of the individual disadvantages.

The question immediately arises as to the composition of multiple deprivation. At one level multiple deprivation exists in the way in which it is experienced by the individuals or social groups concerned. Clearly, not all individuals or social groups will view their disadvantages in the same way. Nevertheless there is a surprising degree of unanimity in the way in which people evaluate what constitutes the principal elements in the quality of life or well being. One survey in the 1970s[2] found that the most highly rated components of social well being were the following:

- your state of health
- family life
- housing conditions
- a stable and secure society
- job satisfaction
- financial situation
- neighbourhood quality.

Such surveys are important in highlighting the most significant perceived elements in well being. However, they do not explain why there are systematic variations in the distribution of multiple deprivation and social disadvantages. This requires an analysis of the constraints on life chances. Multiple deprivation arises from an inability to gain access to those resources which have the greatest influence on life chances: these are employment, housing and education. In turn the ability to gain this access is influenced by social class, gender, race and location.

The most systematic empirical research on multiple deprivation has probably been carried out by Berthoud[3] using special tabulations from the 1975 General Household Survey. Although somewhat dated, it has not been replicated with more recent data and the results are still important. Berthoud's index of multiple deprivation is based on six main elements which are linked to the main dimensions of inequality upon which we have focused: these are −

- Education (no qualifications)
- Family (lone parents or separated or four or more children)
- Housing (more than one person per room or lacking basic facilities)
- Income (below 140 per cent of supplementary benefit entitlement)
- Sickness (long-term illness or not working through sickness)
- Work (non-skilled manual, unemployed or low earnings).

Nearly one family in eleven experienced more than one half of these problems and 50,000 experienced all six of them. Therefore, Berthoud sees the population falling into three groups. In the middle are a large number of persons suffering from one, two or even three disadvantages who certainly face important inequalities. However, this is less significant than is the polarisation between the one quarter of the population who suffer from no disadvantages and the one in eleven who suffer from at least four. This polarisation has undoubtedly increased since 1975.

The results also show that the larger the number of single indicators in terms of which a family is deprived, then the greater the probability that it will suffer from any of the other problems; in other words, disadvantages are cumulative. The seriously disadvantaged are often multiply disadvantaged. Multiple disadvantage is most severe amongst

Table 7.1 The experience of disadvantage in the UK in 1975

Experience of specific problem	% experiencing four of five other problems
Income	65
Work	84
Education	71
Family	31
Housing	36
Sickness	36

Source: R. Berthoud, 'Who suffers social disadvantage?', in M. Brown (ed.), *The Structure of Disadvantage* (London: Heinemann, 1983)

those who experience income, work or educational disadvantage (Table 7.1). They are twice as likely to suffer four or five other forms of disadvantage as are those who experience specific inequalities in terms of the family, housing or sickness. This strongly underlines the class basis of the multiple deprivation in the UK.

Berthoud's work is useful because the analysis is taken a stage further to consider the incidence of multiple disadvantage amongst particular social groups. Age is certainly an important criterion and the elderly are highly prone to illness, low incomes and poor housing. Those aged over 75 are eight times more likely to suffer from multiple disadvantage than are those aged less than 59 (see Table 7.2). There is also a high risk of disadvantage amongst children and during early adulthood, especially with respect to overcrowding and low incomes (in single parent families). However, this is not as great as the substantial disadvantages of old age. Some of these disadvantages may be unavoidable, such as sickness. However the experience of old age is conditioned by that of class. The ability to buy private medical care or private home nursing can ease some of the difficulties associated with sickness. Low incomes and poor housing are also not inevitable in old age; much depends on the type of tenure occupied, on the availability of occupational or private pensions and on the accumulation of wealth. What this suggests is that poverty and multiple disadvantage are class-based, but that the symptoms are probably more painfully exposed in later life and retirement than they are even during earlier adulthood and in a person's working life.

Women are also more prone to multiple disadvantage than are men especially if they have children (see Table 7.2). Not least this is because the great majority of single parents are women, and lone

Table 7.2   Vulnerability to multiple disadvantage, 1975

	% experiencing disadvantage
By age	
Up to 59	1
60–64	2
64–74	5
Over 74	8
By sex: non-married people under 60	
Men without children	19
Men with children	44
Women without children	31
Women with children	78
By occupation	
Professional/managerial	6
Other non-manual	11
Skilled manual	15
Semi-skilled manual	23
Unskilled manual	32
By region	
South West	19
West Midlands	19
South East	20
North West	22
Scotland	22
Yorkshire	24
East Midlands	26
North	29
Wales	29
East Anglia	30
By ethnic group	
White	22
West Indian	41
Other non-white	26

Source: R. Berthoud, op cit. (see Table 7.1)

mothers are especially vulnerable to multiple disadvantage. This constrains their employment possibilities and further exaggerates the inequalities that most women experience with respect to jobs and incomes. Again, any such conclusions have to be modified to take into account the prevalent influence of social class. It is unusual for even single-parent, middle-class mothers to experience multiple disadvantage. They may well suffer from a number of social disadvantages but they do usually have the cushion of education and higher incomes (perhaps in the form of a paternity contribution from a middle-class husband). Working-class single mothers have no such cushion.

There is also a racial dimension to multiple disadvantage. West Indian families are twice as likely as white families to suffer from this (see Table 7.2). Housing problems, low incomes and poor educational achievements are not only widespread amongst West Indians but also tend to coincide. They are almost as prone to multiple disadvantage as are the very elderly. Berthoud's analysis did not identify such a high risk of multiple disadvantage amongst Asian families. While this is partly a function of the limited data available on race, it also reflects the considerable polarisation which exists between different sub-groups of Asian families, especially those of Indian versus those of Bangladeshi origin. There is a growing number of middle class Asian families whose experiences are very different to those of the multiply-disadvantaged majority of working-class Asians.

One thing that emerges strongly, then, is powerful evidence of an association between social class and multiple disadvantage. Berthoud's analysis is based on occupational status rather than class in the strict sense but there is a strong inverse relationship between this and multiple disadvantage. Not only is this true of multiple disadvantage but also of every separate measure of disadvantage. Consequently '. . . no theory about the nature and causation of social disadvantage can be held valid without an explicit explanation of the role of social class'.[3]

The UK is a socially-polarised country and this has strong spatial manifestations. As there are North–South class differences, it is to be expected that there are regional variations in the incidence of multiple disadvantage. The greatest difference is between Northern Ireland and the rest of the UK but there is inadequate data to consider this systematically. However, Berthoud's index did show that the lowest levels were in the South-East, the South-West and the West Midlands (but it is doubtful whether the latter would hold in the 1980s). In contrast, Wales, the North and East Anglia (but again probably not in the 1980s) had the highest levels. There are indisputable differences between North and South but inner cities are the locales with which multiple disadvantage or deprivation are usually associated.

The inner cities: the visible scars of multiple deprivation

Discussions of the UK's inner cities often invoke images of poverty, deprivation and physical decay. 'Inner-city problems' are not a creation of the 1980s for they have been recorded and analysed in a number of reports dating from the 1960s. However, the civil disturbances in the inner cities in the 1980s, especially in 1981 and 1985, brought these areas to greater prominence in the debate about poverty and inequality in the UK.

Spatial concentrations of poverty are more obvious than is poverty which is more widely diffused throughout the population. But do geographical concentrations exacerbate the conditions in any way? It can be argued that they represent an intensification of deprivation; the inhabitants of these areas experience collective deprivation. 'It is not a matter of multiple deprivation – of many people having many problems separately. It is rather an accumulated form of deprivation experienced by those living in inner-city areas, psychic as well as material. Collective deprivation starts with inner-city residents' perceptions of their environment'.[4] The image and, often, the reality is of neglect and dereliction in the physical landscape. This is exacerbated by the widening gap between residents' awareness of conditions elsewhere in the city or society and the conditions which they see around them.

The emphasis on inner cities does not imply that only small numbers of people are involved, living in isolated pockets within the conurbations. As many as four million people may be living in the inner city areas, approximately one in every fourteen of the population.[5] A substantial proportion of the population live in areas where multiple deprivation is considered to be the norm, even if there are many relatively well-off individuals. They all suffer from the same poor environment, lack of jobs and educational opportunities and services in these areas. Whether or not this leads to a self-reproducing culture of poverty is debatable; but it certainly leads to a collective awareness of living in a deprived area. Their residents become categorised as impoverished and deprived in the eyes of the rest of the urban community, irrespective of their personal circumstances. This leads to disadvantage in terms of applying for jobs, houses or credit.

The most systematic study of urban deprivation used a number of indicators for parliamentary constituencies in Britain.[6] This is a scale which allows inner and outer urban areas to be distinguished. Different types of deprivation are found in different parts of the UK (see Figure 7.2). However, there is considerable overlapping of different types of deprivation in inner London constituencies such as Brent, Hackney and Hammersmith. Glasgow also suffers from a marked overlapping of different types of deprivation. This does not necessarily imply that there is either multiple or collective deprivation in these areas but it suggests that it is likely. Other cities which feature prominently in terms of deprivation are Liverpool, Manchester and Birmingham. Northern Ireland was not included in this particular study but there is ample evidence elsewhere. Belfast is not only the most deprived city in the UK but also, with the possible exception of Naples, in the whole of Western Europe.

Although the inner areas of the metropolitan cities are the locales which are most severely affected by deprivation, there are some notable concentrations in outer urban areas. Places such as Knowsley North in Merseyside have very high unemployment as do parts of outer

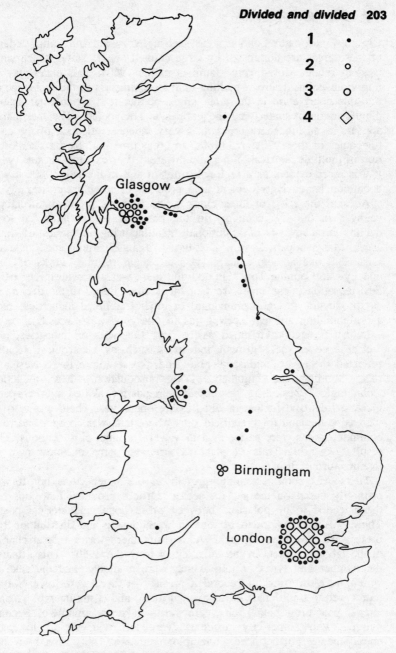

Figure 7.2 Deprivation in British cities, 1981 (Parliamentary constituencies figuring in one or more lists of highly ranked deprived areas; (after D. Sim, 'Urban deprivation: Not just the inner city', *Area*, 16 (1984), pp. 299–300)

Glasgow, and outer London areas such as Norwood and Ealing. Many of these areas are dominated by large council house estates which were used to rehouse low-income families in the 1960s. This underlines an important point. There is nothing unique or timeless in the incidence of multiple deprivation in the inner cities. Rather it is a particular spatial manifestation of underlying inequalities in UK society. The fact that it appears as an inner-city problem is very much a reflection of the contingencies of the 1970s and 1980s. In other time periods the manifestation of multiple deprivation may be different. For example, in the 1930s it was more evident as a regional problem and in the late 1980s it was becoming increasingly evident as a problem in outer urban areas.

At heart the crisis of inner cities is an economic problem. Structural changes in the UK economy in the post-war period have led to a decline in many of the traditional manufacturing industries of these areas. Many industries were dock-based, as in Liverpool and London's East End; one notable example was the sugar refining works of Tate and Lyle in Canning Town. In addition there was also widespread deindustrialisation in the inner areas of other cities linked to the decline of car production (as in Birmingham) or other traditional industries, such as shipbuilding and engineering (as in Glasgow or Newcastle).

Industrial decline stemmed partly from the types of industries, and the absence of new growth industries such as electronics. It also reflected the age of industrial plant and a past failure to reinvest and renew buildings and equipment, via the introduction of new production technologies. Deskilling decreased demand for skilled workers and increased demand for cheap and flexible operatives. There was also an increasing demand for greenfield sites where land was cheaper and road communications were easier than they were in inner-city locations. The result was a high rate of plant closure and some out-movement of manufacturing firms.

There was some economic growth in the inner cities but it was primarily based on the service sector. Offices provided new jobs but these tended to be polarised between professional and clerical posts. There was also a growth of jobs in warehousing and distribution but these were mostly poorly paid. As a result there was a radical change in the labour markets in the inner cities from the 1960s. This affected the number and types of jobs which were available, and the salaries which were on offer. In general it meant that there were lower wages (compared to traditional skilled manual jobs), and rising unemployment. Higher paid professional jobs were mostly taken by middle-class commuters, while inner-city residents were left with no or low-paid employment. Furthermore, unemployment was not spread evenly throughout the community. The most severely affected were young school leavers, middle-aged and elderly men, the unskilled and black people. As a result, a large group of young people in the inner cities in the 1970s and 1980s were or had been unemployed for a substantial period of time. In absolute terms most were white but there was disproportionately high unemployment amongst black youth. This was an important contributory factor to the civil disturbances of 1981 and 1985.

Economic and social decline in the inner cities led to a high rate of out-migration. Many of those who could move out to the more prosperous suburbs with better job opportunities and more attractive environments did so. In some of the more favoured inner areas – such as Islington in London – their places were taken by inmigrant middle class families and individuals. This process is known as gentrification and it is commonly associated with the growth of Yuppies and Dinkies (Double Income No Kids) as distinct social groups. The social changes have been particularly spectacular in East London's docklands; one of the most prominent of this group of inmigrants is David Owen, the SDP leader, who bought a house adjoining the Thames in Limehouse in the early stages of its gentrification. The arrival of such middle-class newcomers powerfully underlines the differences in life chances and wealth between them and the traditional residents of these areas. It also emphasises that inner-city 'problems' are firmly grounded in absolute and relative inequalities.

Not all inner city residents had the option of out-migration, even if they had wished to move. Instead, poor access to housing – one of the most important aspects of their restricted life chances – meant that many families were caught in a housing 'trap'. High house prices and low incomes excluded them from home ownership and they therefore became dependent on renting. The stock of private dwellings is limited, declining and largely confined to older houses in inner cities. In addition, local authority tenants are mostly restricted to moving to other council properties located in the same municipality. In the metropolitan areas this means that there are few opportunities to move to the outer areas. Both sets of tenants are therefore restricted in their abilities to 'escape' the inner cities.

Social polarisation in UK cities has had serious implications for the distribution of multiple deprivation and for the life chances of those who live in these areas. The result has been that '. . . a pattern has emerged of a more unequal society as between a majority in a secure attachment to a still prosperous country and a minority in marginal economic and social conditions – the former moving into the suburban locations of the newer economy of a "green and pleasant land", the latter tending to be trapped into the old provincial industrial cities and their displaced fragments of peripheral council estates'.[7]

The inner-city areas of collective deprivation are certainly not the creation of Thatcherism. But have the extent and the depth of such problems increased or decreased in the 1980s? There is a lack of precise data to answer this question. However, the discussion elsewhere in this book has shown that inequalities have increased with respect to

Table 7.3 Multiple deprivation in London in 1981 (Rank order of London wards)

	Unemployed	Over-crowded	Not home owners	Not car owners
		(Percentages)		
Most deprived				
1. Spitafields (Tower Hamlets)	21.9	28.3	96.5	79.6
2. St Mary (Tower Hamlets)	19.5	16.5	95.2	74.0
Least deprived				
754 Selsdon (Croydon)	2.6	0.5	6.7	13.5
755 Cranham West (Havering)	3.2	0.9	4.1	12.4

Source: Peter Townsend, *Poverty and Labour in London* (London: Low Pay Unit, 1987)

several of the separate dimensions of inequality. Homelessness has increased, the most desirable council house properties have been sold and real incomes have polarised. This has to be seen alongside diverging standards of provision in public and private health care and education. It is therefore impossible to escape the conclusion that multiple deprivation has increased during the Thatcher administrations.

The factor which has contributed more than any other to an increase in multiple deprivation is unemployment. Unemployment rates have risen in the UK in response to global economic conditions and deliberate government policy. This meant, for example, that the number of unemployed living in the inner cities increased considerably in the 1980s. It also meant that the proportion who were long-term unemployed (over one year) increased from 25 per cent in 1979 to 41 per cent in 1985. Unemployment, and especially long-term unemployment, are often at the root of multiple deprivation and multiple inequality. In this respect the conclusion that inner-city multiple inequalities have increased is unavoidable.

Some concrete data to confirm this general conclusion are presented in a Low Pay Unit study of London.[8] The extent of multiple deprivation in London was considerable even in the early 1980s. Furthermore the variations between the most privileged and the most disadvantaged areas of London were enormous; this is illustrated by a comparison of wards in terms of four indicators of deprivation (see Table 7.3). At one extreme are wards such as Spitalfields and St Mary (in Tower Hamlets) where one fifth of the population is unemployed, between one sixth and one quarter of households are over-crowded, three-quarters lack cars and less than one in twenty are home-owners. In contrast there are the outer-London wards such as Selsdon and Cranham West where there is virtually no unemployment or overcrowding, almost everyone owns their homes and only one in eight households lacks a car.

Given the context noted above, it is alarming to note that the standards of living of the poor and the rich diverged in London more quickly than they had in the rest of the UK in the 1970s. Not only was there a divergence in relative terms but there was also a fall in the real spending power of the poorest quarter of the population during the first two Thatcher administrations. Between 1979 and 1985 the gross household incomes of the poorest tenth of London's population fell by 17 per cent. Even the gross household incomes of the poorest tenth of the population fell by 8 per cent.

The impoverishment of a large proportion of London's population was linked to high rates of unemployment. With 400,000 unemployed in 1986, London had the largest concentration of unemployment of any major city in the industrial world. This was not distributed evenly within London. At the level of the Boroughs, unemployment rates varied from 5.9 per cent in Kingston to 22.7 per cent in Hackney. But at ward level some areas, such as Angell in Lambeth, had unemployment rates as high as 36 per cent. Moreover, the gap between areas had grown considerably during the Thatcher years. In 1979 the unemployment rate in the worst-affected ward was 2.4 times higher than in the best-off ward; by 1986 this ratio had widened to 3.8. In other words, the probability of being unemployed was almost four times higher in parts of inner London than in parts of outer London. Social class and labour market position are again the keys to life chances and multiple disadvantage.

Deprivation need not be urban: the rural areas of the UK

The publicity given to urban deprivation in the 1970s and 1980s has tended to obscure the fact that multiple disadvantages are not confined to towns and cities. The underlying roots of multiple disadvantage are to be found in the way in which society is organised, especially its class nature. Multiple disadvantage is experienced by individuals and families and where they live influences the precise form of this rather than its root causes. This can be illustrated by considering rural areas although, it must be emphasised, we could equally well have looked at suburban areas.

Until the 1970s rural areas were often portrayed as idyllic, attractive and prosperous. This view was coloured by the romanticism which is attached to rural areas, which were often contrasted with the real and imagined horrors of urban areas. This romanticism is to be found in literature from the nineteenth century onwards, in government reports and in the popular press. It has serious consequences in two ways. First, the seeming absence of poverty in rural areas reinforces the idea

Table 7.4 Multiple deprivation in Scotland in the late 1970s (%)

Area type	All Scottish households	Multiply-deprived households	Multiply-deprived areas
Major cities	37	61	65
Other urban settlements	40	25	31
Rural areas	23	14	4
Total	100	100	100

Source: A.R. Millar, *A Study of Multiply-Deprived Households in Scotland* (Edinburgh: Scottish Office, 1980)

that multiple inequality is a specifically urban rather than a general feature of society. Secondly, it leads to there being hidden poverty and deprivation in rural areas. Because such areas are not seen to be experiencing the same degree or intensity of visible poverty as are urban areas, there is a mistaken assumption that there is no deprivation in the countryside.

The most useful research on rural deprivation has been undertaken on Scotland,[9] using both area-level and individual household data (Table 7.4). Small-area data from the population census suggested that the level of multiple deprivation in rural areas was 4 per cent, but a household level analysis showed that they contained about 14 per cent of *all* the multiply deprived. Given that these areas only contained 23 per cent of all households, this represents a high incidence of deprivation. Although not highly visible, multiple deprivation was widespread.

Many of the symptoms of deprivation in rural areas are similar to those observed in urban areas. The affected zones have experienced economic decline, population losses, reduced service provision, a lack of investment, the operation of housing 'traps' and low morale. In addition several other symptoms of deprivation are commonplace in rural areas. These include inaccessibility and isolation and a lack of infrastructure.

Opportunity deprivation is pervasive in rural areas. Opportunities are much fewer than elsewhere in the UK in relation to education, health and social services, jobs, shops and information. Closures of village schools and shops have actually led to a decline in the availability of such services in the post-war period. Even if the services are available, they are likely to be of poor quality and to lack choice compared to urban areas. The extent of the problem is considerable. In England and Wales alone there are some 3.3 million people living in settlements with less than 1,000 population: of these some 1.4 million live more than ten miles from their nearest main town. Many of the difficulties result from central and local government policies which have sought to 'rationalise' service provision in the face of public expenditure restrictions and, sometimes, declining populations. They also result from mobility limitations.

Mobility deprivation is the most distinctive form of rural deprivation. It can affect a community as a whole, as for example when a rail or bus service is closed. However, depending on their access to private transport, some individuals are more affected than others. This is partly a matter of income and the ability to buy access to shops, doctors and leisure facilities in distant towns. However, this is only one dimension of transport poverty. For the 'transport poor' also include the elderly, housewives and young people who lack access to cars during all or part of the day. This reinforces one of our earlier conclusions: class, income and unemployment may be the keys to multiple disadvantages, but these are most acutely experienced by women and by certain age groups, especially the elderly.

Given the emphasis on accessibility and isolation in rural deprivation, remote areas are usually characterised as being deprived. However, severely deprived households also exist in accessible and attractive rural areas, such as Sussex and Suffolk, which are normally characterised as the loci of middle class individualised consumption. These people are deprived because of their position in the class system and in the labour market, or because of their age or gender. Living in the accessible countryside does not necessarily ameliorate these basic conditions. Indeed, the very presence of the new middle-class residents with their individualistic and privatised consumption patterns can exacerbate the problem. Most obviously they can outbid locals in the housing market. Furthermore, if they send their children to private schools or use private medical care, this may lead to a more rapid withdrawal of public services. There is therefore a direct link between the activities of the middle-class and the multiple deprivation of some working-class households. This can be seen in the overall distribution of income and in their competing interests within a given area.

Multiple Deprivation Matters

Multiple deprivation matters because many people in the UK face a number of inter-linked barriers blocking their access to improved life chances. It also matters because, judging from the evidence on class mobility, it may be transmitted between generations.

The evidence on transmitted deprivation is patchy but largely unequivocal.[10] Low incomes tend to be transmitted between generations and this is linked to the way in which class conditions educational achievements and employment prospects. Children are seven times more likely to leave school without qualifications if their parents had only an elementary school education than if they had had post-secondary school education. Moreover, the inheritance of wealth –

especially housing – is also a major channel for transmitting inequalities between generations. The expansion of home ownership in the post-1945 period, coupled with house price inflation in the 1970s and 1980s, has had a particularly strong influence in this respect.

Class also influences the transmission of life chances in other ways. There is, for example, continuity in housing deprivation. While 11 per cent of the adult children of parents living in houses lacking basic amenities also lacked such amenities themselves, only 4 per cent of the adult children of parents who had not lacked basic housing amenities did so. Mental and physical health are also influenced by inter-generational transmission for both social and genetic reasons.

These is no data on the inter-generational transmission of *multiple* deprivation or *multiple* disadvantage per se. However, multiple disadvantage has been shown to be strongly related to social class, and social class is strongly transmitted between generations. Therefore, those born into multiply disadvantaged households are themselves disproportionately likely to become multiply disadvantaged in adulthood.

It does not automatically follow that the same individuals suffer from all these forms of disadvantage and that therefore there is a strong degree of inter-generational transmission of multiple disadvantage. However, the way in which each of these indicators is linked to social class makes it difficult to reach any other conclusion. This reinforces the evidence that deprivation has strong roots in the structural inequalities in UK society. It is, then, all the more relevant to consider the policies which the state has adopted to ameliorate multiple deprivation.

Multiple Deprivation And State Policies: Remedies And Gestures

Although the Beveridge report had not highlighted multiple deprivation as such to be a problem, it recognised that there was a strong inter-linking of different individual needs. Its target for the welfare state was the elimination of what it saw as five major areas of blight: want, ignorance, idleness, illness and squalor.

The response of the 1945 Labour government was to establish a number of new and revamped forms of social provision. These included income supplements and sickness insurance, the National Health Service, educational reforms, a large-scale public housing programme and macro-economic regulation of the economy to minimise unemployment. Although the full programme was less comprehensive than that recommended by the Beveridge report, it was a radical and impressive array of measures. It was, without doubt, the single most important landmark in the creation of the UK's welfare state. At the time it had no rival in Western Europe in terms of its scope and egalitarian tendencies.

In the 1950s and early 1960s there was no serious attempt to question either the legitimacy or the efficiency of the welfare state (although some Conservative voices queried its cost). Indeed, there was an assumption that it was well on the way to eliminating poverty and deprivation, if not social inequalities. There was broad consensus concerning the importance of these achievements. These were only really challenged in the 1960s when growing difficulties in the national economy became translated into stresses within UK society, especially as the result of rising unemployment. The publication of reports such as Abel-Smith's and Townsend's 'The Poor and the Poorest' played no small part in the rediscovery of poverty.

The state and, in particular, the Labour government, could have reacted to these new social challenges in various ways. More resources could have been ear-marked for welfare needs. But in the face of growing economic difficulties there was already strong pressure to reduce public expenditure. Another way to meet the challenge was greater selectivity within the welfare state, concentrating resources on those in greatest need. However, this implied greater reliance on means testing and a move away from the principle of universalism.

Selectivism had long been opposed by those in the Labour Party who had long and bitter memories of the harsh use of the means test during the inter-war years. As the main aim of such tests is to exclude applicants, the poor are more likely to be seen as the needy seeking charity rather than as individuals receiving their rights in a just society. Not surprisingly the Labour Party was unwilling to accept any substantial shift to greater selectivism. Instead Harold Wilson's government opted for the spatial targeting of policies. As poverty and deprivation had been identified as being particularly acute in urban areas in the 1960s, this led to the development of specifically urban policies. Any such approach implicitly, and wrongly, implies that deprivation has a limited spatial distribution and exclusiveness.

Urban policy assumed a number of forms, all characterised by the concentration of additional resources on particular (inner) urban areas. Educational Priority Areas were introduced in 1968 along with the Urban Aid Programme. Area-based policies were also introduced into housing provision: especially General Improvement Areas (1969) and Housing Action Areas (1974). The most important of the urban policies introduced before 1979 was probably the 1977 Policy For the Inner Cities. There were to be three tiers of special assistance to deprived urban areas, most notably seven inner-city partnerships in London and the major conurbations. This was important in two ways. First, the political weight attached to the launch of the programme underlined the considerable priority which was now attached to area-based policies. Secondly, the inner-city partnerships in the metropolitan areas were established as joint ventures between local and central government. This was to be a portent of a more radical attack on local autonomy by the Thatcher administration.

How are we to evaluate area-based policies? On the one hand they are preferable to greater selectivism. Welfare provision is still seen as a matter of social rights. It reaches deprived individuals by virtue of their being resident in a priority area, not because they as individuals have been subject to means testing.

In practice, however, area-based policies were often inspired by the objectives of limiting public expenditure while allowing governments to appear to be active in combatting poverty. In other words this approach had great political appeal. More fundamental was the implicit assumption that multiple deprivation was a localised and geographically concentrated phenomenon. This is patently misleading. Deprived people live outside the priority areas and non-deprived people live within them. Indeed, deprivation is so widespread that, in order to delimit areas which encompassed even one half of all deprived people, it would be necessary to include almost one half of all the areas in the UK. Above all, this exposes the weakness of trying to tackle structural inequalities via area-based policies.

Inner Cities And The Policies Of Thatcherism

At first sight the policies of Mrs Thatcher's governments could be seen as a continuation of those which had been developed by previous Tory and Labour administrations. It can be argued that if the political rhetoric of Thatcherism is stripped away then the most obvious of the 'urban' policies of the 1980s – such as Enterprise Zones – are continuations of the policies of the 1970s. Such a judgement would be profoundly wrong: there has been a decisive reshaping of inner-city policies under Thatcherism.

Inner cities have been deeply affected by two of the major ideological planks of Thatcherism, individualism and deregulation. These are translated into a belief that the 'problem' of the inner cities is the lack of individual self-help and initiative. Except for Keith Joseph, no government minister has tried to relate this explicitly to the idea of the culture of poverty, which implies that individuals are socialised into low expectations and failure. Instead Mrs Thatcher's governments have emphasised the need to remove constraints on individual initiative. This is associated with arguments about the need to reduce public intervention and to allow free enterprise and market forces to revive the inner cities.

It is within this context that Thatcherite area-based policies must be seen. The most important of these are the Enterprise Zones, Free Ports and Urban Development Corporations (UDCs). Enterprise Zones, introduced in 1981, were envisaged as special economic areas which offered less regulated environments for firms. Planning controls were reduced in these areas and there was also a benevolent financial environment with, for example, firms being excluded from paying rates during their first ten years of operation. Free Ports provided special zones where imported goods could be processed and then re-exported free of customs duties. Finally, UDCs were designated for Merseyside and London Docklands in the first instance, but extended subsequently to other urban areas. These agencies were initially charged with redeveloping derelict industrial areas and later with encouraging employment in them. They were given special exemption from many forms of local government control and planning legislation. In our opinion they are probably better viewed as attempts to bolster speculative property development than as specific policies to deal with multiple deprivation in British cities.

Each of these programmes can be criticised in terms of its specific objectives and it is debatable to what extent these have been achieved. They have all been designed to create deregulated economic environments for private enterprise. It is assumed that this will lead to economic growth, the benefits of which will percolate down eventually to all members of the community in the form of increased opportunities for individuals. This makes a number of assumptions about the types of jobs created and the type of labour which is demanded to fill them; it is probably not provided by the multiply-deprived who live in the inner cities. These policies also represent a shift away from the previous attempt to tackle inner-city problems via an array of social and economic policies. In other words, there is even less explicit recognition of structural inequalities than there had been in the area-based policies of the 1970s.

Enterprise Zones, Free Ports and Development Corporations have in common the fact that they by-pass traditional local authority influence on development and public expenditure within their areas. This has to be seen in context of the systematic attack on local government autonomy under the Thatcher administration. It is part of the process of political centralisation which removes one of the checks that local communities have on the power of the executive. This is seen most starkly in the way in which the London Docklands Corporation has often proceeded to redevelop east London in the face of strong opposition from Labour-controlled local authorities. This is a struggle not only between central and local power but also between the interests of developers and the local community.

These are not the only instruments of centralisation, and centralisation has not been the sole prerogative of Conservative governments. There were substantial cut-backs in public expenditure and a move to reduce local authority financial autonomy under the Labour government in the 1970s. In particular, cash limits and the curtailment of Rate Support Grant supplements were imposed on local authorities in 1975. However, Mrs Thatcher's governments have been far more active in their attack on local autonomy. Quite apart from a stream of political rhetoric aimed at 'wasteful' (Labour) councils, metropolitan counties and the GLC have been abolished. In addition, financial limits have been imposed on borrowing and spending, and these have been reinforced by 'rate capping', a system of financial penalties. Some of the major victims of these cuts and of centralism have been local authority expenditure on housing, education and special community programmes. Yet these are essential in any attempt to tackle urban poverty.

Cuts in local authority expenditure to counter poverty have been matched by cuts in many of the programmes directly controlled by central government. The most important of these are the social benefits administered by the DHSS, and the most significant development has been the 1988 reform of benefits. The National Association of Citizens Advice Bureaux considered that by November of that same year, more than 80 per cent of claimants had become worse off. In particular, changes in housing benefits and in the loss of free school meals exceeded whatever gains most families had obtained via the family credit scheme.

By 1989 the government was exploring the possibilities for further shifts from public to private provision of welfare benefits. Ministers emphasised that there was a moral obligation on those who had benefited from government economic policies to support voluntary and charity groups. At the time individual donations to charity totalled only about £1.5 billion, less than 1 per cent of total household disposable income. There would have to be an enormous increase in individual donations if the charities were to be able to compensate, significantly, for past or planned reductions in public expenditure on welfare. Even if such a large-scale transfer of resources to the charities did take place, this would represent a shift away from providing benefits as of right to having to apply for charity. There would also be no guarantees about the ways in which these resources would be used. The priorities and resource allocation of the charities would not necessarily adequately reflect the needs of the multiply-deprived living in the inner cities.

If we look beyond welfare and urban policies, then the policies of Mrs Thatcher's governments are seen to have been even more damaging to the inner cities. Thatcherite economic policies in the early 1980s deliberately used unemployment as an instrument of economic and social policy, to weaken the power of labour and to combat inflation. The cost in terms of unemployment was felt especially strongly in the inner cities. While economic growth recovered in the later 1980s, especially in 1986–88, unemployment continued at high rates in the inner cities. Given that there is such a strong association between unemployment and multiple deprivation, it is an unavoidable conclusion that Thatcherite economic policies increased the misery of the inner cities.

Multiple disadvantage and the needs of the inner cities are not high priorities for Mrs Thatcher's government. The emphasis on individual initiative either made the government blind to the many real structural inequalities in UK society, or has allowed it deliberately to ignore these. The main thrusts of government policies have been directed towards individuals, both in terms of means testing individual benefits and in terms of increasing market opportunities for individuals. Beyond this Thatcherism has had little to offer the inner cities and the victims of multiple deprivation except attacks on the welfare state, a narrow interpretation of the virtues of citizenship and racist-tinged immigration policies.

Notes

1. Discussed in A. Mama, 'Black women and the economic crisis', in Feminist Review (ed.), *Waged Work: A Reader* (London: Virago, 1986).
2. P.L. Knox, *Social Priorities For Social Indicators: A Survey Approach*, Occasional Paper No. 4, Department of Geography, University of Dundee, 1976.
3. R. Berthoud, 'Who suffers social disadvantage?', in M. Brown (ed.), *The Structure of Disadvantage'* (London: Heinemann, 1983).
4. H.W.E. Davies, 'The Inner City In Britain', in G.C. Schwartz (ed.), *Advanced Industrialisation and the Inner City* (Lexington: Lexington Books, 1981).
5. D.M. Smith, 'Inner city deprivation: problems and policies in advanced capitalist countries', *Geoforum*, 10 (1979), pp. 297–310.
6. D. Sim, 'Urban deprivation: not just the inner city', *Area*, 16 (1984), pp. 299–306.
7. A.H. Halsey in *Social Trends* 17, CSO: HMSO, 1987.
8. Low Pay Unit. *Poverty and Labour in London* (London: LPU, 1987).
9. A.R. Millar, *A Study Of Multiply Deprived Households In Scotland* (Edinburgh: Scottish Office, 1980).
10. Berthoud, op. cit., discusses this issue.

Further Reading

A general introduction to inequality is provided in M. Brown (ed), *The Structure of Disadvantage* (London: Heinemann, 1983).

Multiple deprivation is discussed in R. Berthoud, 'Who suffers social disadvantage' in M. Brown, op. cit. Indicators of multiple deprivation and the quality of life are reviewed in B.E. Coates, R.J. Johnston and P.L. Knox, *Geography and Inequality* (Oxford: Oxford University Press, 1977).

The nature of inner-city 'problems' is considered in R. Hudson and A. Williams, The United Kingdom (London: Harper & Row, 1986).

The specific case of London is analysed in Low Pay Unit, *Poverty and Labour in London* (London, 1987).

Rural deprivation is discussed in D. Phillips and A. Williams, *Rural Britain* (Oxford: Blackwell, 1984); P. Lowe, T. Bradley, and S. Wright, *Deprivation and Welfare in Rural Areas* (Norwich: GeoBooks, 1987).

8
Divided forever?

Introduction

It has been demonstrated, we think beyond any reasonable doubt, that UK society has become more deeply divided since 1979 as a result of Thatcherite policies. Moreover, the growing divisions are a deliberate rather than an inadvertent consequence of those policies. In claiming this, we do not deny that prior to 1979 there were already deep divisions in UK society. Nor do we wish to suggest that existing inequalities have simply been widened. Rather, the dimensions of division have been selectively reworked, redefined *and* magnified at one and the same time. Divisions by class, gender, race and space are more pronounced than they were in 1979 but at the same time the pattern of inequalities has been altered. Sometimes these changes have been subtle and on other occasions they have been more obvious.

The question that we must now consider is this: is the future inevitably one of persisting, even deepening, divisions? To what extent would a change of prime minister, and a switch from Thatcherite policies, produce a less divided, or perhaps a differently divided, society? Posing the question differently, we need to ask to what extent divisions are structurally inscribed in UK society, and to what extent they have taken a particular contingent form because of the specific policies and politics of Thatcherism?

We attempt to give an answer to these questions by considering the possibilities for change over three time horizons: the immediate future; the medium-term alternatives; and the longer-term prospects.

The Immediate Future

For the foreseeable future, and indeed for as long as Thatcherism remains the dominant political philosophy in the UK, the *only* realistic scenario is one of continuing, indeed widening, inequalities. It is a future of 'more of the same', and of unremitting divisiveness. The politics of Thatcherism revolve around creating social divisions, rewarding those who succeed through the market and punishing those who do not.

With Mrs Thatcher in office, the political agenda will continue to be dominated by what are now familiar themes. Further regressive income and wealth tax changes will go hand in hand with a weakening of the welfare state. Further privatisation of nationalised industries and public services, at knock-down prices, is also likely. This reinforces the illusion of a people's capitalism through widening what is still a thin veneer of personal share ownership. The virtues of the enterprise culture and the promotion of small firms will continue to be glorified. There is likely to be a still greater, though ever more selective, reliance on the market as the mechanism through which goods and services are to be provided. Not all the public sector will disappear but there will be intensified pressures on the remaining rump of public sector industries and services to behave as if they were in the private sector. In practice this will mean further reducing the access to and the quality of provision of health and welfare services. The chosen economic strategy will continue to centre around 'casino' capitalism, meeting the demands of internationally-orientated commercial and financial capital rather than addressing the need to reconstruct the productive base of the national economy.

In short, the government will continue to pursue the same sorts of economic and social policies as it has done over the last decade. This will be done in pursuit of Mrs Thatcher's holy grail, which she sees as the destruction of socialism but many others see as the destruction of a civilised society. At the same time we see no reason to anticipate any lessening of the ugly authoritarianism which has characterised Thatcherism – whether dealing with trades unions, broadcasters or local authorities.

Changes such as these will further widen class differences in income, wealth, health and living conditions. The processes of class reformation and of a redefinition to the boundaries between classes will continue for such changes are central to the Thatcherite project. Capitalism, by definition, requires a working class. The specification of this class, who is seen to be in it and who is not, is a matter of vital political concern. One of the central aims of the Thatcherite programme has been to reform the working class as one that is passively subservient, and that bows with little protest to the changing demands of capitalist production. This helps recreate conditions for profitable accumulation within the UK.

It is equally difficult to foresee any significant reduction in ethnic or gender inequalities. Not least, this is because they are strongly related to, though they are certainly not reducible to, those of class. Mrs Thatcher's term as Prime Minister has been more notable for an unprecedented centralisation of power in her person in 10 Downing Street than it has been for any marked improvement in the position of the vast majority of women in the UK. Ethnic divisions remain as marked, if not more so, than they were in 1979. There are now black MPs in Parliament but no black politician has yet to attain the rank of Cabinet minister. Furthermore, with an aging population, inequalities between different age groups will probably widen. The elderly are already more subject to multiple deprivation than any other social group. Such age divisions will continue and become more complex. Agism will join sexism and racism as one of the defining dimensions of the divided society in the 1990s and into the twenty-first century.

There is no doubt either that spatial inequalities will become more pronounced. This is because the spatial segregation of UK society is another integral part of the Thatcherite project. It involves effectively ghettoising not just small areas of cities but whole swathes of the North in a geography that separates the haves from the have-nots.

Not least, by creating two political nations, the North and the South, Thatcherite policies have created a new social and political landscape which is likely to bring Mrs Thatcher continuing electoral success. This will be enough to ensure the survival of her government for some time to come. The importance of this and other social divisions was underlined by a MORI opinion poll taken immediately after the 1987 general election. Few voters expected her to improve welfare services, reduce unemployment, or narrow the gap between rich and poor. What they did expect were more tax cuts and continuing low rates of infla-tion. These expectations appealed strongly to the affluent majority (in the South), many of whom were willing to accept the consequences of greater inequalities. Looking beyond the ballot box, it is inconceivable that there could be a sufficiently broadly-based and sustained extra-parliamentary challenge to Thatcherism on the streets or in the work places of the UK to displace it. Even if such a challenge was mounted, it would doubtless be met by the full force of the armed forces and the police. As events such as the 1984–85 miners' strike clearly demonstrated, a Thatcher government has no hesitation in releasing the forces of 'law and order' on those who dare to challenge its view of what UK society ought to become.

A scenario can be unfolded whereby national economic policy and selective government expenditure have created enough of an affluent South for it to continue to vote Conservative. Labour will remain domi-nant in the North but will probably continue to trail more than one hundred seats behind the government in the House of Commons. The SLD vote will continue to be diluted over the national territory while pockets of nationalist support will remain confined to the Celtic fringes. Given this scenario, the only hope for the country to escape the grip of Thatcherism, and for the opposition parties to accede to power, would be via electoral reform to establish proportional representation.

The prospect of Mrs Thatcher's government agreeing to this is, to say the least, remote. This is not to say that the Conservative South versus Labour North will remain as a simple dichotomous division. There may be localised rebellions in the South, based on environmental arguments as, for example, over the route of the Channel Tunnel rail link. There is also, for example, the Govan by-election shock result in 1988, when Jim Sillars overturned a massive Labour majority. This provided a sharp reminder that the combination of a Conservative government seen as hostile to Scotland and a massive Labour majority in Scotland that is powerless to change this, might yet upset this North/South division of the political map. But this may occur in ways that are much more damaging to Labour than to the Conservatives. Indeed, they may reinforce Mrs Thatcher's position by further fragmenting an already divided opposition.

A Medium-Term Political Alternative?

However it may appear at present, one could argue that Thatcherism will at some point in the future cease to be the dominant political philosophy. At some point in the future Mrs Thatcher will have to cease to be Prime Minister. The question then is, to what extent will Thatcherism outlive Thatcher? Gaullism certainly managed to outlive de Gaulle so why shouldn't Thatcherism outlive Thatcher? In some senses it undoubtedly will, for the changes that have already been wrought over the last decade penetrate deeply into the fabric of society. At best they will take many years to reverse.

Nevertheless, although to some it has at times appeared as a seamless web, Thatcherism as a political and economic philosophy is riddled with contradictions. For example, one has only to consider how the government stridently proclaims the need for a market-driven energy policy. Yet in practice it selectively intervenes to prevent market forces eliminating nuclear power stations! Consequently, one could argue, Thatcherism will collapse under the weight of its own internal contradictions. It might then be replaced by a new dominant political viewpoint. Just what this alternative might be is far from clear. Presumably it would bear some resemblance to the doctrines of former 'one nation' consensus Tory politics. It is difficult to anticipate the possibility of anything radically to the left of this. Even so, such a modest change would surely usher in an era of narrowing inequalities in terms of all the main dimensions of division?

There is definitely some evidence to support such a claim if one examines the historical record. Over the post-war period inequalities in incomes and wealth became more muted. There was greater public-sector provision of health and educational services, which removed their provision from the ability to pay. Other parts of the welfare state provided some sort of a safety net for the old, the sick and the unemployed. But even here, although they were 'unintended', there was evidence of widening class divisions in access to and benefits from public sector provision of education and health care.

Despite a long period of regional and then urban policies, spatial divisions did not disappear. It is salutary to recall that, despite the proclaimed good intentions of Conservative and Labour governments alike to tackle the 'regional problem', public expenditure per capita in the South-East in 1978 was well above the national average. Although comprehensive data on the regional distribution of public expenditure are not available for the 1980s, there is no doubt that the selective concentration of public expenditure into the South has increased further. But the point that we wish to stress here is that the polarisation between North and South was already heavily underpinned by public spending policies before 1979. This is a point with profound implications for any serious attempt to narrow, if not eliminate, the North/South divide.

More generally, there is an abundance of evidence that points to the persistence of inequalities – between classes, between ethnic groups, between men and women – in an era of consensus, mildly socially-democratic reformist policies and politics prior to 1979. In part, such divisions remained because of, rather than despite, the implementation of avowedly reformist policies. The actual effects of policies often diverged from what was intended: in short, there were policy-reinforced inequalities.

Therefore, inequalities persisted despite a very different and, in many respects, much more propitious political and economic environment. International competition was generally much less pronounced on world markets, the internationalisation of capital was yet to reach the heights that it was to attain in the 1980s, and the national economy seemed to be much more closed than it was subsequently to become. In short, there still appeared to be a basis for managing the economy on broadly Keynesian lines. Since 1979 much of this basis has been quite deliberately demolished by government policies. For example, restrictions on the movement of capital have been abolished. The subsequent further increase in the internationalisation of what could once reasonably be regarded as UK-based capital has made it much less amenable to influence, let alone control, by government. Deregulation and privatisation have also resulted in important areas of the economy being placed beyond the reach of direct government influence. Such changes have been reflected in and compounded by national economic policy. This is based on engineering a further switch from an economy based on manufacturing and productive activity to one based on services. But within the service sector, internationally-competitive financial services centred on the City of London are juxtaposed with domestically-oriented low skill, low productivity and low wage service activities. It is difficult to see how many of these changes could be reversed, except over a fairly long period.

Even with this qualification, the prognosis is not a promising one. For post-war consensus politics were based on attempting to influence, not control, private capital. They were not very successful then. The environment in which 'influence' could be exerted is now much less promising than it was before 1979. For example, the possibilities for 'control' over the dominant multinational conglomerates are even less now than they were in 1979; and even then they were limited.

In some ways, our medium-term prognosis is even gloomier. Mrs Thatcher's policies have made the UK a more divided society and future generations will have to live with the consequences of this. The sale of public assets, inadequate investment in health and education, and council house sales have all lessened the possibilities for future governments to provide better facilities and opportunities for the poor and deprived. Furthermore, a polarisation of wealth and a reduction in inheritance taxes have made for even greater inequalities in the inter-generational transfer of wealth. Therefore the foundations for deep divisions in the next and succeeding generations have already been laid in the 1980s.

So is the UK Divided Forever?

The short answer to this question is 'yes, for as long as UK society remains a capitalist one'. Materially and ideologically, Thatcherism has powerfully both reinforced and altered the character of capitalism in the UK. For the foreseeable future, we have to rule out the possibility of any significant move to the left, let alone a socialist 'revolution'. Indeed, it is by no means obvious what a move to the left would mean at present. For the Labour Party continues to move rightwards to occupy the space left by Thatcherism, which itself continues its long march yet further right. In this sense, Thatcherism has redefined the political terrain in a way that seemed impossible only a few years ago. This is not to say that the terrain cannot again be redefined to accommodate a socialist project that would attract sufficient support to result in a government with very different priorities to those of Mrs Thatcher. But it is to say that such a transformation is beyond the present bounds of possibility.

So if the future is to be a capitalist one, and social inequality is endemic to capitalism, then the UK must remain divided. Class inequalities are structurally inscribed into capitalist societies. Capitalism simply cannot exist without the capital-labour class relation, however this is or seems to be mediated by the emergence of the 'middle classes'. Ethnic and gender divisions are not unavoidable in capitalist societies in the same sense as are divisions between classes, but they are closely related to the latter. Hence they are unlikely to disappear in the UK. There are strong links between racial inequalities and class, and between patriarchy and class, for example. Similarly, locational divisions are not necessary in the same way as are those of class but capitalist development has served to widen existing divisions and create new ones. Cleavages along the planes of class, ethnicity, gender and location have become intertwined in complex ways which makes them all the more resistant to progressive change. This isn't to say that the pattern of divisions will remain unaltered. It will not. Nor should it be said that, within the limits defined by capitalist social relations, there is not scope for progressive changes that would at least narrow some of the existing inequalities. There is. And it is important, politically and ideologically, that such possibilities be developed wherever there is a chance to do so. Not least, it must continue to be demonstrated that there *are* alternatives and that, however unpromising the circumstances, these can be kept alive. There is scope, for example, for forms of cooperative development that prove that such alternatives *do* exist. Foundations for a more profound transformation towards a more egalitarian society could begin to be laid. But for the moment, and indeed for the foreseeable future, such developments will at best nibble at the margins of inequality. The divisions will remain deep, in all probability becoming deeper. The UK will indeed remain divided.

Finally, it seems appropriate to end by paraphrasing the remarks with which Mrs Thatcher entered 10 Downing Street in May 1979. During the past decade, her governments have brought discord where there was harmony and despair where there was hope.

Index